STEALTH HEALTH MEAL PREP COOKBOOK

THE ULTIMATE GUIDE
TO HEALTHY AND CONVENIENT MEAL PREP

Index

INTRODUCTION

Welcome to Stealth Health

Welcome to the world of Stealth Health, where eating healthy becomes simple and delicious, without compromising on taste or time. You are about to embark on a culinary journey that will revolutionize the way you think about meal prepping, making it an art accessible to everyone, regardless of your cooking skill level.

Why "Stealth Health"?

Our unique approach, "Stealth Health," is built on a fundamental concept: making health an integrated and almost invisible part of your daily routine. Many of us want to eat healthily, but we often face obstacles like lack of time, perceived high costs, and the fear of losing flavor in our favorite dishes. Stealth Health was created to overcome these barriers.

With this book, you'll discover how to integrate nutritious ingredients and healthy cooking techniques into your everyday recipes, without sacrificing flavor or convenience. Whether you aim to lose weight, build muscle, or simply maintain a healthy lifestyle, you'll find the answers and inspiration you need right here.

The Goals of This Book

1. **Ease and Convenience**: Our recipes are designed to be easy to follow, with clear instructions and common ingredients. Each recipe is crafted to optimize your time in the kitchen, allowing you to prepare healthy meals without stress.
2. **Nutritional Balance**: Every dish is balanced to provide an optimal combination of proteins, complex carbohydrates, and healthy fats, along with a generous portion of vegetables. Detailed nutritional information helps you monitor calorie intake and macronutrients.
3. **Variety and Creativity**: We offer a wide range of recipes for breakfasts, lunches, dinners, snacks, and desserts, ensuring you never get bored and always find something new and interesting to try.
4. **Adaptability**: We understand that everyone has different dietary needs. Therefore, many of our recipes include variations for vegetarian, vegan, gluten-free, and low-carb options. You'll find tips on how to customize recipes to meet your specific needs.
5. **Strategic Meal Plans**: We don't just provide recipes; we also help you plan your weekly meals with detailed guides. Our meal plans will save you time and money, reduce food waste, and ensure you always have healthy, tasty meals on hand.

How to Use This Book

The "Stealth Health Meal Prep Cookbook" is structured to guide you step-by-step into the world of meal prepping. Each chapter is designed to provide practical tools and delicious recipes that will accompany you throughout your day. Start with the initial sections to understand the fundamental principles of meal prep and meal planning. Then, explore the various categories of recipes, all accompanied by enticing photographs and detailed nutritional information.

A Fusion of Health and Flavor

Health and flavor do not have to be in conflict. In this book, you will learn to combine them harmoniously, discovering that eating healthy can be just as gratifying and delicious as indulging in your favorite dishes. Through simple techniques and natural ingredients, you'll prepare meals that nourish your body and delight your taste buds.

Join the Stealth Health Journey

As you embark on this journey, you will find that healthy eating can seamlessly fit into your lifestyle. The recipes and meal plans in this book are designed to make meal prepping easy, enjoyable, and effective. Let's get ready to transform the way we cook and live, one healthy meal at a time.

The Benefits of Meal Prep

Meal prepping has become a cornerstone of healthy living for many, and for good reason. By dedicating a few hours each week to preparing your meals in advance, you can reap numerous benefits that make a positive impact on your health, wallet, and overall well-being. Let's explore the key advantages of meal prep and how they align perfectly with the Stealth Health philosophy.

1. Time-Saving Efficiency

One of the most significant benefits of meal prep is the time it saves. Instead of cooking every day, you can prepare multiple meals in one go. This means fewer evenings spent in the kitchen and more time for yourself, your family, and your hobbies. By planning and preparing your meals in advance, you can streamline your weeknight dinners, pack your lunches effortlessly, and even have breakfast ready to go each morning.

The recipes and meal plans in this cookbook are designed for efficiency. We provide step-by-step guides to help you batch-cook and store your meals properly, ensuring you maximize your time without compromising on quality or taste.

2. Healthier Eating Habits

Meal prep puts you in control of your nutrition. By planning your meals, you can ensure that each dish is balanced and aligns with your dietary goals. Whether you're aiming to lose weight, build muscle, or simply maintain a healthy diet, meal prep helps you avoid the pitfalls of last-minute unhealthy choices.

Each recipe is crafted with nutrition in mind, offering balanced portions of protein, carbohydrates, and healthy fats. We also provide nutritional information for each recipe, so you can keep track of your intake and make informed choices.

3. Cost-Effective Solutions

Eating out and ordering takeout can quickly add up. Meal prepping allows you to buy ingredients in bulk, reducing your overall food costs. Plus, having your meals ready means you're less likely to spend money on spontaneous, and often expensive, dining options.

Our shopping tips and meal plans are designed to be budget-friendly. We focus on using common, affordable ingredients and provide strategies for making the most out of your grocery budget. You'll find that eating healthy doesn't have to be costly.

4. Reducing Food Waste

When you plan your meals and shop with a list, you're less likely to buy unnecessary items that end up going to waste. Meal prepping encourages you to use all the ingredients you purchase, leading to less food waste and a more sustainable kitchen.

We emphasize the importance of smart shopping and offer tips on how to repurpose leftovers creatively. You'll learn how to store your food properly to extend its shelf life and reduce waste.

5. Stress Reduction

Knowing what you're going to eat every day takes the guesswork out of mealtime. Meal prep eliminates the daily stress of deciding what to cook, making your life more organized and less hectic. With a well-thought-out plan, you can approach each day with confidence and calm.

Our meal prep plans are designed to provide structure and simplicity. By following our guides, you can reduce daily mealtime stress and focus on enjoying your food and your time.

6. Portion Control

Meal prepping allows you to control your portions more effectively. This is particularly beneficial if you're working towards specific health goals, such as weight loss or muscle gain. By pre-portioning your meals, you can avoid overeating and ensure you're consuming the right amount of nutrients.

Each recipe includes portion sizes and nutritional breakdowns, helping you to portion your meals correctly and stay on track with your dietary goals.

7. Culinary Variety

Contrary to the belief that meal prep is monotonous, it actually encourages culinary creativity. By prepping different ingredients, you can mix and match to create a variety of meals throughout the week. This keeps your diet interesting and enjoyable.

We provide a diverse range of recipes that cater to different tastes and dietary preferences. From quick breakfast options to elaborate dinners, you'll find a variety of delicious and nutritious meals that keep your palate excited.

Understanding the benefits of meal prep is the first step towards embracing a healthier lifestyle. In the following sections, we'll guide you through the basics of getting started with meal prep, including essential tools, planning strategies, and shopping tips. You'll learn how to streamline your kitchen routine and set yourself up for success with our comprehensive meal prep plans and delicious recipes.

Embrace the benefits of meal prep and start your journey to a healthier, more organized, and enjoyable way of eating with Stealth Health.

How to Use This Cookbook

Whether you are a seasoned meal prepper or a beginner looking to streamline your kitchen routine, this cookbook is designed to guide you every step of the way. Here's how to make the most out of this resource and fully embrace the benefits of meal prepping.

Structure of the Cookbook

This cookbook is organized into several key sections, each tailored to different aspects of meal prepping and healthy eating. Here's a quick overview:

1. **Introduction**
   - Overview of the meal prep concept and its benefits.
   - Essential tools and equipment for successful meal prep.
2. **Getting Started with Meal Prep**
   - Basics of meal planning and preparation.
   - Shopping tips and food storage guidelines.
3. **Recipe Sections**
   - Breakfast Boosters: Quick and nutritious options to start your day.
   - Lunches on the Go: Convenient meals for busy days.
   - Dinners Made Easy: Simple yet satisfying dinner recipes.
   - Snack Smart: Healthy snacks to keep you energized.
   - Desserts without the Guilt: Sweet treats that are healthy and delicious.
   - Batch Cooking Basics: Recipes that form the foundation of multiple meals.
   - Special Diets and Preferences: Vegetarian, vegan, gluten-free, and more.
4. **Meal Prep Plans**
   - Step-by-step guides for weekly meal prep.
   - Customizable templates to fit your schedule and dietary goals.
5. **Nutritional Information**
   - Detailed breakdowns for each recipe.
   - Tips on understanding and tracking your nutritional intake.

Navigating the Recipes

Each recipe in this book is designed to be easy to follow and packed with flavor. Here's how to navigate the recipe sections effectively:

- **Ingredients List**: The ingredients are listed in the order of use. Make sure to read through the list before starting to ensure you have everything you need.
- **Step-by-Step Instructions**: Each recipe includes clear and concise instructions. Follow them sequentially for the best results.
- **Nutritional Information**: At the end of each recipe, you'll find a detailed nutritional breakdown, helping you to track your intake and make informed decisions.

- **Tips and Variations**: Look out for additional tips and variations at the bottom of the recipes. These suggestions offer ways to customize the dish to your taste or dietary needs.

Utilizing Meal Prep Plans

Our meal prep plans are designed to simplify your weekly cooking routine. Here's how to make the most of them:

- **Beginner to Advanced Plans**: Start with the beginner plans if you're new to meal prepping and gradually move to more advanced plans as you become comfortable.
- **Flexible and Customizable**: The plans are flexible. Feel free to mix and match recipes according to your preferences and dietary needs.
- **Shopping Lists**: Each plan comes with a comprehensive shopping list to streamline your grocery trips.
- **Batch Cooking Tips**: Learn how to efficiently prepare multiple meals in one go, saving time and reducing kitchen stress.

Essential Tools and Equipment

To make meal prepping as smooth as possible, having the right tools and equipment is essential. Here's what you'll need:

- **Containers**: Invest in high-quality, airtight containers of various sizes for storing your meals. Glass containers are ideal as they are durable and microwave-safe.
- **Cooking Tools**: Basic kitchen tools such as sharp knives, cutting boards, measuring cups, and spoons are a must.
- **Appliances**: Useful appliances include a slow cooker, instant pot, blender, and food processor. These can greatly speed up your meal prep process.
- **Labels and Markers**: Use labels and markers to date and identify your prepped meals, ensuring nothing goes to waste.

Tips for Success

- **Plan Ahead**: Take a few minutes each week to plan your meals and make a shopping list. This will save you time and reduce stress during the week.
- **Stay Organized**: Keep your kitchen organized and maintain a clean workspace. This makes the meal prep process more enjoyable and efficient.
- **Be Flexible**: Life can be unpredictable, so allow yourself some flexibility. It's okay to adjust your meal prep plans as needed.
- **Enjoy the Process**: Meal prepping is not just about the end result; it's about enjoying the process of creating nourishing meals for yourself and your loved ones.

Embracing Stealth Health

Using this cookbook is about more than just following recipes; it's about adopting a lifestyle that prioritizes health and convenience. Each section is designed to build on the previous one, gradually enhancing your meal prep skills and knowledge. By the end of this book, you'll not only have a repertoire of delicious recipes but also the confidence and tools to maintain a healthy, balanced diet effortlessly.

Dive into the Stealth Health Meal Prep Cookbook and start transforming your approach to cooking and eating today.

Essential Tools and Equipment

Having the right tools and equipment is crucial for effective and enjoyable meal prepping. With the right gear, you can streamline your process, reduce preparation time, and ensure your meals are stored safely and remain fresh throughout the week. In this section, we'll cover the essential tools and equipment that will help you become a meal prep pro.

1. Storage Containers

Investing in high-quality storage containers is perhaps the most important step in meal prepping. Here are some key types you should consider:

- **Glass Containers**: These are durable, microwave-safe, and do not retain odors or stains. They are perfect for storing a variety of foods and can be used for both cooking and reheating.
- **Plastic Containers**: Look for BPA-free options. These are lightweight and convenient for on-the-go meals.
- **Mason Jars**: Ideal for salads and parfaits, mason jars help keep ingredients fresh and are great for portion control.
- **Silicone Bags**: These reusable bags are excellent for storing snacks, fruits, and liquids. They are flexible, space-saving, and eco-friendly.

2. Cooking Tools

A well-equipped kitchen makes meal prep easier and more efficient. Ensure you have the following basic tools:

- **Sharp Knives**: A good set of sharp knives, including a chef's knife, paring knife, and serrated knife, is essential for chopping, slicing, and dicing.
- **Cutting Boards**: Have separate boards for vegetables, meats, and fruits to avoid cross-contamination. Opt for sturdy, non-slip boards.
- **Measuring Cups and Spoons**: Accurate measurements are key to recipe success. Invest in a good set of measuring cups and spoons.
- **Mixing Bowls**: A variety of mixing bowls in different sizes is useful for preparing ingredients and mixing recipes.
- **Wooden Spoons and Spatulas**: These tools are gentle on cookware and are versatile for stirring, mixing, and serving.
- **Tongs**: Useful for flipping and serving food, tongs are a must-have in any kitchen.

3. Small Appliances

Certain appliances can significantly speed up your meal prep process and expand your cooking options:

- **Slow Cooker**: Ideal for set-it-and-forget-it recipes, a slow cooker allows you to prepare large batches of stews, soups, and roasts with minimal effort.
- **Instant Pot**: This multifunctional appliance can pressure cook, slow cook, steam, sauté, and more, making it a versatile tool for quick and efficient meal prep.
- **Blender**: A high-powered blender is perfect for smoothies, soups, sauces, and even batters.
- **Food Processor**: Great for chopping, slicing, grating, and pureeing, a food processor can save you a lot of time in the kitchen.
- **Rice Cooker**: Simplifies the process of cooking rice and grains, ensuring they turn out perfectly every time.

4. Bakeware and Cookware

Quality bakeware and cookware are essential for preparing a variety of meals:

- **Sheet Pans**: Perfect for roasting vegetables, baking sheet pan meals, and making snacks like granola.
- **Baking Dishes**: Glass or ceramic baking dishes are great for casseroles, lasagnas, and baked desserts.
- **Non-Stick Pans**: These are ideal for cooking eggs, pancakes, and other foods that tend to stick.
- **Dutch Oven**: A versatile pot that can be used on the stovetop or in the oven for soups, stews, and braised dishes.

5. Miscellaneous Tools

These additional tools can further enhance your meal prep efficiency and food storage:

- **Labels and Markers**: Use labels to date and identify your prepped meals, which helps in keeping track of freshness and contents.
- **Digital Kitchen Scale**: For precise measurements, especially useful if you're tracking your macros or portion sizes.
- **Salad Spinner**: Quickly dries your greens, making them ready to store and ensuring they stay fresh longer.
- **Mandoline Slicer**: Helps in slicing vegetables quickly and uniformly, perfect for salads and stir-fries.

Tips for Organizing Your Kitchen

- **Designate Specific Areas**: Assign specific areas in your kitchen for meal prep activities. Have a dedicated space for chopping, mixing, and assembling.
- **Keep Tools Accessible**: Store frequently used tools and equipment within easy reach to streamline your prep process.
- **Maintain a Clean Workspace**: Clean as you go to keep your kitchen organized and efficient. This reduces clutter and makes the meal prep process more enjoyable.

Bringing It All Together

With the right tools and equipment, meal prepping becomes a seamless and efficient process. The investment you make in these essential items will pay off in time saved, stress reduced, and meals that are both delicious and nutritious. As you proceed through this cookbook, you'll see how these tools come into play in various recipes and meal prep plans, making your journey towards Stealth Health smooth and enjoyable.

Meal Prep 101: Basics and Benefits

Welcome to Meal Prep 101! If you're new to meal prepping or looking to refine your skills, this section will provide you with a solid foundation. We'll cover the basics of meal prep, highlight its numerous benefits, and set you up for success. By the end of this chapter, you'll be ready to dive into the practical aspects of planning, shopping, and preparing your meals with confidence.

What is Meal Prep?

Meal prepping involves preparing meals or meal components in advance, making it easier to enjoy nutritious, home-cooked food throughout the week. This approach can vary from preparing full meals ahead of time to simply prepping ingredients that can be quickly assembled later. The goal is to save time, reduce stress, and ensure that you always have healthy options available.

The Basics of Meal Prep

1. **Planning Your Meals**:
   - **Assess Your Schedule**: Start by looking at your week ahead. Identify busy days when you'll need quick meals and days when you might have more time to cook.
   - **Choose Your Recipes**: Select recipes that fit your schedule and dietary goals. Aim for a balance of proteins, carbs, and fats, and include plenty of vegetables.
   - **Create a Meal Plan**: Outline your meals for the week, including breakfast, lunch, dinner, and snacks. Write down your plan to keep yourself organized.
2. **Shopping Smart**:
   - **Make a Shopping List**: Based on your meal plan, create a comprehensive shopping list. Group items by category (produce, dairy, meats, etc.) to make your shopping trip more efficient.
   - **Shop in Bulk**: Buy ingredients in bulk when possible, especially pantry staples like grains, beans, and nuts. This saves money and ensures you always have essential items on hand.
   - **Choose Fresh and Seasonal**: Opt for fresh, seasonal produce. It's often more affordable and nutritious.
3. **Preparing Your Ingredients**:
   - **Batch Cooking**: Cook large batches of staples like grains, proteins, and vegetables. These can be mixed and matched throughout the week to create different meals.
   - **Pre-Cutting and Pre-Washing**: Wash and cut vegetables in advance. Store them in airtight containers to maintain freshness.
   - **Portioning**: Use your storage containers to portion out meals and snacks. This helps with portion control and makes it easy to grab meals on the go.

The Benefits of Meal Prep

1. **Time-Saving**:

- o **Efficiency**: Spend a few hours once or twice a week prepping your meals, and save time each day. This frees up your schedule for other activities.
- o **Quick Meals**: Having prepped ingredients or ready-made meals means you can have a nutritious meal on the table in minutes, even on the busiest days.

2. **Healthier Eating**:
   - o **Control Over Ingredients**: By preparing your meals, you control what goes into your food. This allows you to avoid processed ingredients and focus on whole, nutrient-dense foods.
   - o **Balanced Nutrition**: Prepping meals in advance helps ensure your diet is balanced and varied. You can plan to include a mix of proteins, healthy fats, and complex carbohydrates in each meal.

3. **Cost-Effective**:
   - o **Reduce Takeout**: By having meals ready, you're less likely to order takeout or dine out, which can be expensive and less healthy.
   - o **Bulk Purchasing**: Buying ingredients in bulk and in season can save money. Meal prepping also reduces food waste as you plan exactly what you need.

4. **Stress Reduction**:
   - o **Eliminate Last-Minute Decisions**: With meals planned and prepped, you eliminate the daily stress of deciding what to cook.
   - o **Consistent Routine**: Establishing a meal prep routine brings consistency and structure to your week, reducing anxiety around mealtime.

5. **Better Portion Control**:
   - o **Manage Intake**: Pre-portioned meals help you manage your food intake, which is particularly beneficial for those with specific dietary goals such as weight loss or muscle gain.
   - o **Nutritional Tracking**: Having meals planned and portioned makes it easier to track your nutritional intake, ensuring you meet your dietary needs.

Steps to Successful Meal Prep

1. **Start Small**: If you're new to meal prepping, start with prepping a few meals or snacks. Gradually increase as you become more comfortable.
2. **Stay Organized**: Keep your kitchen, pantry, and fridge organized. This makes meal prep more efficient and enjoyable.
3. **Be Flexible**: Allow some flexibility in your meal plan. Life happens, and it's okay to adjust your plan as needed.
4. **Keep It Fun**: Try new recipes and experiment with different ingredients to keep your meals exciting.

Meal prepping is a powerful tool that can transform your eating habits and simplify your life. As you progress through this cookbook, you'll find detailed guides, practical tips, and delicious recipes that will make meal prepping an integral and enjoyable part of your routine. Let's get started on your journey to healthier, more efficient cooking with Stealth Health!

Planning Your Meals

Effective meal planning is the cornerstone of successful meal prepping. By taking the time to plan your meals, you can save time, reduce stress, and ensure a balanced and nutritious diet. This section will guide you through the essential steps of meal planning, providing practical tips and strategies to help you create a meal plan that fits your lifestyle and dietary goals.

Assess Your Schedule

The first step in planning your meals is to assess your weekly schedule. Consider the following:

- **Identify Busy Days**: Note the days when you are likely to be busiest. These are the days when you'll benefit most from having pre-prepared meals.
- **Consider Meal Types**: Think about the types of meals you need. Do you need quick breakfasts, portable lunches, or easy-to-assemble dinners?
- **Allocate Time for Prep**: Choose one or two days during the week when you have some free time to dedicate to meal prep. Many people find Sunday and Wednesday work well.

Set Your Dietary Goals

Before you start planning specific meals, it's important to set your dietary goals. These might include:

- **Weight Loss**: Focus on calorie control and balanced nutrition. Plan meals that are low in unhealthy fats and sugars but high in fiber and protein.
- **Muscle Building**: Prioritize protein-rich meals and include complex carbohydrates and healthy fats.
- **Maintenance and General Health**: Aim for a variety of foods that provide all essential nutrients. Ensure each meal includes a mix of proteins, carbs, and fats.

Choose Your Recipes

With your schedule and dietary goals in mind, it's time to choose your recipes. Here's how to do it:

- **Diverse Selection**: Select a mix of recipes to keep your meals interesting. Include different proteins (chicken, beef, fish, tofu), vegetables, grains, and legumes.
- **Batch-Friendly Recipes**: Opt for recipes that can be easily scaled up to make multiple servings. Casseroles, soups, stews, and grain bowls are great options.
- **Balance and Variety**: Ensure your meal plan includes a balance of macronutrients and a variety of foods to cover all your nutritional bases. Rotate different cuisines and ingredients to avoid monotony.

Create a Meal Plan Template

A meal plan template is a useful tool to keep you organized. Here's how to create and use one:

- **Weekly Layout**: Divide your template into days of the week and meals (breakfast, lunch, dinner, snacks).

- **Recipe Assignments**: Fill in the template with your chosen recipes. Make sure to plan for leftovers and consider incorporating them into different meals to minimize waste.
- **Flexibility**: Allow some flexibility in your plan. Life can be unpredictable, so it's helpful to have a few backup options like quick-cook meals or healthy frozen dinners.

Develop a Shopping List

A well-organized shopping list is crucial for efficient grocery shopping. Here's how to create one:

- **Categorize Items**: Group your list by categories (produce, dairy, meat, pantry staples, etc.). This makes your shopping trip quicker and more organized.
- **Check Your Inventory**: Before heading to the store, check what you already have at home. This prevents buying duplicates and helps you use up what's on hand.
- **Stick to the List**: Avoid impulse buys by sticking to your list. This not only keeps you on budget but also ensures you only buy what you need.

Tips for Effective Meal Planning

1. **Start Simple**: If you're new to meal planning, start with a few days at a time. Gradually work your way up to planning for a full week.
2. **Incorporate Leftovers**: Plan to use leftovers creatively. For example, roasted chicken from dinner can be used in salads or wraps for lunch the next day.
3. **Prep Ingredients**: Sometimes, it's easier to prep ingredients rather than full meals. Wash and chop vegetables, cook grains, and portion out snacks in advance.
4. **Stay Flexible**: Life happens, and plans change. Be flexible and adjust your meal plan as needed. Having a few quick and easy recipes on hand can be a lifesaver.
5. **Enjoy the Process**: Make meal planning a fun and enjoyable process. Involve your family or roommates in planning and prepping. Experiment with new recipes and cuisines to keep things exciting.

Planning your meals is a proactive step towards a healthier, more organized lifestyle. By dedicating a little time each week to planning, you can save hours in the kitchen, reduce stress, and ensure you're eating nutritious, balanced meals. As you move forward, the strategies and recipes in this book will guide you in creating meal plans that work for you, making meal prep a seamless and rewarding part of your routine.

Shopping Smart: Tips and Tricks

Shopping smart is an essential component of effective meal prep. By mastering the art of grocery shopping, you can save time, reduce costs, and ensure you have all the ingredients you need for a week of healthy, delicious meals. In this section, we'll cover practical tips and tricks to help you shop efficiently and strategically.

Create a Comprehensive Shopping List

A well-organized shopping list is your roadmap to a successful grocery trip. Here's how to create one that works:

1. **Use Categories**: Divide your list into categories such as produce, dairy, meats, grains, and pantry staples. This helps you navigate the store more efficiently and ensures you don't miss anything.
2. **Check Inventory**: Before you head to the store, take a quick inventory of what you already have at home. This prevents overbuying and helps you use up existing items.
3. **Stick to the List**: Once you're at the store, stick to your list to avoid impulse purchases. This not only keeps you on budget but also ensures you're buying what you need for your meal plan.

Shop Seasonally and Locally

Buying seasonal and local produce has several benefits:

1. **Cost-Effective**: Seasonal produce is often cheaper because it's more abundant. Local farmers' markets can offer great deals on fresh, seasonal items.
2. **Nutrient-Rich**: Fruits and vegetables are most nutritious when they are in season and haven't traveled long distances.
3. **Support Local Economy**: Purchasing from local farmers supports your community and promotes sustainable agriculture.

Buy in Bulk

Certain items are more cost-effective when bought in bulk. Consider the following:

1. **Pantry Staples**: Items like rice, quinoa, beans, lentils, nuts, and seeds are great to buy in bulk. They have a long shelf life and can be used in various recipes.
2. **Meat and Poultry**: Buying larger quantities of meat and poultry can save money. Portion and freeze them for future use.
3. **Spices and Herbs**: Spices and dried herbs are often cheaper when bought in larger quantities. Store them properly to maintain freshness.

Take Advantage of Sales and Discounts

Maximize your savings by taking advantage of sales and discounts:

1. **Weekly Flyers**: Check store flyers and online promotions for weekly deals. Plan your meals around what's on sale.
2. **Loyalty Programs**: Join store loyalty programs to earn points, receive member discounts, and access special promotions.
3. **Coupons**: Use coupons for additional savings. Many stores offer digital coupons that can be easily added to your account.

Choose Generic Brands

Generic or store brands often offer the same quality as name brands but at a lower price. Compare labels and ingredients to ensure you're getting a good product.

Reduce Food Waste

Minimize food waste by being mindful of what you buy and how you store it:

1. **Buy What You Need**: Avoid buying perishable items in bulk unless you're sure you can use them before they spoil.
2. **Proper Storage**: Store fruits and vegetables correctly to extend their shelf life. Use airtight containers and freezer bags to keep ingredients fresh.
3. **Repurpose Leftovers**: Plan to use leftovers creatively. Yesterday's roasted vegetables can become today's salad topping or stir-fry ingredient.

Stock Up on Essentials

Having a well-stocked pantry ensures you always have the basics on hand. Here are some essentials to keep:

1. **Grains and Legumes**: Rice, quinoa, pasta, oats, lentils, and beans.
2. **Canned Goods**: Tomatoes, beans, coconut milk, broth, and tuna.
3. **Spices and Condiments**: Salt, pepper, garlic powder, onion powder, olive oil, vinegar, soy sauce, and hot sauce.
4. **Baking Supplies**: Flour, sugar, baking powder, baking soda, and cocoa powder.
5. **Frozen Foods**: Vegetables, fruits, and meats that you can use in a pinch.

Plan for Flexibility

While it's great to have a detailed shopping list, it's also important to stay flexible:

1. **Substitute Ingredients**: If an item on your list is unavailable or too expensive, be prepared to substitute it with a similar ingredient.
2. **Adjust Quantities**: If you find a great deal on a particular item, consider buying extra and adjusting your meal plan to incorporate it.

Utilize Technology

Make your shopping experience even smoother with technology:

1. **Shopping Apps**: Use grocery apps to create and organize your shopping list, find coupons, and track your budget.
2. **Online Shopping**: Many stores offer online shopping and delivery services. This can save time and help you avoid impulse buys.
3. **Meal Planning Tools**: Digital meal planning tools can help you create a shopping list directly from your meal plan, ensuring you don't forget any ingredients.

Shopping smart is about planning ahead, staying organized, and making strategic choices that align with your meal prep goals. By following these tips and tricks, you can make your grocery shopping trips more efficient, cost-effective, and enjoyable. With your ingredients in hand, you'll be well-prepared to dive into the meal prep process, creating healthy and delicious meals for the week ahead. Happy shopping!

Food Safety and Storage Guidelines

Ensuring food safety and proper storage is crucial for maintaining the quality and longevity of your meal preps. By following these guidelines, you can prevent foodborne illnesses, reduce waste, and keep your meals fresh and nutritious. This section covers essential tips and best practices for food safety and storage, from handling ingredients to storing finished meals.

Handling Ingredients Safely

Proper handling of ingredients from the moment you purchase them to the time you store them can prevent contamination and spoilage:

1. **Cleanliness**: Always wash your hands with soap and water before handling food. Clean and sanitize countertops, cutting boards, and utensils before and after use.
2. **Separate Raw and Cooked Foods**: Avoid cross-contamination by using separate cutting boards and utensils for raw meats, poultry, and seafood. Keep raw foods away from cooked foods and ready-to-eat items.
3. **Rinse Produce**: Wash fruits and vegetables under running water before cutting or cooking. This removes dirt, bacteria, and potential pesticides.

Cooking Temperatures

Cooking food to the right temperature is vital for killing harmful bacteria. Use a food thermometer to ensure your food reaches the safe internal temperature:

1. **Poultry**: 165°F (74°C)
2. **Ground Meats**: 160°F (71°C)
3. **Beef, Pork, Lamb, and Veal (steaks, chops, and roasts)**: 145°F (63°C) with a 3-minute rest time
4. **Fish and Shellfish**: 145°F (63°C)
5. **Leftovers and Casseroles**: 165°F (74°C)

Cooling and Storing Food

Proper cooling and storage are key to maintaining the safety and quality of your meals:

1. **Cool Quickly**: To prevent bacterial growth, cool cooked food quickly. Divide large portions into smaller, shallow containers to speed up cooling. Place them in the refrigerator or freezer within two hours of cooking.
2. **Refrigeration**: Store perishable foods in the refrigerator at or below 40°F (4°C). This includes cooked meats, dairy products, and cut fruits and vegetables.
3. **Freezing**: Freeze foods at 0°F (-18°C) or lower. This is ideal for preserving meats, cooked grains, and prepared meals for longer periods.
4. **Labeling**: Label containers with the date and contents to keep track of when you prepared and stored the food. This helps you use the oldest items first and reduces waste.

Storage Duration

Knowing how long different foods can be safely stored helps in planning your meal preps:

1. **Refrigerated Foods**:
   - o Cooked poultry, meat, and fish: 3-4 days
   - o Cooked vegetables and grains: 3-5 days
   - o Soups and stews: 3-4 days
2. **Frozen Foods**:
   - o Cooked poultry, meat, and fish: 2-6 months
   - o Cooked vegetables and grains: 2-3 months
   - o Soups and stews: 2-3 months

Reheating Guidelines

Reheating food properly ensures it is safe to eat and retains its quality:

1. **Reheat Thoroughly**: Reheat leftovers to an internal temperature of 165°F (74°C). Use a food thermometer to check.
2. **Microwave Safety**: When reheating in the microwave, cover food with a microwave-safe lid or wrap to retain moisture and ensure even heating. Stir and rotate food halfway through cooking.
3. **Avoid Repeated Reheating**: Only reheat the portion you plan to eat. Repeated reheating can degrade food quality and safety.

Best Practices for Different Food Types

Different food types have specific storage needs to maintain their freshness and safety:

1. **Dairy Products**: Store dairy products like milk, cheese, and yogurt in the coldest part of the refrigerator. Keep them sealed to prevent exposure to air and bacteria.
2. **Meat and Poultry**: Store raw meat and poultry on the bottom shelf of the refrigerator to prevent their juices from dripping onto other foods. Keep them in their original packaging until use.
3. **Fruits and Vegetables**: Store fruits and vegetables separately. Some fruits produce ethylene gas, which can cause vegetables to spoil faster. Use perforated bags or containers to maintain humidity levels.
4. **Grains and Legumes**: Store dry grains and legumes in airtight containers in a cool, dark place. Cooked grains can be refrigerated for up to a week or frozen for several months.

Maintaining Kitchen Hygiene

A clean kitchen is essential for food safety. Here are some tips to keep your kitchen hygienic:

1. **Regular Cleaning**: Clean your kitchen surfaces, utensils, and appliances regularly with hot, soapy water. Disinfect areas that come into contact with raw foods.
2. **Dishwashing**: Wash dishes, pots, and pans promptly after use. Avoid leaving dirty dishes in the sink for extended periods.
3. **Trash Management**: Empty trash bins regularly and keep them covered to prevent attracting pests and spreading bacteria.

By following these food safety and storage guidelines, you can ensure that your meal preps are not only convenient and nutritious but also safe to eat. Proper handling, cooking, cooling, and storing practices are essential components of meal prepping that contribute to your overall health and well-being. With these practices in place, you can confidently enjoy the meals you've prepared, knowing they are fresh, safe, and delicious.

Energizing Smoothies and Bowls

Starting your day with a nutritious breakfast is essential for maintaining energy levels, focus, and overall well-being. Energizing smoothies and bowls are perfect breakfast options that provide a balanced mix of nutrients, giving you the boost you need to tackle your daily tasks. This section will introduce you to the benefits of smoothies and bowls, provide tips for creating the perfect blend, and offer a variety of recipes to get you started.

Introduction to Energizing Smoothies and Bowls

Smoothies and bowls are versatile, quick to prepare, and packed with nutrients. Whether you prefer a refreshing smoothie to sip on the go or a hearty bowl to savor at home, these breakfast boosters can be customized to fit your taste preferences and dietary needs.

Benefits of Smoothies and Bowls

1. **Nutrient-Dense**: Smoothies and bowls are an excellent way to pack a lot of nutrients into a single meal. By blending or mixing various fruits, vegetables, and superfoods, you get a concentrated dose of vitamins, minerals, and antioxidants.
2. **Convenience**: They are quick to prepare, making them an ideal choice for busy mornings. Most recipes can be made in under 10 minutes, and you can even prep ingredients the night before to save more time.
3. **Versatility**: The combinations are endless. You can tailor your smoothies and bowls to your taste preferences and dietary needs. Whether you prefer a green smoothie for detox or a protein-packed bowl for muscle recovery, there's a recipe for everyone.
4. **Hydration**: Many smoothie and bowl recipes include a liquid base such as water, coconut water, or almond milk, which helps keep you hydrated.
5. **Digestive Health**: Including ingredients like yogurt, kefir, chia seeds, and flaxseeds can aid digestion and promote gut health.

Tips for Making the Perfect Smoothie or Bowl

1. **Balance Your Ingredients**: Aim for a balance of fruits, vegetables, protein, and healthy fats. This ensures you get a well-rounded meal that keeps you full and energized.
2. **Choose a Liquid Base**: Depending on your preference, you can use water, milk (dairy or plant-based), coconut water, or juice. The liquid base helps blend the ingredients smoothly and adds to the nutritional value.
3. **Add Protein**: Incorporate protein sources like Greek yogurt, protein powder, or nut butter to make your smoothie or bowl more satisfying and to support muscle maintenance and growth.
4. **Incorporate Healthy Fats**: Healthy fats from sources like avocado, nuts, and seeds provide sustained energy and help absorb fat-soluble vitamins.
5. **Boost with Superfoods**: Enhance the nutritional profile by adding superfoods like chia seeds, flaxseeds, spirulina, maca powder, or acai berries.
6. **Texture and Toppings**: For smoothie bowls, aim for a thicker consistency that can hold up toppings. Add a variety of textures with toppings like granola, fresh fruit, nuts, seeds, and coconut flakes.

GREEN ENERGY SMOOTHIE

PREP TIME
5 MINUTES

COOK TIME
0 MINUTES

DIFFICULTY

SE4VES
1

INGREDIENTS

- 1 cup spinach
- 1 frozen banana
- 1/2 cup pineapple chunks
- 1/2 avocado
- 1 cup coconut water
- 1 tablespoon chia seeds

INSTRUCTIONS

1. Combine all ingredients in a blender.
2. Blend until smooth.
3. Pour into a glass and enjoy immediately.

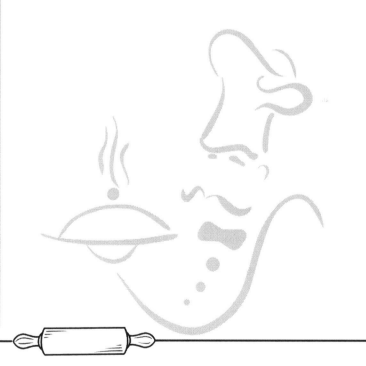

Nutritional Information (per serving):

CALORIES: 250	PROTEIN: 4G	CARBOHYDRATES: 38G	FIBER: 10G	SUGARS: 18G	FAT: 11G	SATURATED FAT: 1.5G
SODIUM: 60MG	POTASSIUM: 960MG	VITAMIN A: 150% DV	VITAMIN C: 120% DV	CALCIUM: 10% DV	IRON: 15% DV	

BERRY PROTEIN SMOOTHIE BOWL

PREP TIME
10 MINUTES

COOK TIME
0 MINUTES

DIFFICULTY

SE4VES
1

INGREDIENTS

- 1 cup frozen mixed berries
- 1/2 cup Greek yogurt
- 1 scoop vanilla protein powder
- 1/2 cup almond milk
- 1 tablespoon almond butter

Toppings:
- Fresh berries
- Granola
- Chia seeds
- Sliced almonds

INSTRUCTIONS

1. Combine the frozen berries, Greek yogurt, protein powder, almond milk, and almond butter in a blender.
2. Blend until thick and smooth.
3. Pour into a bowl.
4. Top with fresh berries, granola, chia seeds, and sliced almonds.
5. Serve immediately with a spoon.

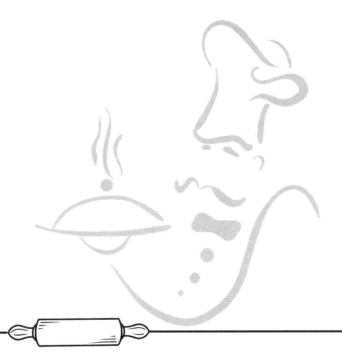

Nutritional Information (per serving):

CALORIES: 400	PROTEIN: 28G	CARBOHYDRATES: 45G	FIBER: 12G	SUGARS: 22G	FAT: 15G	SATURATED FAT: 2G
SODIUM: 150MG	POTASSIUM: 700MG	VITAMIN A: 10% DV	VITAMIN C: 50% DV	CALCIUM: 30% DV	IRON: 15% DV	

TROPICAL SUNSHINE SMOOTHIE

ENERGIZING SMOOTHIES AND BOWLS

PREP TIME
5 MINUTES

COOK TIME
0 MINUTES

DIFFICULTY

SE4VES
1

INGREDIENTS

- 1 cup mango chunks
- 1/2 cup pineapple chunks
- 1/2 banana
- 1 cup orange juice
- 1/2 cup Greek yogurt
- 1 tablespoon flaxseeds

INSTRUCTIONS

1. Combine all ingredients in a blender.
2. Blend until smooth.
3. Pour into a glass and enjoy immediately.

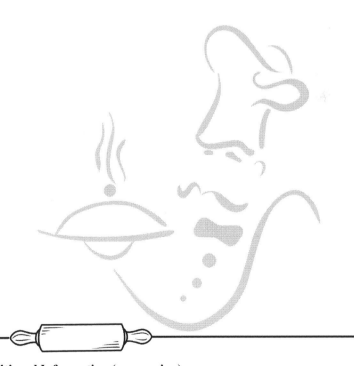

Nutritional Information (per serving):

CALORIES: 300	PROTEIN: 9G	CARBOHYDRATES: 60G	FIBER: 8G	SUGARS: 45G	FAT: 5G	SATURATED FAT: 0.5G
SODIUM: 50MG	POTASSIUM: 900MG	VITAMIN A: 80% DV	VITAMIN C: 220% DV	CALCIUM: 20% DV	IRON: 8% DV	

CHOCOLATE PEANUT BUTTER SMOOTHIE BOWL

ENERGIZING SMOOTHIES AND BOWLS

PREP TIME
10 MINUTES

COOK TIME
0 MINUTES

DIFFICULTY

SE4VES
1

INGREDIENTS

- 1 frozen banana
- 1/2 cup Greek yogurt
- 1 tablespoon cocoa powder
- 1 tablespoon peanut butter
- 1/2 cup almond milk
- 1 scoop chocolate protein powder

Toppings:
- Sliced banana
- Cacao nibs
- Chopped peanuts
- Shredded coconut

INSTRUCTIONS

1. Combine the frozen banana, Greek yogurt, cocoa powder, peanut butter, almond milk, and protein powder in a blender.
2. Blend until thick and smooth.
3. Pour into a bowl.
4. Top with sliced banana, cacao nibs, chopped peanuts, and shredded coconut.
5. Serve immediately with a spoon.

Nutritional Information (per serving):

CALORIES: 450	PROTEIN: 30G	CARBOHYDRATES: 45G	FIBER: 10G	SUGARS: 25G	FAT: 20G	SATURATED FAT: 4G
SODIUM: 200MG	POTASSIUM: 900MG	VITAMIN A: 6% DV	VITAMIN C: 15% DV	CALCIUM: 25% DV		IRON: 20% DV

Quick and Healthy Muffins

Muffins can be a nutritious breakfast or snack option when made with wholesome ingredients. They are portable, easy to make in batches, and can be stored for several days or frozen for longer periods. This section introduces you to the benefits of incorporating muffins into your meal prep routine, provides tips for making the perfect muffin, and offers a variety of recipes to get you started.

Benefits of Quick and Healthy Muffins

1. **Convenient**: Muffins are perfect for busy mornings. You can bake a batch over the weekend and enjoy them throughout the week.
2. **Nutritious**: By using whole grains, fruits, nuts, and seeds, you can make muffins that are both delicious and packed with nutrients.
3. **Portable**: Muffins are easy to take on the go, making them a great option for breakfast at your desk, in the car, or wherever your day takes you.
4. **Customizable**: You can tailor muffins to your dietary needs and preferences, whether you need gluten-free, vegan, low-sugar, or high-protein options.

Tips for Making the Perfect Muffin

1. **Choose Whole Grains**: Use whole wheat flour, oat flour, or other whole grain flours to increase fiber content and make your muffins more filling.
2. **Sweeten Naturally**: Opt for natural sweeteners like honey, maple syrup, or mashed bananas instead of refined sugar.
3. **Add Fruits and Vegetables**: Incorporate fruits and vegetables like berries, apples, carrots, and zucchini to boost the nutritional value and add moisture.
4. **Include Healthy Fats**: Use healthy fats like olive oil, coconut oil, or nut butters to add richness and flavor.
5. **Mix in Protein**: Add Greek yogurt, protein powder, or nuts to increase the protein content and make your muffins more satisfying.
6. **Don't Overmix**: When combining wet and dry ingredients, mix until just combined to avoid tough, dense muffins.

BANANA OAT MUFFINS

PREP TIME
10 MINUTES

COOK TIME
25 MINUTES

DIFFICULTY

SE4VES
12 MUFFINS

INGREDIENTS

- 2 ripe bananas, mashed
- 1 cup rolled oats
- 1/2 cup whole wheat flour
- 1/4 cup honey or maple syrup
- 1/4 cup Greek yogurt
- 1 egg
- 1 teaspoon baking powder
- 1/2 teaspoon baking soda
- 1/2 teaspoon cinnamon
- 1/4 teaspoon salt

INSTRUCTIONS

1. Preheat the oven to 350°F (175°C) and line a muffin tin with paper liners.
2. In a large bowl, combine the mashed bananas, honey, Greek yogurt, and egg.
3. In a separate bowl, mix the oats, whole wheat flour, baking powder, baking soda, cinnamon, and salt.
4. Gradually add the dry ingredients to the wet ingredients, stirring until just combined.
5. Divide the batter evenly among the muffin cups.
6. Bake for 20-25 minutes, or until a toothpick inserted into the center comes out clean.
7. Allow to cool before serving.

Nutritional Information (per serving):

CALORIES: 110	PROTEIN: 3G	CARBOHYDRATES: 20G	FIBER: 2G	SUGARS: 8G	FAT: 2G	SATURATED FAT: 0.5G
SODIUM: 100MG	POTASSIUM: 150MG	VITAMIN A: 2% DV	VITAMIN C: 4% DV	CALCIUM: 4% DV	IRON: 4% DV	

BLUEBERRY ALMOND MUFFINS

 **QUICK AND HEALTHY MUFFINS**

PREP TIME
10 MINUTES

COOK TIME
25 MINUTES

★☆☆☆☆

DIFFICULTY

SE4VES
12 MUFFINS

INGREDIENTS

- 1 cup whole wheat flour
- 1/2 cup almond flour
- 1/2 cup rolled oats
- 1/2 cup honey or maple syrup
- 1 cup Greek yogurt
- 2 eggs
- 1 teaspoon baking powder
- 1/2 teaspoon baking soda
- 1/2 teaspoon vanilla extract
- 1/2 teaspoon almond extract
- 1 cup fresh or frozen blueberries
- 1/4 cup sliced almonds

INSTRUCTIONS

1. Preheat the oven to 350°F (175°C) and line a muffin tin with paper liners.
2. In a large bowl, whisk together the Greek yogurt, honey, eggs, vanilla extract, and almond extract.
3. In a separate bowl, mix the whole wheat flour, almond flour, rolled oats, baking powder, and baking soda.
4. Gradually add the dry ingredients to the wet ingredients, stirring until just combined.
5. Gently fold in the blueberries.
6. Divide the batter evenly among the muffin cups.
7. Sprinkle the tops with sliced almonds.
8. Bake for 20-25 minutes, or until a toothpick inserted into the center comes out clean.
9. Allow to cool before serving.

Nutritional Information (per serving):

CALORIES: 160	PROTEIN: 5G	CARBOHYDRATES: 25G	FIBER: 4G	SUGARS: 12G	FAT: 5G	SATURATED FAT: 1G
SODIUM: 150MG	POTASSIUM: 200MG	VITAMIN A: 2% DV	VITAMIN C: 4% DV	CALCIUM: 6% DV	IRON: 6% DV	

CARROT APPLE MUFFINS

QUICK AND HEALTHY MUFFINS

PREP TIME
15 MINUTES

COOK TIME
25 MINUTES

 ★☆☆☆☆
DIFFICULTY

SE4VES
12 MUFFINS

INGREDIENTS

- 1 cup whole wheat flour
- 1/2 cup rolled oats
- 1/2 cup grated carrots
- 1/2 cup grated apple
- 1/3 cup honey or maple syrup
- 1/3 cup unsweetened applesauce
- 2 eggs
- 1/4 cup coconut oil, melted
- 1 teaspoon baking powder
- 1/2 teaspoon baking soda
- 1/2 teaspoon ground cinnamon
- 1/4 teaspoon ground nutmeg
- 1/4 teaspoon salt
- 1/4 cup chopped walnuts (optional)
- 1/4 cup raisins (optional)

INSTRUCTIONS

1. Preheat the oven to 350°F (175°C) and line a muffin tin with paper liners.
2. In a large bowl, whisk together the honey, applesauce, eggs, and melted coconut oil.
3. In a separate bowl, mix the whole wheat flour, rolled oats, baking powder, baking soda, cinnamon, nutmeg, and salt.
4. Gradually add the dry ingredients to the wet ingredients, stirring until just combined.
5. Fold in the grated carrots and apple. If using, also fold in the chopped walnuts and raisins.
6. Divide the batter evenly among the muffin cups.
7. Bake for 20-25 minutes, or until a toothpick inserted into the center comes out clean.
8. Allow to cool before serving.

Nutritional Information (per serving):

CALORIES: 140	PROTEIN: 3G	CARBOHYDRATES: 23G	FIBER: 4G	SUGARS: 12G	FAT: 5G	SATURATED FAT: 2G
SODIUM: 120MG	POTASSIUM: 150MG	VITAMIN A: 25% DV	VITAMIN C: 4% DV	CALCIUM: 6% DV	IRON: 4% DV	

LEMON POPPY SEED MUFFINS

PREP TIME
10 MINUTES

COOK TIME
25 MINUTES

DIFFICULTY

SE4VES
12 MUFFINS

INGREDIENTS

- 1 cup whole wheat flour
- 1/2 cup almond flour
- 1/2 cup rolled oats
- 1/2 cup honey or maple syrup
- 1 cup Greek yogurt
- 2 eggs
- 1/4 cup coconut oil, melted
- 2 tablespoons poppy seeds
- 1 tablespoon lemon zest
- 1/4 cup fresh lemon juice
- 1 teaspoon baking powder
- 1/2 teaspoon baking soda
- 1/2 teaspoon vanilla extract
- 1/4 teaspoon salt

INSTRUCTIONS

1. Preheat the oven to 350°F (175°C) and line a muffin tin with paper liners.
2. In a large bowl, whisk together the Greek yogurt, honey, eggs, melted coconut oil, lemon zest, lemon juice, and vanilla extract.
3. In a separate bowl, mix the whole wheat flour, almond flour, rolled oats, baking powder, baking soda, poppy seeds, and salt.
4. Gradually add the dry ingredients to the wet ingredients, stirring until just combined.
5. Divide the batter evenly among the muffin cups.
6. Bake for 20-25 minutes, or until a toothpick inserted into the center comes out clean.
7. Allow to cool before serving.

Nutritional Information (per serving):

CALORIES: 160	PROTEIN: 5G	CARBOHYDRATES: 23G	FIBER: 4G	SUGARS: 12G	FAT: 6G	SATURATED FAT: 3G
SODIUM: 150MG	POTASSIUM: 100MG	VITAMIN A: 2% DV	VITAMIN C: 4% DV	CALCIUM: 8% DV	IRON: 4% DV	

Overnight Oats and Chia Puddings

Overnight oats and chia puddings are perfect for those busy mornings when you need a nutritious breakfast ready to go. These recipes are incredibly versatile, allowing you to customize them to your taste and dietary needs. They are packed with fiber, protein, and essential nutrients, ensuring you start your day off right.

Benefits of Overnight Oats and Chia Puddings

1. **Time-Saving**: Prepare these breakfasts the night before, and they are ready to eat in the morning. No cooking required!
2. **Nutrient-Dense**: Both oats and chia seeds are excellent sources of fiber, protein, and omega-3 fatty acids.
3. **Customizable**: You can add a variety of fruits, nuts, seeds, and flavorings to suit your taste preferences and dietary requirements.
4. **Portable**: Store them in jars or containers for an easy grab-and-go breakfast.

Tips for Making Perfect Overnight Oats and Chia Puddings

1. **Choose Your Base Liquid**: Use milk (dairy or plant-based), yogurt, or a combination of both as your liquid base. This adds creaminess and enhances the nutritional value.
2. **Sweeten Naturally**: Add natural sweeteners like honey, maple syrup, or mashed fruit to avoid refined sugars.
3. **Add Protein**: Incorporate protein-rich ingredients like Greek yogurt, protein powder, or nuts to make your breakfast more satisfying.
4. **Layer for Texture**: Layering ingredients like fruits, nuts, and seeds can add delightful textures and flavors.
5. **Let It Sit**: Allow your oats or chia seeds to soak for at least 4 hours, but preferably overnight, to absorb the liquid and soften.

VANILLA ALMOND OVERNIGHT OATS

PREP TIME
5 MINUTES

COOK TIME
4 HOURS OR OVERNIGHT

DIFFICULTY

SE4VES
1

INGREDIENTS

- 1/2 cup rolled oats
- 1/2 cup almond milk
- 1 tablespoon chia seeds
- 1 teaspoon vanilla extract
- 1 tablespoon almond butter
- 1 teaspoon honey or maple syrup (optional)

Toppings:
- Sliced almonds
- Fresh berries
- Banana slices

INSTRUCTIONS

1. In a jar or container, combine the rolled oats, almond milk, chia seeds, vanilla extract, almond butter, and honey.
2. Stir well to ensure all ingredients are mixed.
3. Cover and refrigerate for at least 4 hours, preferably overnight.
4. In the morning, stir the oats again and add a splash of almond milk if needed to reach desired consistency.
5. Top with sliced almonds, fresh berries, and banana slices before serving.

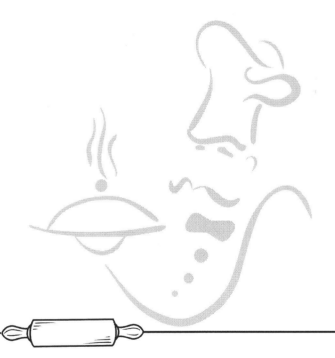

Nutritional Information (per serving):

CALORIES: 300	PROTEIN: 8G	CARBOHYDRATES: 42G	FIBER: 9G	SUGARS: 12G	FAT: 12G	SATURATED FAT: 1G
SODIUM: 60MG	POTASSIUM: 400MG	VITAMIN A: 2% DV	VITAMIN C: 10% DV	CALCIUM: 20% DV	IRON: 10% DV	

BERRY BLISS OVERNIGHT OATS

PREP TIME
5 MINUTES

COOK TIME
4 HOURS OR OVERNIGHT

DIFFICULTY

SE4VES
1

INGREDIENTS

- 1/2 cup rolled oats
- 1/2 cup almond milk
- 1/4 cup Greek yogurt
- 1 tablespoon chia seeds
- 1 teaspoon vanilla extract
- 1/2 cup mixed berries (fresh or frozen)
- 1 teaspoon honey or maple syrup (optional)

Toppings:
- Fresh berries
- Granola
- Chopped nuts

INSTRUCTIONS

1. In a jar or container, combine the rolled oats, almond milk, Greek yogurt, chia seeds, vanilla extract, mixed berries, and honey.
2. Stir well to ensure all ingredients are mixed.
3. Cover and refrigerate for at least 4 hours, preferably overnight.
4. In the morning, stir the oats again and add a splash of almond milk if needed to reach desired consistency.
5. Top with fresh berries, granola, and chopped nuts before serving.

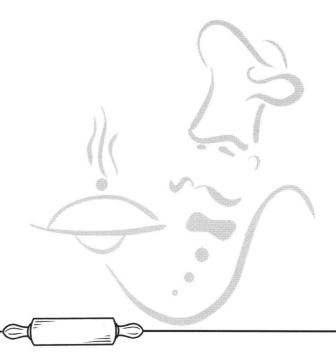

Nutritional Information (per serving):

CALORIES: 320	PROTEIN: 10G	CARBOHYDRATES: 50G	FIBER: 9G	SUGARS: 20G	FAT: 8G	SATURATED FAT: 1G
SODIUM: 70MG	POTASSIUM: 450MG	VITAMIN A: 2% DV	VITAMIN C: 30% DV	CALCIUM: 25% DV	IRON: 10% DV	

CHOCOLATE BANANA CHIA PUDDING

PREP TIME
5 MINUTES

COOK TIME
4 HOURS OR OVERNIGHT

★☆☆☆☆
DIFFICULTY

SE4VES
2

INGREDIENTS

- 1 cup almond milk
- 1/4 cup chia seeds
- 2 tablespoons unsweetened cocoa powder
- 1 tablespoon honey or maple syrup
- 1 teaspoon vanilla extract
- 1 ripe banana, mashed

Toppings:
- Sliced banana
- Shaved dark chocolate
- Chopped nuts

INSTRUCTIONS

1. In a mixing bowl, whisk together the almond milk, chia seeds, cocoa powder, honey, vanilla extract, and mashed banana until well combined.
2. Divide the mixture into two jars or containers.
3. Cover and refrigerate for at least 4 hours, preferably overnight, until the pudding has thickened.
4. Before serving, stir the pudding and top with sliced banana, shaved dark chocolate, and chopped nuts.

Nutritional Information (per serving):

CALORIES: 250	PROTEIN: 6G	CARBOHYDRATES: 40G	FIBER: 12G	SUGARS: 18G	FAT: 9G	SATURATED FAT: 1.5G
SODIUM: 60MG	POTASSIUM: 480MG	VITAMIN A: 2% DV	VITAMIN C: 10% DV	CALCIUM: 25% DV	IRON: 15% DV	

MANGO COCONUT CHIA PUDDING

PREP TIME
5 MINUTES

COOK TIME
4 HOURS OR OVERNIGHT

★☆☆☆☆
DIFFICULTY

SE4VES
2

INGREDIENTS

- 1 cup coconut milk
- 1/4 cup chia seeds
- 1 tablespoon honey or maple syrup
- 1 teaspoon vanilla extract
- 1/2 cup mango chunks (fresh or frozen)

Toppings:
- Fresh mango slices
- Shredded coconut
- Chopped macadamia nuts

INSTRUCTIONS

1. In a mixing bowl, whisk together the coconut milk, chia seeds, honey, and vanilla extract until well combined.
2. Fold in the mango chunks.
3. Divide the mixture into two jars or containers.
4. Cover and refrigerate for at least 4 hours, preferably overnight, until the pudding has thickened.
5. Before serving, stir the pudding and top with fresh mango slices, shredded coconut, and chopped macadamia nuts.

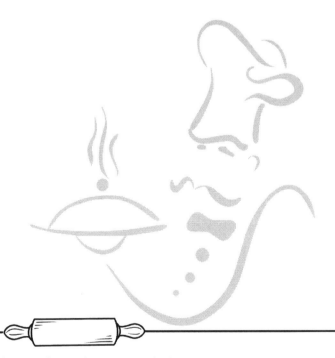

Nutritional Information (per serving):

CALORIES: 270	PROTEIN: 5G	CARBOHYDRATES: 30G	FIBER: 10G	SUGARS: 18G	FAT: 15G	SATURATED FAT: 10G
SODIUM: 30MG	POTASSIUM: 350MG	VITAMIN A: 15% DV	VITAMIN C: 60% DV	CALCIUM: 15% DV		IRON: 15% DV

High-Protein Breakfast Burritos

High-protein breakfast burritos are an excellent way to start your day with a satisfying and nutritious meal. Packed with protein, fiber, and healthy fats, these burritos provide the energy and nutrients needed to fuel your morning activities. They are also highly customizable, easy to prepare in advance, and perfect for meal prepping.

Benefits of High-Protein Breakfast Burritos

1. **Protein-Packed**: Each burrito contains a significant amount of protein, which is essential for muscle repair, growth, and overall satiety. This makes them an excellent choice for those who engage in regular physical activity or are looking to maintain a balanced diet.
2. **Convenient**: Breakfast burritos are easy to make in large batches and can be stored in the refrigerator or freezer for quick, grab-and-go meals throughout the week.
3. **Balanced Nutrition**: By including a variety of ingredients such as lean meats, eggs, vegetables, and whole grains, breakfast burritos offer a balanced mix of macronutrients and micronutrients.
4. **Customizable**: These burritos can be tailored to meet individual dietary preferences and needs. Whether you prefer vegetarian, low-carb, or gluten-free options, you can adjust the ingredients accordingly.
5. **Portable**: Ideal for busy mornings, breakfast burritos can be easily wrapped and taken on the go, making them a practical option for those who need a nutritious meal on the move.

Tips for Making the Perfect High-Protein Breakfast Burrito

1. **Choose High-Quality Protein Sources**: Incorporate lean meats like turkey or chicken sausage, eggs or egg whites, tofu, or beans to boost the protein content.
2. **Incorporate Vegetables**: Add a variety of vegetables such as spinach, bell peppers, tomatoes, and onions to increase the fiber content and add essential vitamins and minerals.
3. **Use Whole Grains**: Opt for whole wheat tortillas or other whole grain options to provide complex carbohydrates that offer sustained energy and additional fiber.
4. **Add Healthy Fats**: Include healthy fats from sources like avocado, cheese, or nuts to enhance the flavor and provide satiety.
5. **Season Well**: Use herbs, spices, and seasonings to add flavor without extra calories or sodium. Common choices include cilantro, cumin, paprika, and black pepper.
6. **Prep and Store Properly**: Prepare your burritos in advance and wrap them individually in foil or parchment paper. Store them in the refrigerator for up to 4 days or in the freezer for up to 3 months. Reheat in the microwave or oven when ready to eat.

SPINACH AND EGG WHITE BURRITO

HIGH-PROTEIN BREAKFAST BURRITOS

PREP TIME
10 MINUTES

COOK TIME
10 MINUTES

DIFFICULTY

SE4VES
2

INGREDIENTS

- 1 cup egg whites
- 1 cup fresh spinach, chopped
- 1/2 bell pepper, diced
- 1/4 cup shredded low-fat cheese (optional)
- 1/4 cup salsa
- 2 whole wheat tortillas
- 1 tablespoon olive oil
- Salt and pepper to taste

INSTRUCTIONS

1. Heat the olive oil in a non-stick skillet over medium heat.
2. Add the diced bell pepper to the skillet and sauté for 3-4 minutes until softened.
3. Add the chopped spinach to the skillet and cook for another 2 minutes until wilted.
4. Pour the egg whites into the skillet, season with salt and pepper, and cook, stirring gently, until the egg whites are set.
5. Warm the whole wheat tortillas in a separate skillet or microwave.
6. Divide the egg white and vegetable mixture evenly between the two tortillas.
7. Sprinkle shredded cheese over the filling (if using).
8. Top with salsa.
9. Roll up the tortillas, folding in the sides, to form a burrito.
10. Serve immediately or wrap in foil for later

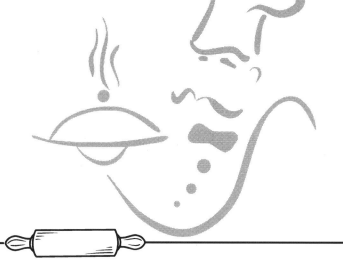

Nutritional Information (per serving):

CALORIES: 210	PROTEIN: 18G	CARBOHYDRATES: 25G	FIBER: 4G	SUGARS: 3G	FAT: 6G	SATURATED FAT: 1.5G
SODIUM: 450MG	POTASSIUM: 400MG	VITAMIN A: 50% DV	VITAMIN C: 60% DV		CALCIUM: 15% DV	IRON: 10% DV

TURKEY SAUSAGE AND VEGGIE BURRITO

PREP TIME
10 MINUTES

COOK TIME
10 MINUTES

DIFFICULTY

SE4VES
2

INGREDIENTS

- 4 ounces turkey sausage, crumbled
- 1/2 cup egg whites
- 1/2 cup diced bell pepper
- 1/2 cup diced zucchini
- 1/4 cup shredded low-fat cheese (optional)
- 1/4 cup salsa
- 2 whole wheat tortillas
- 1 tablespoon olive oil
- Salt and pepper to taste

INSTRUCTIONS

1. Heat the olive oil in a non-stick skillet over medium heat.
2. Add the crumbled turkey sausage to the skillet and cook until browned and cooked through, about 5-7 minutes.
3. Add the diced bell pepper and zucchini to the skillet and sauté for 3-4 minutes until softened.
4. Pour the egg whites into the skillet, season with salt and pepper, and cook, stirring gently, until the egg whites are set.
5. Warm the whole wheat tortillas in a separate skillet or microwave.
6. Divide the turkey sausage and veggie mixture evenly between the two tortillas.
7. Sprinkle shredded cheese over the filling (if using).
8. Top with salsa.
9. Roll up the tortillas, folding in the sides, to form a burrito.
10. Serve immediately or wrap in foil for later.

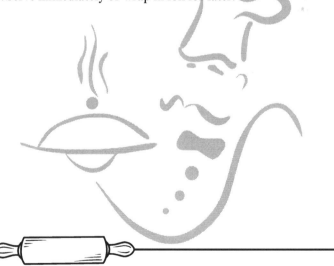

Nutritional Information (per serving):

CALORIES: 300	PROTEIN: 25G	CARBOHYDRATES: 28G	FIBER: 4G	SUGARS: 4G	FAT: 10G	SATURATED FAT: 2.5G
SODIUM: 600MG	POTASSIUM: 500MG	VITAMIN A: 35% DV	VITAMIN C: 70% DV	CALCIUM: 15% DV	IRON: 15% DV	

BLACK BEAN AND AVOCADO BURRITO

HIGH-PROTEIN BREAKFAST BURRITOS

PREP TIME
10 MINUTES

COOK TIME
5 MINUTES

DIFFICULTY

SE4VES
2

INGREDIENTS

- 1 cup canned black beans, drained and rinsed
- 1/2 avocado, diced
- 1/2 cup diced tomatoes
- 1/4 cup diced red onion
- 1/4 cup shredded low-fat cheese (optional)
- 1/4 cup salsa
- 2 whole wheat tortillas
- 1 tablespoon olive oil
- 1 teaspoon cumin
- 1 teaspoon chili powder
- Salt and pepper to taste
- Fresh cilantro, chopped (optional)

INSTRUCTIONS

1. Heat the olive oil in a non-stick skillet over medium heat.
2. Add the diced red onion to the skillet and sauté for 2-3 minutes until softened.
3. Add the black beans, cumin, and chili powder to the skillet. Cook for another 2-3 minutes until heated through, stirring occasionally.
4. Warm the whole wheat tortillas in a separate skillet or microwave.
5. Divide the black bean mixture evenly between the two tortillas.
6. Top each tortilla with diced avocado, diced tomatoes, shredded cheese (if using), salsa, and fresh cilantro (if using).
7. Roll up the tortillas, folding in the sides, to form a burrito.
8. Serve immediately or wrap in foil for later.

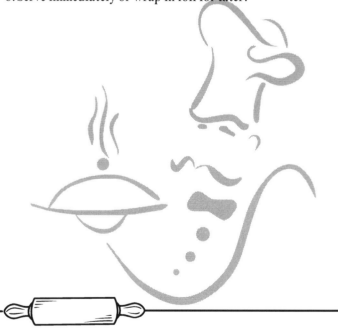

Nutritional Information (per serving):

CALORIES: 350	PROTEIN: 13G	CARBOHYDRATES: 50G	FIBER: 14G	SUGARS: 4G	FAT: 12G	SATURATED FAT: 2.5G
SODIUM: 480MG	POTASSIUM: 800MG	VITAMIN A: 15% DV	VITAMIN C: 25% DV	CALCIUM: 15% DV	IRON: 20% DV	

Wholesome Salads with a Twist

Wholesome salads are a fantastic option for lunch on the go. They are not only nutritious and satisfying but also incredibly versatile. By incorporating a variety of ingredients, you can create salads that are flavorful, filling, and packed with essential nutrients. This section introduces you to the benefits of wholesome salads and provides tips for creating salads that are anything but boring.

Benefits of Wholesome Salads

1. **Nutrient-Dense**: Salads can be loaded with a variety of vegetables, lean proteins, healthy fats, and whole grains, making them a nutrient-dense meal.
2. **Hydrating**: Many salad ingredients, such as cucumbers, lettuce, and tomatoes, have high water content, which helps keep you hydrated.
3. **Customizable**: You can easily tailor salads to your taste preferences and dietary needs. Whether you prefer a vegetarian option, a protein-packed salad, or a low-carb choice, there's a salad for everyone.
4. **Portable**: Salads can be easily packed in containers, making them a convenient option for lunch at work, school, or on the go.
5. **Quick and Easy**: With a bit of prep, salads can be assembled quickly, allowing you to enjoy a healthy meal without spending too much time in the kitchen.

Tips for Making the Perfect Wholesome Salad

1. **Start with Fresh Greens**: Use a variety of fresh greens such as spinach, kale, arugula, or mixed lettuce as the base of your salad. This provides a range of textures and nutrients.
2. **Add Protein**: Incorporate lean proteins like grilled chicken, turkey, tofu, beans, or chickpeas to make your salad more filling and balanced.
3. **Include Healthy Fats**: Add healthy fats from sources like avocado, nuts, seeds, or olive oil to enhance the flavor and provide satiety.
4. **Incorporate Whole Grains**: Adding whole grains like quinoa, brown rice, or farro can increase the fiber content and make your salad more satisfying.
5. **Mix in Colorful Vegetables**: Use a variety of colorful vegetables such as bell peppers, carrots, tomatoes, cucumbers, and beets to boost the nutritional value and make your salad visually appealing.
6. **Use Flavorful Dressings**: Choose dressings that complement the ingredients of your salad. Opt for homemade dressings to control the ingredients and avoid added sugars and unhealthy fats.
7. **Add Texture**: Include crunchy elements like nuts, seeds, croutons, or crispy chickpeas to add texture and interest to your salad.

MEDITERRANEAN QUINOA SALAD

PREP TIME
15 MINUTES

COOK TIME
15 MINUTES

DIFFICULTY

SE4VES
4

INGREDIENTS

- 1 cup quinoa
- 2 cups water
- 1 cup cherry tomatoes, halved
- 1 cucumber, diced
- 1/2 red onion, finely chopped
- 1/2 cup Kalamata olives, pitted and sliced
- 1/2 cup feta cheese, crumbled
- 1/4 cup fresh parsley, chopped
- 1/4 cup fresh mint, chopped (optional)

Dressing:
- 1/4 cup olive oil
- 2 tablespoons lemon juice
- 1 tablespoon red wine vinegar
- 1 clove garlic, minced
- 1 teaspoon dried oregano
- Salt and pepper to taste

INSTRUCTIONS

1. Rinse the quinoa under cold water. In a medium saucepan, combine the quinoa and water and bring to a boil.
2. Reduce the heat to low, cover, and simmer for about 15 minutes or until the quinoa is tender and the water is absorbed. Fluff with a fork and let it cool.
3. In a large bowl, combine the cooled quinoa, cherry tomatoes, cucumber, red onion, Kalamata olives, feta cheese, parsley, and mint (if using).
4. In a small bowl, whisk together the olive oil, lemon juice, red wine vinegar, minced garlic, dried oregano, salt, and pepper.
5. Pour the dressing over the salad and toss to combine.
6. Serve immediately or refrigerate for later.

Nutritional Information (per serving):

CALORIES: 280	PROTEIN: 8G	CARBOHYDRATES: 28G	FIBER: 5G	SUGARS: 4G	FAT: 15G	SATURATED FAT: 4G
SODIUM: 400MG	POTASSIUM: 400MG	VITAMIN A: 10% DV	VITAMIN C: 25% DV		CALCIUM: 15% DV	IRON: 10% DV

ASIAN SESAME CHICKEN SALAD

WHOLESOME SALADS WITH A TWIST

PREP TIME
20 MINUTES

COOK TIME
10 MINUTES

DIFFICULTY

SE4VES
4

INGREDIENTS

- 2 cups cooked chicken breast, shredded
- 4 cups mixed greens (such as romaine, spinach, and arugula)
- 1 cup shredded red cabbage
- 1 cup shredded carrots
- 1 red bell pepper, thinly sliced
- 2 green onions, chopped
- 1/4 cup fresh cilantro, chopped
- 2 tablespoons sesame seeds
- 1/4 cup sliced almonds
- 1/2 cup mandarin orange segments (optional)

Dressing:
- 1/4 cup soy sauce (low sodium)
- 2 tablespoons rice vinegar
- 2 tablespoons sesame oil
- 1 tablespoon honey
- 1 tablespoon fresh ginger, grated
- 1 clove garlic, minced
- 1 tablespoon water (if needed to thin)

INSTRUCTIONS

1. In a large bowl, combine the mixed greens, shredded red cabbage, shredded carrots, red bell pepper, green onions, fresh cilantro, sesame seeds, and sliced almonds.
2. Add the shredded chicken and mandarin orange segments (if using) to the bowl.
3. In a small bowl, whisk together the soy sauce, rice vinegar, sesame oil, honey, grated ginger, minced garlic, and water (if needed) until well combined.
4. Pour the dressing over the salad and toss to combine.
5. Serve immediately or refrigerate for later.

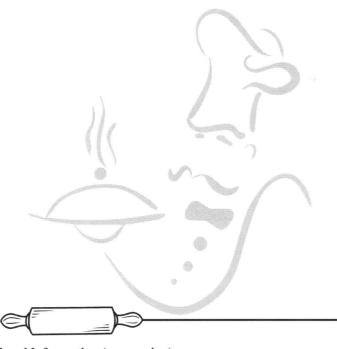

Nutritional Information (per serving):

CALORIES: 320	PROTEIN: 22G	CARBOHYDRATES: 18G	FIBER: 5G	SUGARS: 9G	FAT: 18G	SATURATED FAT: 2.5G
SODIUM: 600MG	POTASSIUM: 750MG	VITAMIN A: 120% DV	VITAMIN C: 100% DV	CALCIUM: 15% DV	IRON: 15% DV	

SOUTHWEST BLACK BEAN AND CORN SALAD

PREP TIME
15 MINUTES

COOK TIME
5 MINUTES

DIFFICULTY

SE4VES
4

INGREDIENTS

- 1 can (15 oz) black beans, drained and rinsed
- 1 cup corn kernels (fresh, frozen, or canned)
- 1 red bell pepper, diced
- 1 avocado, diced
- 1/2 red onion, finely chopped
- 1 cup cherry tomatoes, halved
- 1/4 cup fresh cilantro, chopped
- 1 jalapeño, seeded and finely chopped (optional)
- 1/4 cup cotija cheese, crumbled (optional)

Dressing:
- 3 tablespoons olive oil
- 2 tablespoons lime juice
- 1 tablespoon apple cider vinegar
- 1 teaspoon ground cumin
- 1/2 teaspoon smoked paprika
- Salt and pepper to taste

INSTRUCTIONS

1. In a large bowl, combine the black beans, corn kernels, red bell pepper, avocado, red onion, cherry tomatoes, fresh cilantro, and jalapeño (if using).
2. In a small bowl, whisk together the olive oil, lime juice, apple cider vinegar, ground cumin, smoked paprika, salt, and pepper until well combined.
3. Pour the dressing over the salad and toss to combine.
4. Top with crumbled cotija cheese (if using).
5. Serve immediately or refrigerate for later.

Nutritional Information (per serving):

CALORIES: 250	PROTEIN: 7G	CARBOHYDRATES: 28G	FIBER: 10G	SUGARS: 5G	FAT: 14G	SATURATED FAT: 2G
SODIUM: 220MG	POTASSIUM: 750MG	VITAMIN A: 25% DV	VITAMIN C: 60% DV	CALCIUM: 8% DV	IRON: 15% DV	

KALE AND APPLE SALAD WITH WALNUTS

PREP TIME
15 MINUTES

COOK TIME
0 MINUTES

DIFFICULTY

SE4VES
4

INGREDIENTS

- 4 cups kale, stems removed and leaves chopped
- 1 apple, thinly sliced
- 1/2 cup walnuts, toasted
- 1/4 cup dried cranberries
- 1/4 cup feta cheese, crumbled (optional)
- 1/4 red onion, thinly sliced

Dressing:
- 1/4 cup olive oil
- 2 tablespoons apple cider vinegar
- 1 tablespoon honey or maple syrup
- 1 teaspoon Dijon mustard
- Salt and pepper to taste

INSTRUCTIONS

1. In a large bowl, combine the chopped kale, sliced apple, toasted walnuts, dried cranberries, feta cheese (if using), and red onion.
2. In a small bowl, whisk together the olive oil, apple cider vinegar, honey or maple syrup, Dijon mustard, salt, and pepper until well combined.
3. Pour the dressing over the salad and toss to combine.
4. Serve immediately or refrigerate for later.

Nutritional Information (per serving):

CALORIES: 250	PROTEIN: 4G	CARBOHYDRATES: 22G	FIBER: 5G	SUGARS: 13G	FAT: 18G	SATURATED FAT: 3G
SODIUM: 150MG	POTASSIUM: 450MG	VITAMIN A: 100% DV	VITAMIN C: 70% DV	CALCIUM: 15% DV		IRON: 8% DV

SPINACH AND STRAWBERRY SALAD WITH FETA

WHOLESOME SALADS WITH A TWIST

PREP TIME
10 MINUTES

COOK TIME
0 MINUTES

★☆☆☆☆
DIFFICULTY

SE4VES
4

INGREDIENTS

- 4 cups fresh spinach leaves
- 1 cup strawberries, hulled and sliced
- 1/4 red onion, thinly sliced
- 1/4 cup feta cheese, crumbled
- 1/4 cup sliced almonds, toasted

Dressing:
- 3 tablespoons balsamic vinegar
- 2 tablespoons olive oil
- 1 tablespoon honey or maple syrup
- 1 teaspoon Dijon mustard
- Salt and pepper to taste

INSTRUCTIONS

1. In a large bowl, combine the fresh spinach leaves, sliced strawberries, red onion, feta cheese, and toasted almonds.
2. In a small bowl, whisk together the balsamic vinegar, olive oil, honey or maple syrup, Dijon mustard, salt, and pepper until well combined.
3. Pour the dressing over the salad and toss to combine.
4. Serve immediately or refrigerate for later.

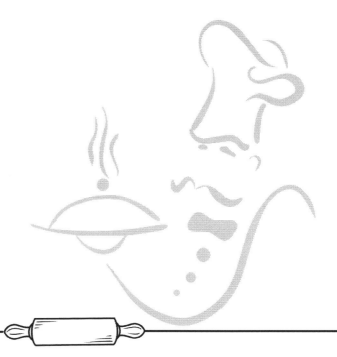

Nutritional Information (per serving):

CALORIES: 180	PROTEIN: 4G	CARBOHYDRATES: 14G	FIBER: 3G	SUGARS: 9G	FAT: 13G	SATURATED FAT: 3G
SODIUM: 180MG	POTASSIUM: 450MG	VITAMIN A: 60% DV	VITAMIN C: 90% DV	CALCIUM: 10% DV	IRON: 8% DV	

Delicious Wraps and Sandwiches

Wraps and sandwiches are perfect for lunches on the go. They are easy to prepare, highly portable, and can be packed with a variety of nutritious ingredients. This section introduces you to the benefits of incorporating wraps and sandwiches into your meal prep routine, provides tips for making them healthy and satisfying, and offers a variety of recipes to get you started.

Benefits of Delicious Wraps and Sandwiches

1. **Convenient**: Wraps and sandwiches are quick to assemble and can be made in advance, making them an ideal choice for busy weekdays.
2. **Portable**: They are easy to pack and carry, making them perfect for lunch at work, school, or on the go.
3. **Customizable**: You can tailor wraps and sandwiches to suit your dietary needs and preferences, including options for vegetarian, vegan, gluten-free, and high-protein diets.
4. **Balanced Nutrition**: By including a mix of proteins, vegetables, and whole grains, wraps and sandwiches can provide a balanced and nutritious meal.
5. **Variety**: The combinations are endless, allowing you to enjoy different flavors and textures with each meal.

Tips for Making Healthy and Satisfying Wraps and Sandwiches

1. **Choose Whole Grains**: Use whole grain or whole wheat wraps and bread to increase fiber content and make your meal more filling.
2. **Include Lean Proteins**: Opt for lean proteins such as turkey, chicken, tuna, tofu, or beans to keep the calorie count low and the nutrition high.
3. **Add Plenty of Vegetables**: Load up on vegetables like lettuce, spinach, tomatoes, cucumbers, bell peppers, and avocado to add vitamins, minerals, and fiber.
4. **Healthy Fats**: Include healthy fats from sources like avocado, hummus, nuts, and seeds to provide satiety and flavor.
5. **Watch the Condiments**: Be mindful of the condiments you use. Opt for healthier options like mustard, hummus, avocado spread, or light vinaigrettes instead of high-fat, high-sugar dressings.
6. **Portion Control**: Keep an eye on portion sizes to ensure your wraps and sandwiches are balanced and not overly calorie-dense.

TURKEY AVOCADO WRAP

PREP TIME
10 MINUTES

COOK TIME
0 MINUTES

DIFFICULTY

SE4VES
2

INGREDIENTS

- 4 whole wheat tortillas
- 8 ounces sliced turkey breast
- 1 avocado, sliced
- 1 cup baby spinach leaves
- 1/2 cup shredded carrots
- 1/4 cup red bell pepper, thinly sliced
- 1/4 cup hummus
- Salt and pepper to taste
- 1 tablespoon olive oil (optional, for a richer taste)

INSTRUCTIONS

1. Lay out the whole wheat tortillas on a clean surface.
2. Spread a thin layer of hummus on each tortilla.
3. Divide the turkey slices evenly among the tortillas, placing them in the center.
4. Add slices of avocado on top of the turkey.
5. Layer with baby spinach leaves, shredded carrots, and red bell pepper slices.
6. Season with salt and pepper to taste. If using olive oil, drizzle a small amount over the ingredients.
7. Roll up each tortilla tightly, folding in the sides as you go to form a secure wrap.
8. Cut each wrap in half diagonally and serve immediately or wrap in foil for later.

Nutritional Information (per serving):

CALORIES: 380	PROTEIN: 25G	CARBOHYDRATES: 35G	FIBER: 10G	SUGARS: 4G	FAT: 15G	SATURATED FAT: 2G
SODIUM: 750MG	POTASSIUM: 800MG	VITAMIN A: 60% DV	VITAMIN C: 40% DV		CALCIUM: 10% DV	IRON: 15% DV

HUMMUS AND VEGGIE WRAP

PREP TIME
10 MINUTES

COOK TIME
0 MINUTES

★☆☆☆☆
DIFFICULTY

SE4VES
2

INGREDIENTS

- 4 whole wheat tortillas
- 1 cup hummus
- 1 cup mixed greens (such as spinach, arugula, or lettuce)
- 1/2 cucumber, thinly sliced
- 1/2 red bell pepper, thinly sliced
- 1/2 yellow bell pepper, thinly sliced
- 1 small carrot, shredded
- 1/4 red onion, thinly sliced
- 1/4 cup crumbled feta cheese (optional)
- 1 tablespoon olive oil (optional)
- Salt and pepper to taste

INSTRUCTIONS

1. Lay out the whole wheat tortillas on a clean surface.
2. Spread a generous layer of hummus on each tortilla.
3. Divide the mixed greens evenly among the tortillas, placing them in the center.
4. Add slices of cucumber, red bell pepper, yellow bell pepper, shredded carrot, and red onion.
5. Sprinkle with crumbled feta cheese if using.
6. Drizzle with a small amount of olive oil if desired, and season with salt and pepper to taste.
7. Roll up each tortilla tightly, folding in the sides as you go to form a secure wrap.
8. Cut each wrap in half diagonally and serve immediately or wrap in foil for later.

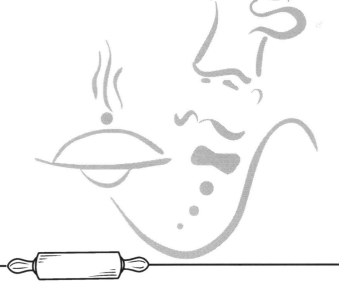

Nutritional Information (per serving):

CALORIES: 340	PROTEIN: 10G	CARBOHYDRATES: 42G	FIBER: 12G	SUGARS: 5G	FAT: 15G	SATURATED FAT: 2G
SODIUM: 580MG	POTASSIUM: 700MG	VITAMIN A: 120% DV	VITAMIN C: 150% DV	CALCIUM: 10% DV		IRON: 15% DV

GRILLED CHICKEN CAESAR WRAP

PREP TIME
10 MINUTES

COOK TIME
10 MINUTES

★★☆☆☆

DIFFICULTY

SE4VES
2

INGREDIENTS

- 2 whole wheat tortillas
- 1 cup grilled chicken breast, sliced
- 2 cups romaine lettuce, chopped
- 1/4 cup grated Parmesan cheese
- 1/4 cup Caesar dressing (preferably low-fat)
- 1/4 cup cherry tomatoes, halved (optional)
- Salt and pepper to taste

INSTRUCTIONS

1. Lay out the whole wheat tortillas on a clean surface.
2. In a large bowl, combine the chopped romaine lettuce, grated Parmesan cheese, and Caesar dressing. Toss until the lettuce is well coated.
3. Divide the Caesar salad mixture evenly among the tortillas, placing it in the center.
4. Add the sliced grilled chicken breast on top of the salad mixture.
5. Add cherry tomatoes if using, and season with salt and pepper to taste.
6. Roll up each tortilla tightly, folding in the sides as you go to form a secure wrap.
7. Cut each wrap in half diagonally and serve immediately or wrap in foil for later.

Nutritional Information (per serving):

CALORIES: 350	PROTEIN: 28G	CARBOHYDRATES: 28G	FIBER: 6G	SUGARS: 3G	FAT: 15G	SATURATED FAT: 4G
SODIUM: 750MG	POTASSIUM: 750MG	VITAMIN A: 80% DV	VITAMIN C: 15% DV		CALCIUM: 20% DV	IRON: 10% DV

TUNA SALAD SANDWICH ON WHOLE WHEAT

PREP TIME
10 MINUTES

COOK TIME
0 MINUTES

DIFFICULTY

SE4VES
2

INGREDIENTS

- 1 can (5 oz) tuna, drained
- 2 tablespoons Greek yogurt (or mayonnaise)
- 1 tablespoon Dijon mustard
- 1 celery stalk, finely chopped
- 1/4 red onion, finely chopped
- 1 tablespoon fresh parsley, chopped
- 1 teaspoon lemon juice
- Salt and pepper to taste
- 4 slices whole wheat bread
- 1 cup lettuce leaves
- 1 tomato, sliced

INSTRUCTIONS

1. In a medium bowl, combine the drained tuna, Greek yogurt (or mayonnaise), Dijon mustard, chopped celery, chopped red onion, fresh parsley, lemon juice, salt, and pepper. Mix until well combined.
2. Lay out the whole wheat bread slices on a clean surface.
3. Divide the tuna salad mixture evenly between two slices of bread, spreading it to cover the bread.
4. Top each with lettuce leaves and tomato slices.
5. Place the remaining slices of bread on top to form sandwiches.
6. Cut each sandwich in half diagonally and serve immediately or wrap in foil for later.

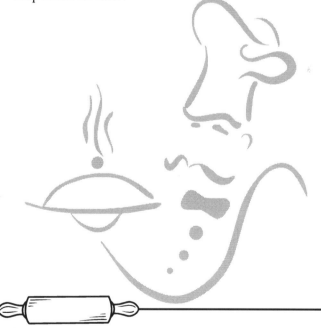

Nutritional Information (per serving):

CALORIES: 300	PROTEIN: 22G	CARBOHYDRATES: 32G	FIBER: 6G	SUGARS: 4G	FAT: 9G	SATURATED FAT: 1.5G
SODIUM: 500MG	POTASSIUM: 500MG	VITAMIN A: 20% DV	VITAMIN C: 15% DV		CALCIUM: 10% DV	IRON: 15% DV

MEDITERRANEAN VEGGIE PITA

PREP TIME
10 MINUTES

COOK TIME
0 MINUTES

DIFFICULTY

SE4VES
2

INGREDIENTS

- 2 whole wheat pita pockets
- 1/2 cup hummus
- 1/2 cup cherry tomatoes, halved
- 1/2 cucumber, diced
- 1/4 red onion, thinly sliced
- 1/4 cup Kalamata olives, pitted and sliced
- 1/4 cup feta cheese, crumbled
- 1/4 cup fresh parsley, chopped
- 1 tablespoon olive oil
- 1 tablespoon lemon juice
- Salt and pepper to taste

INSTRUCTIONS

1. Cut the pita pockets in half to create 4 halves.
2. In a small bowl, combine the cherry tomatoes, cucumber, red onion, Kalamata olives, feta cheese, and fresh parsley.
3. In another small bowl, whisk together the olive oil, lemon juice, salt, and pepper to create the dressing.
4. Pour the dressing over the vegetable mixture and toss to combine.
5. Spread a layer of hummus inside each pita half.
6. Stuff the pita pockets with the vegetable mixture.
7. Serve immediately or wrap in foil for later.

Nutritional Information (per serving):

CALORIES: 320	PROTEIN: 10G	CARBOHYDRATES: 40G	FIBER: 8G	SUGARS: 5G	FAT: 14G	SATURATED FAT: 3G
SODIUM: 600MG	POTASSIUM: 450MG	VITAMIN A: 15% DV	VITAMIN C: 25% DV		CALCIUM: 15% DV	IRON: 15% DV

Hearty Grain Bowls

Hearty grain bowls are a fantastic option for a balanced and nutritious lunch on the go. They combine whole grains, vegetables, proteins, and healthy fats into a single, convenient meal. This section introduces you to the benefits of grain bowls, provides tips for making them delicious and nutritious, and offers a variety of recipes to get you started.

Benefits of Hearty Grain Bowls

1. **Balanced Nutrition**: Grain bowls can be easily customized to include a variety of food groups, providing a balanced mix of carbohydrates, proteins, fats, vitamins, and minerals.
2. **Versatility**: You can use different grains, vegetables, proteins, and dressings to create endless flavor combinations, ensuring you never get bored.
3. **Portability**: Grain bowls are easy to pack and take with you, making them an excellent option for lunch at work, school, or on the go.
4. **Meal Prep Friendly**: Many components of grain bowls can be prepared in advance and stored separately, allowing for quick assembly during the week.
5. **Satiating**: The combination of whole grains, proteins, and healthy fats helps keep you full and satisfied for longer periods.

Tips for Making Delicious and Nutritious Grain Bowls

1. **Choose Whole Grains**: Use whole grains such as quinoa, brown rice, farro, barley, or bulgur to provide a base that is high in fiber and nutrients.
2. **Incorporate a Variety of Vegetables**: Use a mix of raw and cooked vegetables to add different textures, flavors, and nutrients. Think leafy greens, roasted vegetables, and fresh veggies.
3. **Add Lean Proteins**: Include lean proteins such as grilled chicken, tofu, beans, lentils, or fish to make your bowl more satisfying.
4. **Healthy Fats**: Add healthy fats from sources like avocado, nuts, seeds, and olive oil to enhance flavor and satiety.
5. **Flavorful Dressings**: Use homemade dressings made from healthy ingredients like olive oil, vinegar, lemon juice, and herbs to add flavor without extra calories or unhealthy additives.
6. **Season Well**: Don't forget to season your grains and proteins with herbs, spices, and sauces to ensure your grain bowl is flavorful.

BROWN RICE AND EDAMAME BOWL

PREP TIME
15 MINUTES

COOK TIME
30 MINUTES

★★☆☆☆
DIFFICULTY

SE4VES
2

INGREDIENTS

- 1 cup brown rice
- 2 cups water
- 1 cup shelled edamame (fresh or frozen)
- 1 cup shredded carrots
- 1 cup red cabbage, thinly sliced
- 1/2 avocado, sliced
- 2 tablespoons sesame seeds
- 2 green onions, sliced

Dressing:
- 2 tablespoons soy sauce (low sodium)
- 1 tablespoon rice vinegar
- 1 tablespoon sesame oil
- 1 teaspoon honey or maple syrup
- 1 teaspoon fresh ginger, grated
- 1 clove garlic, minced

INSTRUCTIONS

1. Rinse the brown rice under cold water. In a medium saucepan, combine the rice and water, and bring to a boil.
2. Reduce the heat to low, cover, and simmer for about 30 minutes, or until the rice is tender and the water is absorbed. Fluff with a fork and let it cool slightly.
3. While the rice is cooking, prepare the dressing by whisking together the soy sauce, rice vinegar, sesame oil, honey or maple syrup, grated ginger, and minced garlic in a small bowl.
4. In a large bowl, combine the cooked brown rice, shelled edamame, shredded carrots, and red cabbage.
5. Drizzle the dressing over the rice and vegetables, and toss to combine.
6. Divide the mixture between two bowls.
7. Top each bowl with sliced avocado, sesame seeds, and green onions.
8. Serve immediately or refrigerate for later.

Nutritional Information (per serving):

CALORIES: 400	PROTEIN: 12G	CARBOHYDRATES: 56G	FIBER: 10G	SUGARS: 6G	FAT: 14G	SATURATED FAT: 2G
SODIUM: 600MG	POTASSIUM: 700MG	VITAMIN A: 150% DV	VITAMIN C: 50% DV	CALCIUM: 10% DV	IRON: 20% DV	

FARRO AND ROASTED VEGETABLE BOWL

PREP TIME
15 MINUTES

COOK TIME
40 MINUTES

DIFFICULTY

SE4VES
2

INGREDIENTS

- 1 cup farro
- 3 cups water or vegetable broth
- 1 cup cherry tomatoes, halved
- 1 zucchini, diced
- 1 red bell pepper, diced
- 1 red onion, cut into wedges
- 2 tablespoons olive oil
- 1 teaspoon dried oregano
- 1 teaspoon dried thyme
- Salt and pepper to taste
- 1/4 cup crumbled feta cheese (optional)
- 2 tablespoons fresh basil, chopped

Dressing:
- 2 tablespoons balsamic vinegar
- 1 tablespoon olive oil
- 1 teaspoon Dijon mustard
- 1 teaspoon honey or maple syrup
- Salt and pepper to taste

INSTRUCTIONS

1. Preheat the oven to 400°F (200°C).
2. Rinse the farro under cold water. In a medium saucepan, combine the farro and water or vegetable broth, and bring to a boil.
3. Reduce the heat to low, cover, and simmer for about 30 minutes, or until the farro is tender. Drain any excess liquid and let it cool slightly.
4. While the farro is cooking, place the cherry tomatoes, zucchini, red bell pepper, and red onion on a baking sheet. Drizzle with olive oil and sprinkle with dried oregano, dried thyme, salt, and pepper. Toss to coat evenly.
5. Roast the vegetables in the preheated oven for 25-30 minutes, or until tender and lightly browned.
6. In a small bowl, whisk together the balsamic vinegar, olive oil, Dijon mustard, honey or maple syrup, salt, and pepper to make the dressing.
7. In a large bowl, combine the cooked farro and roasted vegetables. Drizzle with the dressing and toss to combine.
8. Divide the mixture between two bowls.
9. Top each bowl with crumbled feta cheese (if using) and chopped fresh basil.
10. Serve immediately or refrigerate for later.

Nutritional Information (per serving):

CALORIES: 450	PROTEIN: 12G	CARBOHYDRATES: 62G	FIBER: 10G	SUGARS: 12G	FAT: 18G	SATURATED FAT: 3G
SODIUM: 400MG	POTASSIUM: 900MG	VITAMIN A: 35% DV	VITAMIN C: 100% DV	CALCIUM: 15% DV	IRON: 15% DV	

BARLEY AND MUSHROOM BOWL

PREP TIME
15 MINUTES

COOK TIME
40 MINUTES

★★☆☆☆
DIFFICULTY

SE4VES
2

INGREDIENTS

- 1 cup pearl barley
- 3 cups vegetable broth or water
- 2 tablespoons olive oil
- 1 onion, finely chopped
- 2 cloves garlic, minced
- 8 ounces mushrooms, sliced (such as cremini, shiitake, or button)
- 1 cup baby spinach
- 1/4 cup grated Parmesan cheese (optional)
- 1 tablespoon fresh thyme, chopped
- Salt and pepper to taste

Dressing:
- 2 tablespoons balsamic vinegar
- 1 tablespoon olive oil
- 1 teaspoon Dijon mustard
- 1 teaspoon honey or maple syrup
- Salt and pepper to taste

INSTRUCTIONS

1. Rinse the pearl barley under cold water. In a medium saucepan, combine the barley and vegetable broth or water, and bring to a boil.
2. Reduce the heat to low, cover, and simmer for about 30-35 minutes, or until the barley is tender. Drain any excess liquid and let it cool slightly.
3. While the barley is cooking, heat the olive oil in a large skillet over medium heat.
4. Add the chopped onion and cook for 3-4 minutes, until softened.
5. Add the minced garlic and sliced mushrooms to the skillet, and cook for another 8-10 minutes, until the mushrooms are tender and browned.
6. Stir in the baby spinach and cook until wilted, about 2 minutes.
7. In a small bowl, whisk together the balsamic vinegar, olive oil, Dijon mustard, honey or maple syrup, salt, and pepper to make the dressing.
8. In a large bowl, combine the cooked barley, mushroom mixture, and grated Parmesan cheese (if using). Drizzle with the dressing and toss to combine.
9. Divide the mixture between two bowls.
10. Top each bowl with fresh thyme.
11. Serve immediately or refrigerate for later.

Nutritional Information (per serving):

CALORIES: 420	PROTEIN: 12G	CARBOHYDRATES: 65G	FIBER: 12G	SUGARS: 8G	FAT: 14G	SATURATED FAT: 2.5G
SODIUM: 600MG	POTASSIUM: 800MG	VITAMIN A: 40% DV	VITAMIN C: 15% DV	CALCIUM: 15% DV	IRON: 20% DV	

QUINOA AND CHICKPEA POWER BOWL

HEARTY GRAIN BOWLS

PREP TIME
15 MINUTES

COOK TIME
20 MINUTES

★☆☆☆☆
DIFFICULTY

SE4VES
2

INGREDIENTS

- 1 cup quinoa
- 2 cups water or vegetable broth
- 1 can (15 oz) chickpeas, drained and rinsed
- 1 cup cherry tomatoes, halved
- 1 cucumber, diced
- 1/4 red onion, finely chopped
- 1/2 cup shredded carrots
- 1 avocado, sliced
- 2 tablespoons fresh parsley, chopped
- 2 tablespoons fresh mint, chopped (optional)

Dressing:
- 3 tablespoons olive oil
- 2 tablespoons lemon juice
- 1 tablespoon tahini
- 1 teaspoon ground cumin
- 1 clove garlic, minced
- Salt and pepper to taste

INSTRUCTIONS

1. Rinse the quinoa under cold water. In a medium saucepan, combine the quinoa and water or vegetable broth, and bring to a boil.
2. Reduce the heat to low, cover, and simmer for about 15 minutes, or until the quinoa is tender and the water is absorbed. Fluff with a fork and let it cool slightly.
3. While the quinoa is cooking, prepare the dressing by whisking together the olive oil, lemon juice, tahini, ground cumin, minced garlic, salt, and pepper in a small bowl.
4. In a large bowl, combine the cooked quinoa, chickpeas, cherry tomatoes, cucumber, red onion, and shredded carrots.
5. Drizzle the dressing over the quinoa and vegetable mixture, and toss to combine.
6. Divide the mixture between two bowls.
7. Top each bowl with sliced avocado and sprinkle with fresh parsley and mint (if using).
8. Serve immediately or refrigerate for later.

Nutritional Information (per serving):

CALORIES: 500	PROTEIN: 15G	CARBOHYDRATES: 58G	FIBER: 14G	SUGARS: 6G	FAT: 25G	SATURATED FAT: 3.5G
SODIUM: 400MG	POTASSIUM: 950MG	VITAMIN A: 120% DV	VITAMIN C: 50% DV	CALCIUM: 10% DV	IRON: 25% DV	

BULGUR WHEAT TABBOULEH BOWL

PREP TIME
15 MINUTES

COOK TIME
15 MINUTES

DIFFICULTY

SE4VES
2

INGREDIENTS

- 1 cup bulgur wheat
- 2 cups water or vegetable broth
- 1 cup cherry tomatoes, quartered
- 1 cucumber, diced
- 1/4 red onion, finely chopped
- 1/2 cup fresh parsley, chopped
- 1/4 cup fresh mint, chopped
- 1/4 cup feta cheese, crumbled (optional)
- 1/4 cup Kalamata olives, pitted and sliced (optional)

Dressing:
- 1/4 cup olive oil
- 3 tablespoons lemon juice
- 1 teaspoon lemon zest
- 1 clove garlic, minced
- Salt and pepper to taste

INSTRUCTIONS

1. In a medium saucepan, bring the water or vegetable broth to a boil. Add the bulgur wheat, cover, and remove from heat. Let it sit for about 15 minutes, or until the bulgur is tender and the liquid is absorbed. Fluff with a fork and let it cool slightly.
2. While the bulgur is cooking, prepare the dressing by whisking together the olive oil, lemon juice, lemon zest, minced garlic, salt, and pepper in a small bowl.
3. In a large bowl, combine the cooked bulgur, cherry tomatoes, cucumber, red onion, fresh parsley, and fresh mint.
4. Drizzle the dressing over the bulgur and vegetable mixture, and toss to combine.
5. Divide the mixture between two bowls.
6. Top each bowl with crumbled feta cheese and sliced Kalamata olives (if using).
7. Serve immediately or refrigerate for later.

Nutritional Information (per serving):

CALORIES: 350	PROTEIN: 10G	CARBOHYDRATES: 45G	FIBER: 10G	SUGARS: 6G	FAT: 15G	SATURATED FAT: 3G
SODIUM: 300MG	POTASSIUM: 650MG	VITAMIN A: 35% DV	VITAMIN C: 50% DV		CALCIUM: 10% DV	IRON: 15% DV

Nutrient-Packed Soups and Stews

Soups and stews are a comforting and nutritious option for lunch on the go. They are easy to prepare in large batches, store well, and can be packed with a variety of healthy ingredients. This section introduces you to the benefits of soups and stews, provides tips for making them delicious and nutritious, and offers a variety of recipes to get you started.

Benefits of Nutrient-Packed Soups and Stews

1. **Nutrient-Dense**: Soups and stews can be packed with a variety of vegetables, lean proteins, and whole grains, providing a balanced mix of nutrients.
2. **Hydrating**: The high liquid content in soups and stews helps keep you hydrated.
3. **Versatile**: You can use different ingredients to create endless flavor combinations, ensuring you never get bored.
4. **Meal Prep Friendly**: Soups and stews are easy to prepare in large batches and store well in the refrigerator or freezer, making them perfect for meal prepping.
5. **Comforting**: Soups and stews are warm, comforting, and satisfying, making them a great choice for any time of the year.

Tips for Making Delicious and Nutritious Soups and Stews

1. **Use a Variety of Vegetables**: Incorporate a mix of vegetables to add different textures, flavors, and nutrients. Think leafy greens, root vegetables, and fresh herbs.
2. **Include Lean Proteins**: Add lean proteins such as chicken, turkey, beans, lentils, or tofu to make your soup or stew more satisfying.
3. **Healthy Carbohydrates**: Use whole grains, legumes, and starchy vegetables to provide complex carbohydrates and fiber.
4. **Flavorful Broths**: Use homemade or low-sodium broths to enhance the flavor without adding excess sodium.
5. **Season Well**: Don't forget to season your soups and stews with herbs, spices, and other seasonings to ensure they are flavorful.
6. **Proper Storage**: Store soups and stews in airtight containers in the refrigerator for up to 4 days or in the freezer for up to 3 months. Reheat gently on the stove or in the microwave.

LENTIL AND VEGETABLE SOUP

PREP TIME
15 MINUTES

COOK TIME
45 MINUTES

DIFFICULTY

SE4VES
4

INGREDIENTS

- 1 cup dried lentils, rinsed and drained
- 1 tablespoon olive oil
- 1 onion, diced
- 2 cloves garlic, minced
- 2 carrots, diced
- 2 celery stalks, diced
- 1 red bell pepper, diced
- 1 zucchini, diced
- 1 can (14.5 oz) diced tomatoes
- 6 cups vegetable broth
- 1 teaspoon ground cumin
- 1 teaspoon dried thyme
- 1 bay leaf
- Salt and pepper to taste
- 2 cups fresh spinach, chopped
- 1/4 cup fresh parsley, chopped
- 1 tablespoon lemon juice

INSTRUCTIONS

1. Heat the olive oil in a large pot over medium heat. Add the diced onion and cook until softened, about 5 minutes.
2. Add the minced garlic and cook for another 1-2 minutes, until fragrant.
3. Add the carrots, celery, red bell pepper, and zucchini to the pot. Cook for about 5-7 minutes, until the vegetables start to soften.
4. Stir in the lentils, diced tomatoes, vegetable broth, ground cumin, dried thyme, bay leaf, salt, and pepper.
5. Bring the mixture to a boil, then reduce the heat to low and simmer for about 30-35 minutes, until the lentils are tender.
6. Remove the bay leaf and discard it.
7. Stir in the fresh spinach, parsley, and lemon juice. Cook for another 2-3 minutes, until the spinach is wilted.
8. Taste and adjust the seasoning with more salt and pepper if needed.
9. Serve immediately or let it cool and refrigerate for later.

Nutritional Information (per serving):

CALORIES: 250	PROTEIN: 12G	CARBOHYDRATES: 40G	FIBER: 15G	SUGARS: 8G	FAT: 6G	SATURATED FAT: 1G
SODIUM: 600MG	POTASSIUM: 900MG	VITAMIN A: 150% DV	VITAMIN C: 60% DV		CALCIUM: 10% DV	IRON: 25% DV

CHICKEN AND WILD RICE SOUP

PREP TIME
15 MINUTES

COOK TIME
45 MINUTES

DIFFICULTY

SE4VES
4

INGREDIENTS

- 1 tablespoon olive oil
- 1 onion, diced
- 2 cloves garlic, minced
- 2 carrots, diced
- 2 celery stalks, diced
- 1 cup mushrooms, sliced
- 1 cup wild rice, rinsed
- 6 cups chicken broth (low sodium)
- 2 cups cooked chicken breast, shredded
- 1 teaspoon dried thyme
- 1 teaspoon dried rosemary
- 1 bay leaf
- Salt and pepper to taste
- 1 cup baby spinach, chopped
- 1/4 cup fresh parsley, chopped
- 1/4 cup heavy cream or coconut milk (optional)

INSTRUCTIONS

1. Heat the olive oil in a large pot over medium heat. Add the diced onion and cook until softened, about 5 minutes.
2. Add the minced garlic and cook for another 1-2 minutes, until fragrant.
3. Add the carrots, celery, and mushrooms to the pot. Cook for about 5-7 minutes, until the vegetables start to soften.
4. Stir in the wild rice, chicken broth, shredded chicken, dried thyme, dried rosemary, bay leaf, salt, and pepper.
5. Bring the mixture to a boil, then reduce the heat to low and simmer for about 35-40 minutes, until the rice is tender.
6. Remove the bay leaf and discard it.
7. Stir in the chopped spinach and fresh parsley. Cook for another 2-3 minutes, until the spinach is wilted.
8. If using, stir in the heavy cream or coconut milk and heat through.
9. Taste and adjust the seasoning with more salt and pepper if needed.
10. Serve immediately or let it cool and refrigerate for later.

Nutritional Information (per serving):

CALORIES: 300	PROTEIN: 25G	CARBOHYDRATES: 30G	FIBER: 5G	SUGARS: 4G	FAT: 10G	SATURATED FAT: 3G
SODIUM: 500MG	POTASSIUM: 700MG	VITAMIN A: 80% DV	VITAMIN C: 15% DV	CALCIUM: 8% DV	IRON: 15% DV	

MOROCCAN CHICKPEA STEW

PREP TIME
15 MINUTES

COOK TIME
30 MINUTES

DIFFICULTY

SE4VES
4

INGREDIENTS

- 2 tablespoons olive oil
- 1 onion, diced
- 2 cloves garlic, minced
- 2 carrots, diced
- 1 red bell pepper, diced
- 1 zucchini, diced
- 1 can (15 oz) chickpeas, drained and rinsed
- 1 can (14.5 oz) diced tomatoes
- 2 cups vegetable broth
- 1 teaspoon ground cumin
- 1 teaspoon ground coriander
- 1 teaspoon ground cinnamon
- 1/2 teaspoon ground turmeric
- 1/2 teaspoon paprika
- 1/4 teaspoon cayenne pepper (optional)
- Salt and pepper to taste
- 1/4 cup raisins or chopped dried apricots
- 1/4 cup fresh cilantro, chopped
- 1 tablespoon lemon juice

INSTRUCTIONS

1. Heat the olive oil in a large pot over medium heat. Add the diced onion and cook until softened, about 5 minutes.
2. Add the minced garlic and cook for another 1-2 minutes, until fragrant.
3. Add the carrots, red bell pepper, and zucchini to the pot. Cook for about 5-7 minutes, until the vegetables start to soften.
4. Stir in the chickpeas, diced tomatoes, vegetable broth, ground cumin, ground coriander, ground cinnamon, ground turmeric, paprika, cayenne pepper (if using), salt, and pepper.
5. Bring the mixture to a boil, then reduce the heat to low and simmer for about 20 minutes, until the vegetables are tender.
6. Stir in the raisins or chopped dried apricots and cook for another 5 minutes.
7. Stir in the fresh cilantro and lemon juice.
8. Taste and adjust the seasoning with more salt and pepper if needed.
9. Serve immediately or let it cool and refrigerate for later.

Nutritional Information (per serving):

CALORIES: 320	PROTEIN: 9G	CARBOHYDRATES: 50G	FIBER: 12G	SUGARS: 12G	FAT: 10G	SATURATED FAT: 1.5G
SODIUM: 500MG	POTASSIUM: 900MG	VITAMIN A: 150% DV	VITAMIN C: 80% DV	CALCIUM: 10% DV	IRON: 20% DV	

TOMATO BASIL SOUP WITH ORZO

 PREP TIME
10 MINUTES

 COOK TIME
25 MINUTES

 **DIFFICULTY**

 SE4VES
4

INGREDIENTS

- 2 tablespoons olive oil
- 1 onion, diced
- 2 cloves garlic, minced
- 1 can (28 oz) crushed tomatoes
- 4 cups vegetable broth
- 1/2 cup orzo pasta
- 1 teaspoon dried basil
- 1/2 teaspoon dried oregano
- Salt and pepper to taste
- 1/2 cup fresh basil, chopped
- 1/4 cup grated Parmesan cheese (optional)

INSTRUCTIONS

1. Heat the olive oil in a large pot over medium heat. Add the diced onion and cook until softened, about 5 minutes.
2. Add the minced garlic and cook for another 1-2 minutes, until fragrant.
3. Stir in the crushed tomatoes and vegetable broth. Bring to a boil.
4. Add the orzo pasta, dried basil, and dried oregano. Reduce the heat to low and simmer for about 15 minutes, or until the orzo is tender.
5. Season with salt and pepper to taste.
6. Stir in the fresh basil.
7. Serve hot, topped with grated Parmesan cheese if desired.

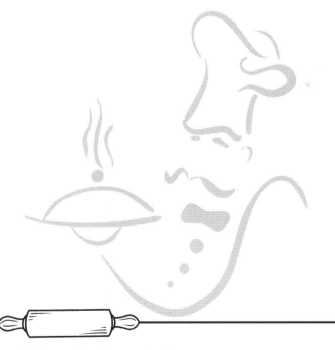

Nutritional Information (per serving):

CALORIES: 220	PROTEIN: 5G	CARBOHYDRATES: 35G	FIBER: 5G	SUGARS: 10G	FAT: 7G	SATURATED FAT: 1G
SODIUM: 600MG	POTASSIUM: 700MG	VITAMIN A: 20% DV	VITAMIN C: 35% DV		CALCIUM: 10% DV	IRON: 15% DV

SWEET POTATO AND BLACK BEAN STEW

NUTRIENT-PACKED SOUPS AND STEWS

PREP TIME
15 MINUTES

COOK TIME
30 MINUTES

DIFFICULTY

SE4VES
4

INGREDIENTS

- 2 tablespoons olive oil
- 1 onion, diced
- 2 cloves garlic, minced
- 2 sweet potatoes, peeled and diced
- 1 red bell pepper, diced
- 1 can (15 oz) black beans, drained and rinsed
- 1 can (14.5 oz) diced tomatoes
- 4 cups vegetable broth
- 1 teaspoon ground cumin
- 1 teaspoon smoked paprika
- 1/2 teaspoon ground coriander
- 1/2 teaspoon ground cinnamon
- Salt and pepper to taste
- 1/4 cup fresh cilantro, chopped
- 1 tablespoon lime juice

INSTRUCTIONS

1. Heat the olive oil in a large pot over medium heat. Add the diced onion and cook until softened, about 5 minutes.
2. Add the minced garlic and cook for another 1-2 minutes, until fragrant.
3. Add the sweet potatoes and red bell pepper to the pot. Cook for about 5-7 minutes, until the vegetables start to soften.
4. Stir in the black beans, diced tomatoes, vegetable broth, ground cumin, smoked paprika, ground coriander, ground cinnamon, salt, and pepper.
5. Bring the mixture to a boil, then reduce the heat to low and simmer for about 20 minutes, until the sweet potatoes are tender.
6. Stir in the fresh cilantro and lime juice.
7. Taste and adjust the seasoning with more salt and pepper if needed.
8. Serve immediately or let it cool and refrigerate for later.

Nutritional Information (per serving):

CALORIES: 300	PROTEIN: 7G	CARBOHYDRATES: 50G	FIBER: 12G	SUGARS: 10G	FAT: 9G	SATURATED FAT: 1.5G
SODIUM: 600MG	POTASSIUM: 900MG	VITAMIN A: 400% DV	VITAMIN C: 70% DV	CALCIUM: 10% DV	IRON: 15% DV	

One-Pan and Sheet-Pan Meals

One-pan and sheet-pan meals are perfect for busy weeknights when you want to enjoy a healthy, home-cooked dinner without spending a lot of time on preparation and cleanup. These meals are convenient, versatile, and can be packed with a variety of nutritious ingredients. This section introduces you to the benefits of one-pan and sheet-pan meals, provides tips for making them delicious and balanced, and offers a variety of recipes to get you started.

Benefits of One-Pan and Sheet-Pan Meals

1. **Convenience**: With everything cooked in one pan or on one sheet, these meals simplify both the cooking and cleaning process.
2. **Versatility**: You can use a wide range of ingredients, including proteins, vegetables, and grains, to create endless flavor combinations.
3. **Balanced Nutrition**: One-pan and sheet-pan meals can easily incorporate a mix of protein, vegetables, and healthy fats to provide a balanced and nutritious dinner.
4. **Time-Saving**: These meals typically require minimal prep and hands-on time, allowing you to relax or attend to other tasks while dinner cooks.
5. **Meal Prep Friendly**: One-pan and sheet-pan meals are great for meal prepping. You can make a large batch and enjoy leftovers for lunch or dinner the next day.

Tips for Making Delicious and Balanced One-Pan and Sheet-Pan Meals

1. **Choose the Right Pan**: Use a heavy-duty sheet pan or a large, oven-safe skillet to ensure even cooking and prevent sticking.
2. **Balance Your Ingredients**: Aim to include a mix of lean proteins, a variety of colorful vegetables, and, if desired, a healthy grain or starch.
3. **Season Generously**: Use herbs, spices, marinades, and sauces to add flavor to your ingredients. Don't be afraid to experiment with different seasonings.
4. **Layer for Even Cooking**: Cut ingredients into uniform sizes and layer them appropriately on the pan. Place denser vegetables and proteins that take longer to cook in a single layer, while adding quicker-cooking items later.
5. **Use Parchment Paper or Foil**: Line your sheet pan with parchment paper or foil to make cleanup even easier.
6. **Monitor and Toss**: Keep an eye on your meal as it cooks, and toss or stir ingredients occasionally to ensure even cooking and browning.

SHEET-PAN LEMON GARLIC CHICKEN WITH VEGETABLES

ONE-PAN AND SHEET-PAN MEALS

PREP TIME
15 MINUTES

COOK TIME
35 MINUTES

DIFFICULTY

SE4VES
4

INGREDIENTS

- 4 boneless, skinless chicken breasts
- 1 pound baby potatoes, halved
- 1 cup baby carrots
- 1 red bell pepper, sliced
- 1 yellow bell pepper, sliced
- 1 red onion, sliced
- 2 tablespoons olive oil
- 3 tablespoons lemon juice
- 4 cloves garlic, minced
- 1 teaspoon dried oregano
- 1 teaspoon dried thyme
- Salt and pepper to taste
- 1 lemon, sliced for garnish
- Fresh parsley, chopped for garnish

INSTRUCTIONS

1. Preheat your oven to 400°F (200°C). Line a large sheet pan with parchment paper or lightly grease it.
2. In a small bowl, whisk together the olive oil, lemon juice, minced garlic, dried oregano, dried thyme, salt, and pepper.
3. Place the chicken breasts, baby potatoes, baby carrots, red bell pepper, yellow bell pepper, and red onion on the sheet pan.
4. Pour the lemon garlic mixture over the chicken and vegetables. Toss to coat everything evenly.
5. Arrange the chicken breasts in the center of the sheet pan and spread the vegetables around them in a single layer.
6. Garnish with lemon slices.
7. Bake in the preheated oven for 30-35 minutes, or until the chicken is cooked through and the vegetables are tender.
8. Garnish with chopped fresh parsley before serving.

Nutritional Information (per serving):

CALORIES: 400	PROTEIN: 35G	CARBOHYDRATES: 35G	FIBER: 6G	SUGARS: 6G	FAT: 15G	SATURATED FAT: 2G
SODIUM: 200MG	POTASSIUM: 1100MG	VITAMIN A: 120% DV	VITAMIN C: 180% DV		CALCIUM: 6% DV	IRON: 15% DV

ONE-PAN BALSAMIC CHICKEN AND VEGGIES

PREP TIME
15 MINUTES

COOK TIME
30 MINUTES

DIFFICULTY

SE4VES
4

INGREDIENTS

- 4 boneless, skinless chicken breasts
- 1 cup cherry tomatoes, halved
- 1 cup broccoli florets
- 1 red bell pepper, sliced
- 1 yellow bell pepper, sliced
- 1 red onion, sliced
- 2 tablespoons olive oil
- 3 tablespoons balsamic vinegar
- 2 cloves garlic, minced
- 1 teaspoon dried basil
- 1 teaspoon dried oregano
- Salt and pepper to taste
- Fresh basil, chopped for garnish

INSTRUCTIONS

1. Preheat your oven to 400°F (200°C). Line a large sheet pan with parchment paper or lightly grease it.
2. In a small bowl, whisk together the olive oil, balsamic vinegar, minced garlic, dried basil, dried oregano, salt, and pepper.
3. Place the chicken breasts, cherry tomatoes, broccoli florets, red bell pepper, yellow bell pepper, and red onion on the sheet pan.
4. Pour the balsamic mixture over the chicken and vegetables. Toss to coat everything evenly.
5. Arrange the chicken breasts in the center of the sheet pan and spread the vegetables around them in a single layer.
6. Bake in the preheated oven for 25-30 minutes, or until the chicken is cooked through and the vegetables are tender.
7. Garnish with chopped fresh basil before serving.

Nutritional Information (per serving):

CALORIES: 350	PROTEIN: 30G	CARBOHYDRATES: 20G	FIBER: 6G	SUGARS: 10G	FAT: 15G	SATURATED FAT: 2.5G
SODIUM: 200MG	POTASSIUM: 900MG	VITAMIN A: 35% DV	VITAMIN C: 220% DV	CALCIUM: 6% DV	IRON: 10% DV	

SHEET-PAN SALMON WITH ASPARAGUS AND SWEET POTATOES

ONE-PAN AND SHEET-PAN MEALS

PREP TIME
15 MINUTES

COOK TIME
25 MINUTES

DIFFICULTY

SE4VES
4

INGREDIENTS

- 4 salmon fillets (about 6 oz each)
- 1 pound asparagus, trimmed
- 2 medium sweet potatoes, peeled and cut into 1-inch cubes
- 2 tablespoons olive oil
- 2 tablespoons lemon juice
- 2 cloves garlic, minced
- 1 teaspoon dried dill
- 1 teaspoon paprika
- Salt and pepper to taste
- 1 lemon, sliced for garnish
- Fresh parsley, chopped for garnish

INSTRUCTIONS

1. Preheat your oven to 400°F (200°C). Line a large sheet pan with parchment paper or lightly grease it.
2. In a small bowl, whisk together the olive oil, lemon juice, minced garlic, dried dill, paprika, salt, and pepper.
3. Place the sweet potato cubes on the sheet pan and drizzle with half of the olive oil mixture. Toss to coat evenly.
4. Roast the sweet potatoes in the preheated oven for 15 minutes.
5. Remove the sheet pan from the oven and add the asparagus and salmon fillets to the pan. Drizzle the remaining olive oil mixture over the asparagus and salmon. Toss the asparagus to coat and ensure the salmon is evenly seasoned.
6. Return the sheet pan to the oven and bake for an additional 10-12 minutes, or until the salmon is cooked through and flakes easily with a fork, and the asparagus is tender.
7. Garnish with lemon slices and chopped fresh parsley before serving.

Nutritional Information (per serving):

CALORIES: 450	PROTEIN: 35G	CARBOHYDRATES: 30G	FIBER: 8G	SUGARS: 8G	FAT: 20G	SATURATED FAT: 3.5G
SODIUM: 200MG	POTASSIUM: 1300MG	VITAMIN A: 300% DV	VITAMIN C: 35% DV	CALCIUM: 10% DV	IRON: 15% DV	

ONE-PAN MEXICAN QUINOA

PREP TIME
10 MINUTES

COOK TIME
20 MINUTES

DIFFICULTY

SE4VES
4

INGREDIENTS

- 1 tablespoon olive oil
- 1 onion, diced
- 2 cloves garlic, minced
- 1 cup quinoa, rinsed
- 1 can (15 oz) black beans, drained and rinsed
- 1 cup corn kernels (fresh or frozen)
- 1 red bell pepper, diced
- 1 can (14.5 oz) diced tomatoes
- 2 cups vegetable broth
- 1 teaspoon ground cumin
- 1 teaspoon chili powder
- 1/2 teaspoon paprika
- Salt and pepper to taste
- 1 avocado, diced
- 1/4 cup fresh cilantro, chopped
- 1 lime, cut into wedges

INSTRUCTIONS

1. Heat the olive oil in a large skillet over medium heat. Add the diced onion and cook until softened, about 5 minutes.
2. Add the minced garlic and cook for another 1-2 minutes, until fragrant.
3. Stir in the quinoa, black beans, corn, red bell pepper, diced tomatoes (with their juice), vegetable broth, ground cumin, chili powder, paprika, salt, and pepper.
4. Bring the mixture to a boil, then reduce the heat to low, cover, and simmer for about 20 minutes, or until the quinoa is cooked and the liquid is absorbed.
5. Remove from heat and let it sit, covered, for 5 minutes.
6. Fluff the quinoa with a fork and stir in the chopped fresh cilantro.
7. Divide the quinoa mixture between four bowls. Top each with diced avocado and serve with lime wedges on the side.

Nutritional Information (per serving):

CALORIES: 350	PROTEIN: 12G	CARBOHYDRATES: 50G	FIBER: 12G	SUGARS: 8G	FAT: 12G	SATURATED FAT: 1.5G
SODIUM: 600MG	POTASSIUM: 950MG	VITAMIN A: 50% DV	VITAMIN C: 70% DV	CALCIUM: 6% DV	IRON: 20% DV	

SHEET-PAN SHRIMP FAJITAS

PREP TIME
15 MINUTES

COOK TIME
15 MINUTES

DIFFICULTY

SE4VES
4

INGREDIENTS

- 1 pound large shrimp, peeled and deveined
- 1 red bell pepper, sliced
- 1 yellow bell pepper, sliced
- 1 green bell pepper, sliced
- 1 red onion, sliced
- 2 tablespoons olive oil
- 1 tablespoon lime juice
- 2 cloves garlic, minced
- 1 teaspoon chili powder
- 1 teaspoon ground cumin
- 1/2 teaspoon smoked paprika
- 1/2 teaspoon dried oregano
- Salt and pepper to taste
- Fresh cilantro, chopped for garnish
- Lime wedges, for serving
- 8 small whole wheat tortillas

INSTRUCTIONS

1. Preheat your oven to 400°F (200°C). Line a large sheet pan with parchment paper or lightly grease it.
2. In a large bowl, whisk together the olive oil, lime juice, minced garlic, chili powder, ground cumin, smoked paprika, dried oregano, salt, and pepper.
3. Add the shrimp, sliced bell peppers, and sliced red onion to the bowl. Toss to coat everything evenly with the seasoning mixture.
4. Spread the shrimp and vegetable mixture in a single layer on the prepared sheet pan.
5. Bake in the preheated oven for 10-15 minutes, or until the shrimp are pink and opaque, and the vegetables are tender.
6. Remove from the oven and garnish with chopped fresh cilantro.
7. Warm the whole wheat tortillas in the oven for a few minutes or in a skillet over medium heat.
8. Serve the shrimp and vegetable mixture in the warm tortillas, with lime wedges on the side.

Nutritional Information (per serving):

CALORIES: 350	PROTEIN: 25G	CARBOHYDRATES: 35G	FIBER: 6G	SUGARS: 6G	FAT: 12G	SATURATED FAT: 2G
SODIUM: 700MG	POTASSIUM: 700MG	VITAMIN A: 60% DV	VITAMIN C: 200% DV	CALCIUM: 10% DV	IRON: 20% DV	

ONE-PAN ITALIAN SAUSAGE AND PEPPERS

ONE-PAN AND SHEET-PAN MEALS

PREP TIME
10 MINUTES

COOK TIME
30 MINUTES

★☆☆☆☆
DIFFICULTY

SE4VES
4

INGREDIENTS

- 4 Italian sausages (mild or spicy, as preferred)
- 1 red bell pepper, sliced
- 1 green bell pepper, sliced
- 1 yellow bell pepper, sliced
- 1 red onion, sliced
- 2 cloves garlic, minced
- 2 tablespoons olive oil
- 1 teaspoon dried oregano
- 1 teaspoon dried basil
- 1/2 teaspoon crushed red pepper flakes (optional)
- Salt and pepper to taste
- 1/4 cup fresh parsley, chopped
- 1/4 cup grated Parmesan cheese (optional)

INSTRUCTIONS

1. Preheat your oven to 400°F (200°C). Line a large sheet pan with parchment paper or lightly grease it.
2. In a large bowl, combine the sliced bell peppers, sliced red onion, and minced garlic. Drizzle with olive oil, and season with dried oregano, dried basil, crushed red pepper flakes (if using), salt, and pepper. Toss to coat evenly.
3. Spread the pepper and onion mixture in a single layer on the prepared sheet pan.
4. Arrange the Italian sausages on top of the vegetables.
5. Bake in the preheated oven for 25-30 minutes, or until the sausages are cooked through and the vegetables are tender and slightly caramelized.
6. Remove from the oven and garnish with chopped fresh parsley and grated Parmesan cheese (if using).
7. Serve immediately, optionally with a side of crusty bread or over a bed of rice.

Nutritional Information (per serving):

CALORIES: 450	PROTEIN: 20G	CARBOHYDRATES: 20G	FIBER: 6G	SUGARS: 6G	FAT: 30G	SATURATED FAT: 10G
SODIUM: 900MG	POTASSIUM: 800MG	VITAMIN A: 60% DV	VITAMIN C: 250% DV	CALCIUM: 10% DV		IRON: 15% DV

SHEET-PAN TERIYAKI CHICKEN WITH BROCCOLI

PREP TIME
15 MINUTES

COOK TIME
25 MINUTES

DIFFICULTY

SE4VES
4

INGREDIENTS

- 4 boneless, skinless chicken breasts
- 1 pound broccoli florets
- 1 red bell pepper, sliced
- 1 yellow bell pepper, sliced
- 1 tablespoon olive oil
- 1/4 cup low-sodium soy sauce
- 1/4 cup teriyaki sauce
- 2 tablespoons honey
- 2 cloves garlic, minced
- 1 teaspoon fresh ginger, grated
- 1 tablespoon sesame seeds (optional)
- 2 green onions, sliced
- Cooked brown rice, for serving

INSTRUCTIONS

1. Preheat your oven to 400°F (200°C). Line a large sheet pan with parchment paper or lightly grease it.
2. In a small bowl, whisk together the soy sauce, teriyaki sauce, honey, minced garlic, and grated ginger.
3. Place the chicken breasts on the prepared sheet pan. Arrange the broccoli florets, red bell pepper, and yellow bell pepper around the chicken.
4. Drizzle the olive oil over the vegetables and toss to coat.
5. Pour the teriyaki mixture over the chicken breasts and vegetables, ensuring everything is evenly coated.
6. Bake in the preheated oven for 25-30 minutes, or until the chicken is cooked through and the vegetables are tender.
7. Remove from the oven and sprinkle with sesame seeds (if using) and sliced green onions.
8. Serve immediately with cooked brown rice.

Nutritional Information (per serving):

CALORIES: 400	PROTEIN: 35G	CARBOHYDRATES: 40G	FIBER: 8G	SUGARS: 18G	FAT: 10G	SATURATED FAT: 2G
SODIUM: 800MG	POTASSIUM: 950MG	VITAMIN A: 100% DV	VITAMIN C: 250% DV	CALCIUM: 10% DV	IRON: 15% DV	

ONE-PAN RATATOUILLE

PREP TIME
15 MINUTES

COOK TIME
45 MINUTES

DIFFICULTY

SE4VES
4

INGREDIENTS

- 1 large eggplant, diced
- 1 zucchini, sliced
- 1 yellow squash, sliced
- 1 red bell pepper, diced
- 1 yellow bell pepper, diced
- 1 red onion, diced
- 4 cloves garlic, minced
- 4 tablespoons olive oil
- 1 can (14.5 oz) diced tomatoes
- 1 teaspoon dried thyme
- 1 teaspoon dried oregano
- 1 teaspoon dried basil
- Salt and pepper to taste
- Fresh basil, chopped for garnish
- Fresh parsley, chopped for garnish

INSTRUCTIONS

1. Preheat your oven to 400°F (200°C). Line a large sheet pan with parchment paper or lightly grease it.
2. In a large bowl, combine the diced eggplant, zucchini, yellow squash, red bell pepper, yellow bell pepper, red onion, and minced garlic.
3. Drizzle the vegetables with olive oil and season with dried thyme, dried oregano, dried basil, salt, and pepper. Toss to coat evenly.
4. Spread the vegetable mixture in a single layer on the prepared sheet pan.
5. Pour the diced tomatoes over the vegetables and gently toss to combine.
6. Bake in the preheated oven for 40-45 minutes, or until the vegetables are tender and slightly caramelized, stirring halfway through.
7. Remove from the oven and garnish with chopped fresh basil and parsley.
8. Serve immediately, optionally with crusty bread or over a bed of rice or quinoa.

Nutritional Information (per serving):

CALORIES: 250	PROTEIN: 4G	CARBOHYDRATES: 30G	FIBER: 8G	SUGARS: 14G	FAT: 14G	SATURATED FAT: 2G
SODIUM: 300MG	POTASSIUM: 1200MG	VITAMIN A: 40% DV	VITAMIN C: 150% DV	CALCIUM: 8% DV	IRON: 10% DV	

SHEET-PAN GREEK CHICKEN WITH TZATZIKI

ONE-PAN AND SHEET-PAN MEALS

PREP TIME
20 MINUTES

COOK TIME
25 MINUTES

★★☆☆☆
DIFFICULTY

SE4VES
4

INGREDIENTS

- 4 boneless, skinless chicken breasts
- 1 pound baby potatoes, halved
- 1 red bell pepper, sliced
- 1 yellow bell pepper, sliced
- 1 red onion, sliced
- 1/4 cup olive oil
- 3 tablespoons lemon juice
- 3 cloves garlic, minced
- 1 teaspoon dried oregano
- 1 teaspoon dried thyme
- Salt and pepper to taste
- 1/4 cup crumbled feta cheese (optional)
- Fresh parsley, chopped for garnish

Tzatziki Sauce:
- 1 cup Greek yogurt
- 1 cucumber, grated and drained
- 2 cloves garlic, minced
- 1 tablespoon lemon juice
- 1 tablespoon fresh dill, chopped
- Salt and pepper to taste

INSTRUCTIONS

1. Preheat your oven to 400°F (200°C). Line a large sheet pan with parchment paper or lightly grease it.
2. In a small bowl, whisk together the olive oil, lemon juice, minced garlic, dried oregano, dried thyme, salt, and pepper.
3. Place the chicken breasts, baby potatoes, red bell pepper, yellow bell pepper, and red onion on the sheet pan.
4. Pour the olive oil mixture over the chicken and vegetables. Toss to coat everything evenly.
5. Arrange the chicken breasts in the center of the sheet pan and spread the vegetables around them in a single layer.
6. Bake in the preheated oven for 25-30 minutes, or until the chicken is cooked through and the vegetables are tender.
7. While the chicken and vegetables are baking, prepare the tzatziki sauce. In a medium bowl, combine the Greek yogurt, grated cucumber, minced garlic, lemon juice, fresh dill, salt, and pepper. Mix well and refrigerate until ready to serve.
8. Remove the sheet pan from the oven and garnish with crumbled feta cheese (if using) and chopped fresh parsley.
9. Serve immediately with the tzatziki sauce on the side.

Nutritional Information (per serving):

CALORIES: 450	PROTEIN: 38G	CARBOHYDRATES: 30G	FIBER: 6G	SUGARS: 8G	FAT: 20G	SATURATED FAT: 4G
SODIUM: 450MG	POTASSIUM: 1000MG	VITAMIN A: 50% DV	VITAMIN C: 180% DV	CALCIUM: 15% DV	IRON: 15% DV	

ONE-PAN HONEY GARLIC PORK CHOPS

PREP TIME
10 MINUTES

COOK TIME
25 MINUTES

DIFFICULTY

SE4VES
4

INGREDIENTS

- 4 boneless pork chops
- 1 pound baby potatoes, halved
- 1 cup green beans, trimmed
- 1 cup carrots, sliced
- 2 tablespoons olive oil
- Salt and pepper to taste

Honey Garlic Sauce:
- 1/4 cup honey
- 3 tablespoons soy sauce (low sodium)
- 4 cloves garlic, minced
- 1 tablespoon apple cider vinegar
- 1 teaspoon dried thyme
- 1/2 teaspoon black pepper

INSTRUCTIONS

1. Preheat your oven to 400°F (200°C). Line a large sheet pan with parchment paper or lightly grease it.
2. In a small bowl, whisk together the honey, soy sauce, minced garlic, apple cider vinegar, dried thyme, and black pepper.
3. Place the pork chops, baby potatoes, green beans, and carrots on the sheet pan.
4. Drizzle the olive oil over the vegetables and toss to coat. Season with salt and pepper.
5. Pour half of the honey garlic sauce over the pork chops and vegetables. Toss to coat evenly.
6. Arrange the pork chops in the center of the sheet pan and spread the vegetables around them in a single layer.
7. Bake in the preheated oven for 20-25 minutes, or until the pork chops are cooked through and the vegetables are tender.
8. Remove the sheet pan from the oven and drizzle the remaining honey garlic sauce over the pork chops.
9. Serve immediately.

Nutritional Information (per serving):

CALORIES: 450	PROTEIN: 30G	CARBOHYDRATES: 40G	FIBER: 6G	SUGARS: 18G	FAT: 20G	SATURATED FAT: 4G
SODIUM: 600MG	POTASSIUM: 900MG	VITAMIN A: 120% DV	VITAMIN C: 50% DV	CALCIUM: 6% DV	IRON: 15% DV	

Slow Cooker and Instant Pot Recipes

Slow cooker and Instant Pot recipes are perfect for those who want to enjoy a home-cooked meal without spending hours in the kitchen. These appliances make it easy to prepare delicious and nutritious meals with minimal effort. This section introduces you to the benefits of using a slow cooker and Instant Pot, provides tips for making the most out of these appliances, and offers a variety of recipes to get you started.

Benefits of Slow Cooker and Instant Pot Recipes

1. **Convenience**: Slow cookers and Instant Pots allow you to prepare meals with minimal hands-on time. Simply add your ingredients, set the timer, and let the appliance do the work.
2. **Versatility**: Both appliances can be used to prepare a wide range of dishes, from soups and stews to meats and desserts.
3. **Flavorful Meals**: Slow cooking allows flavors to develop and meld together, while the Instant Pot's pressure cooking feature intensifies flavors quickly.
4. **Nutrient Retention**: Both slow cooking and pressure cooking methods help retain the nutrients in your ingredients, resulting in healthier meals.
5. **Meal Prep Friendly**: These recipes are great for meal prepping. You can make large batches and store leftovers for easy, ready-to-eat meals throughout the week.

Tips for Making the Most Out of Slow Cooker and Instant Pot Recipes

1. **Layering Ingredients**: When using a slow cooker, place denser ingredients like root vegetables at the bottom and lighter ingredients on top for even cooking. In the Instant Pot, always follow the recipe's layering instructions to prevent burning.
2. **Liquid Levels**: Slow cookers require less liquid than stovetop cooking, as the liquid doesn't evaporate as quickly. For the Instant Pot, ensure there is enough liquid to create steam for pressure cooking.
3. **Pre-Browning**: For added flavor, brown meats and sauté aromatics like onions and garlic before adding them to the slow cooker or Instant Pot.
4. **Timing**: Slow cookers have high and low settings, with cooking times ranging from 4 to 10 hours. The Instant Pot significantly reduces cooking time, often preparing meals in under an hour.
5. **Adjusting Recipes**: Traditional recipes can be adapted for the slow cooker or Instant Pot by adjusting cooking times and liquid amounts.

SLOW COOKER BEEF AND BARLEY STEW

PREP TIME
20 MINUTES

COOK TIME
8H (ON LOW) OR 4H (ON HIGH)

DIFFICULTY

SE4VES
6

INGREDIENTS

- 1 1/2 pounds beef stew meat, cut into 1-inch cubes
- 1 cup pearl barley, rinsed
- 4 cups beef broth (low sodium)
- 1 cup water
- 1 large onion, diced
- 3 carrots, diced
- 3 celery stalks, diced
- 2 cloves garlic, minced
- 1 can (14.5 oz) diced tomatoes
- 1 teaspoon dried thyme
- 1 teaspoon dried rosemary
- 2 bay leaves
- Salt and pepper to taste
- 1/4 cup fresh parsley, chopped

INSTRUCTIONS

1. Pre-Browning (Optional): In a large skillet, heat a tablespoon of oil over medium-high heat. Add the beef stew meat and brown on all sides, about 5-7 minutes. This step adds extra flavor but can be skipped for convenience.
2. Transfer the beef stew meat (browned or raw) to the slow cooker.
3. Add the pearl barley, beef broth, water, diced onion, carrots, celery, minced garlic, diced tomatoes (with their juice), dried thyme, dried rosemary, bay leaves, salt, and pepper.
4. Stir to combine all ingredients.
5. Cover and cook on low for 8 hours or on high for 4 hours, until the beef and barley are tender.
6. Remove the bay leaves and discard.
7. Stir in the chopped fresh parsley.
8. Taste and adjust the seasoning with more salt and pepper if needed.
9. Serve hot, garnished with additional fresh parsley if desired.

Nutritional Information (per serving):

CALORIES: 350	PROTEIN: 30G	CARBOHYDRATES: 35G	FIBER: 8G	SUGARS: 5G	FAT: 10G	SATURATED FAT: 3.5G
SODIUM: 600MG	POTASSIUM: 900MG	VITAMIN A: 100% DV	VITAMIN C: 15% DV		CALCIUM: 8% DV	IRON: 25% DV

INSTANT POT CHICKEN TIKKA MASALA

PREP TIME
15 MINUTES

COOK TIME
30 MINUTES

DIFFICULTY

SE4VES
4

INGREDIENTS

- 1 1/2 pounds boneless, skinless chicken thighs, cut into bite-sized pieces
- 1 cup plain Greek yogurt
- 2 tablespoons lemon juice
- 4 cloves garlic, minced (divided)
- 2 tablespoons ginger, grated (divided)
- 2 teaspoons ground cumin (divided)
- 2 teaspoons ground coriander (divided)
- 2 teaspoons ground turmeric (divided)
- 2 teaspoons garam masala (divided)
- 1 teaspoon chili powder
- 1 teaspoon paprika
- 1 tablespoon olive oil
- 1 large onion, diced
- 1 can (14.5 oz) diced tomatoes
- 1 cup heavy cream or coconut milk
- Salt and pepper to taste
- Fresh cilantro, chopped for garnish
- Cooked basmati rice, for serving

INSTRUCTIONS

1. Marinate the Chicken: In a large bowl, combine the Greek yogurt, lemon juice, half of the minced garlic, half of the grated ginger, 1 teaspoon ground cumin, 1 teaspoon ground coriander, 1 teaspoon ground turmeric, 1 teaspoon garam masala, chili powder, and paprika. Add the chicken pieces and mix to coat evenly. Marinate for at least 30 minutes or overnight in the refrigerator for best results.
2. Sauté: Set the Instant Pot to the sauté function. Add the olive oil and diced onion. Cook for 3-4 minutes until the onion is softened.
3. Add the remaining minced garlic, grated ginger, 1 teaspoon ground cumin, 1 teaspoon ground coriander, 1 teaspoon ground turmeric, and 1 teaspoon garam masala. Cook for another 1-2 minutes until fragrant.
4. Add the marinated chicken to the Instant Pot and cook for about 5 minutes, stirring occasionally, until the chicken is browned.
5. Add the diced tomatoes and stir to combine.
6. Pressure Cook: Close the lid and set the Instant Pot to the high-pressure setting for 10 minutes. Ensure the valve is set to the sealing position.
7. Once the cooking time is complete, let the pressure release naturally for 10 minutes, then perform a quick release to release any remaining pressure.
8. Open the lid and stir in the heavy cream or coconut milk. Season with salt and pepper to taste.
9. Set the Instant Pot to the sauté function and cook for an additional 5 minutes, stirring occasionally, until the sauce has thickened.
10. Serve hot, garnished with chopped fresh cilantro, over cooked basmati rice.

Nutritional Information (per serving):

CALORIES: 450	PROTEIN: 35G	CARBOHYDRATES: 20G	FIBER: 3G	SUGARS: 6G	FAT: 25G	SATURATED FAT: 12G
SODIUM: 700MG	POTASSIUM: 900MG	VITAMIN A: 15% DV	VITAMIN C: 20% DV	CALCIUM: 10% DV	IRON: 20% DV	

SLOW COOKER LENTIL SOUP

PREP TIME
15 MINUTES

COOK TIME
6-8 HOURS (ON LOW) OR 3-4 HOURS (ON HIGH)

★☆☆☆☆

DIFFICULTY

SE4VES
6

INGREDIENTS

- 1 1/2 cups dried green or brown lentils, rinsed and drained
- 1 onion, diced
- 3 carrots, diced
- 3 celery stalks, diced
- 4 cloves garlic, minced
- 1 can (14.5 oz) diced tomatoes
- 6 cups vegetable broth (low sodium)
- 1 teaspoon dried thyme
- 1 teaspoon ground cumin
- 1/2 teaspoon smoked paprika
- 1 bay leaf
- Salt and pepper to taste
- 2 cups fresh spinach, chopped
- 1/4 cup fresh parsley, chopped
- 1 tablespoon lemon juice

INSTRUCTIONS

1. Pre-Browning (Optional): If desired, you can sauté the diced onion, carrots, celery, and garlic in a skillet with a tablespoon of olive oil over medium heat until softened, about 5-7 minutes. This step adds extra flavor but can be skipped for convenience.
2. Transfer the onion, carrots, celery, and garlic (raw or sautéed) to the slow cooker.
3. Add the rinsed lentils, diced tomatoes (with their juice), vegetable broth, dried thyme, ground cumin, smoked paprika, bay leaf, salt, and pepper.
4. Stir to combine all ingredients.
5. Cover and cook on low for 6-8 hours or on high for 3-4 hours, until the lentils are tender.
6. About 10 minutes before serving, stir in the chopped spinach and fresh parsley. Cook until the spinach is wilted.
7. Stir in the lemon juice.
8. Remove the bay leaf and discard.
9. Taste and adjust the seasoning with more salt and pepper if needed.
10. Serve hot, garnished with additional fresh parsley if desired.

Nutritional Information (per serving):

CALORIES: 250	PROTEIN: 12G	CARBOHYDRATES: 40G	FIBER: 15G	SUGARS: 7G	FAT: 3G	SATURATED FAT: 0.5G
SODIUM: 600MG	POTASSIUM: 900MG	VITAMIN A: 120% DV	VITAMIN C: 30% DV	CALCIUM: 10% DV	IRON: 25% DV	

INSTANT POT PULLED PORK

PREP TIME
15 MINUTES

COOK TIME
60 MINUTES

DIFFICULTY

SE4VES
6

INGREDIENTS

- 3 pounds boneless pork shoulder (pork butt), cut into 4 pieces
- 1 tablespoon olive oil
- 1 onion, sliced
- 4 cloves garlic, minced
- 1 cup chicken broth (low sodium)
- 1/2 cup apple cider vinegar
- 1/4 cup brown sugar
- 2 tablespoons tomato paste
- 1 tablespoon smoked paprika
- 1 tablespoon chili powder
- 1 teaspoon ground cumin
- 1 teaspoon dried oregano
- 1 teaspoon salt
- 1/2 teaspoon black pepper
- 1 cup barbecue sauce (plus extra for serving)

INSTRUCTIONS

1. Sauté: Set the Instant Pot to the sauté function. Add the olive oil and sliced onion. Cook for 3-4 minutes until the onion is softened.
2. Add the minced garlic and cook for another 1-2 minutes until fragrant.
3. Add the pork shoulder pieces to the Instant Pot and brown on all sides, about 5 minutes.
4. Deglaze: Pour in the chicken broth and apple cider vinegar, scraping up any browned bits from the bottom of the pot.
5. Seasoning: Stir in the brown sugar, tomato paste, smoked paprika, chili powder, ground cumin, dried oregano, salt, and black pepper.
6. Pressure Cook: Close the lid and set the Instant Pot to the high-pressure setting for 60 minutes. Ensure the valve is set to the sealing position.
7. Once the cooking time is complete, let the pressure release naturally for 15 minutes, then perform a quick release to release any remaining pressure.
8. Shred the Pork: Open the lid and transfer the pork to a large bowl. Shred the pork using two forks.
9. Set the Instant Pot to the sauté function and simmer the cooking liquid for 10-15 minutes to reduce and thicken slightly.
10. Return the shredded pork to the Instant Pot and stir to combine with the reduced cooking liquid.
11. Stir in the barbecue sauce.
12. Serve hot on buns with extra barbecue sauce on the side.

Nutritional Information (per serving):

CALORIES: 450	PROTEIN: 35G	CARBOHYDRATES: 20G	FIBER: 1G	SUGARS: 15G	FAT: 25G	SATURATED FAT: 8G
SODIUM: 700MG	POTASSIUM: 750MG	VITAMIN A: 15% DV	VITAMIN C: 10% DV	CALCIUM: 6% DV	IRON: 15% DV	

SLOW COOKER VEGETARIAN CHILI

PREP TIME
15 MINUTES

COOK TIME
6-8 HOURS (ON LOW) OR 3-4 HOURS (ON HIGH)

DIFFICULTY

SE4VES
6

INGREDIENTS

- 1 tablespoon olive oil
- 1 onion, diced
- 3 cloves garlic, minced
- 1 red bell pepper, diced
- 1 yellow bell pepper, diced
- 1 zucchini, diced
- 1 cup corn kernels (fresh or frozen)
- 2 cans (15 oz each) black beans, drained and rinsed
- 1 can (15 oz) kidney beans, drained and rinsed
- 1 can (15 oz) chickpeas, drained and rinsed
- 2 cans (14.5 oz each) diced tomatoes
- 1 can (6 oz) tomato paste
- 2 cups vegetable broth (low sodium)
- 2 tablespoons chili powder
- 1 tablespoon ground cumin
- 1 teaspoon smoked paprika
- 1 teaspoon dried oregano
- 1/2 teaspoon cayenne pepper (optional)
- Salt and pepper to taste
- 1/4 cup fresh cilantro, chopped
- Juice of 1 lime

INSTRUCTIONS

1. Pre-Sauté (Optional): In a large skillet, heat the olive oil over medium heat. Add the diced onion and cook until softened, about 5 minutes. Add the minced garlic and cook for another 1-2 minutes until fragrant.
2. Transfer the onion and garlic (raw or sautéed) to the slow cooker.
3. Add the red bell pepper, yellow bell pepper, zucchini, corn kernels, black beans, kidney beans, chickpeas, diced tomatoes (with their juice), tomato paste, vegetable broth, chili powder, ground cumin, smoked paprika, dried oregano, cayenne pepper (if using), salt, and pepper.
4. Stir to combine all ingredients.
5. Cover and cook on low for 6-8 hours or on high for 3-4 hours, until the vegetables are tender and the flavors have melded together.
6. About 10 minutes before serving, stir in the chopped fresh cilantro and lime juice.
7. Taste and adjust the seasoning with more salt and pepper if needed.
8. Serve hot, garnished with additional fresh cilantro if desired.

Nutritional Information (per serving):

CALORIES: 300	PROTEIN: 12G	CARBOHYDRATES: 50G	FIBER: 15G	SUGARS: 10G	FAT: 6G	SATURATED FAT: 1G
SODIUM: 600MG	POTASSIUM: 1000MG	VITAMIN A: 35% DV	VITAMIN C: 150% DV	CALCIUM: 10% DV	IRON: 25% DV	

INSTANT POT BEEF STROGANOFF

PREP TIME
15 MINUTES

COOK TIME
25 MINUTES

DIFFICULTY

SE4VES
4

INGREDIENTS

- 1 1/2 pounds beef stew meat, cut into bite-sized pieces
- 2 tablespoons olive oil
- 1 onion, diced
- 3 cloves garlic, minced
- 8 ounces mushrooms, sliced
- 1 teaspoon dried thyme
- 1 teaspoon paprika
- Salt and pepper to taste
- 2 tablespoons Worcestershire sauce
- 3 cups beef broth (low sodium)
- 2 tablespoons cornstarch mixed with 2 tablespoons water (slurry)
- 1/2 cup sour cream
- 8 ounces egg noodles, cooked according to package instructions
- Fresh parsley, chopped for garnish

INSTRUCTIONS

1. Sauté: Set the Instant Pot to the sauté function. Add the olive oil and diced onion. Cook for 3-4 minutes until the onion is softened.
2. Add the minced garlic and cook for another 1-2 minutes until fragrant.
3. Add the beef stew meat to the Instant Pot and cook until browned on all sides, about 5-7 minutes.
4. Stir in the sliced mushrooms, dried thyme, paprika, salt, and pepper.
5. Add the Worcestershire sauce and beef broth. Stir to combine.
6. Pressure Cook: Close the lid and set the Instant Pot to the high-pressure setting for 15 minutes. Ensure the valve is set to the sealing position.
7. Once the cooking time is complete, let the pressure release naturally for 10 minutes, then perform a quick release to release any remaining pressure.
8. Open the lid and set the Instant Pot to the sauté function. Stir in the cornstarch slurry and cook for 2-3 minutes, until the sauce has thickened.
9. Stir in the sour cream until well combined.
10. Serve the beef stroganoff over cooked egg noodles, garnished with chopped fresh parsley.

Nutritional Information (per serving):

CALORIES: 500	PROTEIN: 35G	CARBOHYDRATES: 45G	FIBER: 3G	SUGARS: 4G	FAT: 20G	SATURATED FAT: 8G
SODIUM: 700MG	POTASSIUM: 950MG	VITAMIN A: 15% DV	VITAMIN C: 8% DV	CALCIUM: 10% DV	IRON: 25% DV	

SLOW COOKER THAI PEANUT CHICKEN

SLOW COOKER AND INSTANT POT RECIPES

PREP TIME
15 MINUTES

COOK TIME
6-8 HOURS (ON LOW) OR 3-4 HOURS (ON HIGH)

DIFFICULTY

SE4VES
4

INGREDIENTS

- 1 1/2 pounds boneless, skinless chicken thighs
- 1 red bell pepper, sliced
- 1 yellow bell pepper, sliced
- 1 onion, sliced
- 3 cloves garlic, minced
- 1/2 cup natural peanut butter
- 1/4 cup soy sauce (low sodium)
- 1/4 cup chicken broth (low sodium)
- 2 tablespoons lime juice
- 2 tablespoons honey
- 1 tablespoon fresh ginger, grated
- 1 tablespoon rice vinegar
- 1 teaspoon red pepper flakes (optional)
- Salt and pepper to taste
- Fresh cilantro, chopped for garnish
- Chopped peanuts for garnish
- Cooked jasmine rice, for serving

INSTRUCTIONS

1. Place the chicken thighs in the bottom of the slow cooker.
2. Add the sliced red bell pepper, yellow bell pepper, and onion on top of the chicken.
3. In a medium bowl, whisk together the minced garlic, peanut butter, soy sauce, chicken broth, lime juice, honey, grated ginger, rice vinegar, red pepper flakes (if using), salt, and pepper until smooth.
4. Pour the peanut sauce mixture over the chicken and vegetables in the slow cooker.
5. Cover and cook on low for 6-8 hours or on high for 3-4 hours, until the chicken is tender and cooked through.
6. Remove the chicken thighs from the slow cooker and shred them using two forks. Return the shredded chicken to the slow cooker and stir to combine with the sauce.
7. Serve the Thai peanut chicken over cooked jasmine rice, garnished with chopped fresh cilantro and chopped peanuts.

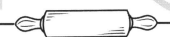

Nutritional Information (per serving):

CALORIES: 450	PROTEIN: 35G	CARBOHYDRATES: 25G	FIBER: 5G	SUGARS: 12G	FAT: 25G	SATURATED FAT: 5G
SODIUM: 800MG	POTASSIUM: 700MG	VITAMIN A: 35% DV	VITAMIN C: 100% DV	CALCIUM: 4% DV	IRON: 15% DV	

INSTANT POT MINESTRONE SOUP

PREP TIME
15 MINUTES

COOK TIME
20 MINUTES

DIFFICULTY

SE4VES
6

INGREDIENTS

- 2 tablespoons olive oil
- 1 onion, diced
- 3 cloves garlic, minced
- 2 carrots, diced
- 2 celery stalks, diced
- 1 zucchini, diced
- 1 yellow squash, diced
- 1 red bell pepper, diced
- 1 can (14.5 oz) diced tomatoes
- 1 can (15 oz) kidney beans, drained and rinsed
- 1 can (15 oz) cannellini beans, drained and rinsed
- 1 cup green beans, trimmed and cut into 1-inch pieces
- 1 cup small pasta (such as ditalini or elbow macaroni)
- 6 cups vegetable broth (low sodium)
- 1 teaspoon dried basil
- 1 teaspoon dried oregano
- 1/2 teaspoon dried thyme
- Salt and pepper to taste
- 2 cups fresh spinach, chopped
- 1/4 cup fresh parsley, chopped
- Grated Parmesan cheese for garnish (optional)

INSTRUCTIONS

1. Sauté: Set the Instant Pot to the sauté function. Add the olive oil and diced onion. Cook for 3-4 minutes until the onion is softened.
2. Add the minced garlic, carrots, celery, zucchini, yellow squash, and red bell pepper. Cook for another 5 minutes, stirring occasionally.
3. Stir in the diced tomatoes, kidney beans, cannellini beans, green beans, pasta, vegetable broth, dried basil, dried oregano, dried thyme, salt, and pepper.
4. Pressure Cook: Close the lid and set the Instant Pot to the high-pressure setting for 5 minutes. Ensure the valve is set to the sealing position.
5. Once the cooking time is complete, perform a quick release to release the pressure.
6. Open the lid and stir in the chopped fresh spinach and parsley.
7. Let the soup sit for a few minutes to allow the spinach to wilt.
8. Taste and adjust the seasoning with more salt and pepper if needed.
9. Serve hot, garnished with grated Parmesan cheese if desired.

Nutritional Information (per serving):

CALORIES: 250	PROTEIN: 10G	CARBOHYDRATES: 40G	FIBER: 10G	SUGARS: 6G	FAT: 6G	SATURATED FAT: 1G
SODIUM: 600MG	POTASSIUM: 900MG	VITAMIN A: 100% DV	VITAMIN C: 60% DV		CALCIUM: 15% DV	IRON: 20% DV

Balanced Stir-Fries and Curries

Stir-fries and curries are versatile and flavorful dishes that can be easily tailored to include a variety of vegetables, proteins, and spices. They are quick to prepare, making them ideal for busy weeknights while still providing a balanced and nutritious meal. This section introduces you to the benefits of stir-fries and curries, provides tips for making them healthy and delicious, and offers a variety of recipes to get you started.

Benefits of Balanced Stir-Fries and Curries

1. **Quick and Easy**: Stir-fries and curries can be prepared in under 30 minutes, making them perfect for quick weeknight dinners.
2. **Nutrient-Dense**: These dishes are packed with a variety of vegetables, providing essential vitamins, minerals, and fiber.
3. **Versatile**: You can easily switch up the proteins and vegetables based on what you have on hand or your dietary preferences.
4. **Flavorful**: The use of fresh herbs, spices, and flavorful sauces makes stir-fries and curries incredibly delicious.
5. **Balanced Nutrition**: By incorporating lean proteins, vegetables, and healthy fats, stir-fries and curries offer a well-rounded meal.

Tips for Making Healthy and Delicious Stir-Fries and Curries

1. **Prep All Ingredients Before Cooking**: Stir-fries cook quickly, so having all your ingredients prepped and ready to go is essential.
2. **Use High-Quality Oils**: Use oils with a high smoke point, such as canola, peanut, or avocado oil, for stir-frying. For curries, coconut oil adds a nice flavor.
3. **Choose Lean Proteins**: Opt for lean cuts of meat, tofu, tempeh, or legumes to keep the dish healthy.
4. **Incorporate a Variety of Vegetables**: Use a mix of colorful vegetables to maximize nutrient intake and add visual appeal.
5. **Balance Flavors**: Use a combination of salty, sweet, sour, and spicy elements to create a well-balanced dish. Soy sauce, honey, lime juice, and chili are common ingredients that can achieve this balance.
6. **Control Portion Sizes**: Serve your stir-fry or curry with a moderate portion of whole grains like brown rice, quinoa, or whole wheat noodles to keep the meal balanced.

CHICKEN AND VEGETABLE STIR-FRY

BALANCED STIR-FRIES AND CURRIES

PREP TIME
15 MINUTES

COOK TIME
15 MINUTES

DIFFICULTY

SE4VES
4

INGREDIENTS

- 1 pound boneless, skinless chicken breasts, sliced into thin strips
- 2 tablespoons canola oil or avocado oil
- 1 red bell pepper, sliced
- 1 yellow bell pepper, sliced
- 1 cup broccoli florets
- 1 cup snap peas
- 1 carrot, julienned
- 3 cloves garlic, minced
- 1 tablespoon fresh ginger, grated
- 3 green onions, sliced
- 1/4 cup low-sodium soy sauce
- 2 tablespoons hoisin sauce
- 1 tablespoon rice vinegar
- 1 teaspoon sesame oil
- 1 tablespoon sesame seeds (optional)
- Cooked brown rice or whole wheat noodles, for serving

INSTRUCTIONS

1. Prep All Ingredients: Have all your ingredients prepped and ready to go before starting to cook, as stir-frying goes quickly.
2. Heat the Oil: In a large skillet or wok, heat the canola or avocado oil over medium-high heat.
3. Cook the Chicken: Add the sliced chicken to the skillet and cook for 5-7 minutes, or until the chicken is cooked through and lightly browned. Remove the chicken from the skillet and set it aside.
4. Cook the Vegetables: In the same skillet, add the red bell pepper, yellow bell pepper, broccoli florets, snap peas, and julienned carrot. Stir-fry for 5-6 minutes, or until the vegetables are tender-crisp.
5. Add Aromatics: Add the minced garlic and grated ginger to the skillet and cook for 1-2 minutes, until fragrant.
6. Combine Chicken and Vegetables: Return the cooked chicken to the skillet and toss to combine with the vegetables.
7. Make the Sauce: In a small bowl, whisk together the soy sauce, hoisin sauce, rice vinegar, and sesame oil.
8. Add the Sauce: Pour the sauce over the chicken and vegetables in the skillet. Toss everything together and cook for another 2-3 minutes, until the sauce is heated through and coats the ingredients evenly.
9. Serve: Serve the chicken and vegetable stir-fry over cooked brown rice or whole wheat noodles. Garnish with sliced green onions and sesame seeds if desired.

Nutritional Information (per serving):

CALORIES: 350	PROTEIN: 30G	CARBOHYDRATES: 25G	FIBER: 5G	SUGARS: 8G	FAT: 12G	SATURATED FAT: 2G
SODIUM: 700MG	POTASSIUM: 900MG	VITAMIN A: 80% DV	VITAMIN C: 150% DV	CALCIUM: 6% DV	IRON: 15% DV	

THAI RED CURRY WITH TOFU

BALANCED STIR-FRIES AND CURRIES

PREP TIME
15 MINUTES

COOK TIME
20 MINUTES

★☆☆☆☆
DIFFICULTY

SE4VES
4

INGREDIENTS

- 1 block (14 oz) firm tofu, drained and cubed
- 2 tablespoons vegetable oil
- 1 onion, diced
- 3 cloves garlic, minced
- 1 tablespoon fresh ginger, grated
- 1 red bell pepper, sliced
- 1 yellow bell pepper, sliced
- 1 zucchini, sliced
- 1 cup snap peas
- 2 tablespoons Thai red curry paste
- 1 can (14 oz) coconut milk
- 1 cup vegetable broth
- 1 tablespoon soy sauce (low sodium)
- 1 teaspoon brown sugar
- 1 tablespoon lime juice
- Fresh basil, chopped for garnish
- Fresh cilantro, chopped for garnish
- Cooked jasmine rice, for serving

INSTRUCTIONS

1. Prep the Tofu: Press the tofu to remove excess moisture. Cut into cubes.
2. Cook the Tofu: In a large skillet or wok, heat 1 tablespoon of vegetable oil over medium-high heat. Add the tofu cubes and cook until golden brown on all sides, about 8-10 minutes. Remove from the skillet and set aside.
3. Sauté Aromatics: In the same skillet, add the remaining tablespoon of vegetable oil. Add the diced onion and cook until softened, about 3-4 minutes. Add the minced garlic and grated ginger and cook for another 1-2 minutes, until fragrant.
4. Cook the Vegetables: Add the red bell pepper, yellow bell pepper, zucchini, and snap peas to the skillet. Cook for 5-6 minutes, until the vegetables are tender-crisp.
5. Add the Curry Paste: Stir in the Thai red curry paste and cook for 1-2 minutes, until the paste is well distributed and fragrant.
6. Add Liquids: Pour in the coconut milk and vegetable broth. Stir to combine. Bring to a simmer.
7. Season the Curry: Add the soy sauce, brown sugar, and lime juice. Stir to combine.
8. Combine and Simmer: Return the tofu to the skillet. Simmer for 5-6 minutes, allowing the flavors to meld together.
9. Serve: Serve the Thai red curry with tofu over cooked jasmine rice. Garnish with chopped fresh basil and cilantro.

Nutritional Information (per serving):

CALORIES: 400	PROTEIN: 15G	CARBOHYDRATES: 35G	FIBER: 7G	SUGARS: 8G	FAT: 25G	SATURATED FAT: 15G
SODIUM: 600MG	POTASSIUM: 700MG	VITAMIN A: 50% DV	VITAMIN C: 120% DV	CALCIUM: 20% DV	IRON: 35% DV	

BEEF AND BROCCOLI STIR-FRY

BALANCED STIR-FRIES AND CURRIES

PREP TIME
15 MINUTES

COOK TIME
15 MINUTES

DIFFICULTY

SE4VES
4

INGREDIENTS

- 1 pound flank steak, thinly sliced against the grain
- 2 tablespoons vegetable oil, divided
- 4 cups broccoli florets
- 1 red bell pepper, sliced
- 3 cloves garlic, minced
- 1 tablespoon fresh ginger, grated
- 3 green onions, sliced
- 1/4 cup low-sodium soy sauce
- 2 tablespoons hoisin sauce
- 1 tablespoon oyster sauce
- 1 tablespoon cornstarch
- 1/4 cup water
- 1 teaspoon sesame oil
- Sesame seeds (optional)
- Cooked jasmine rice or brown rice, for serving

INSTRUCTIONS

1. Prep the Beef: Thinly slice the flank steak against the grain and set aside.
2. Blanch the Broccoli: Bring a pot of water to a boil. Add the broccoli florets and cook for 2-3 minutes until tender-crisp. Drain and set aside.
3. Sauté the Beef: In a large skillet or wok, heat 1 tablespoon of vegetable oil over medium-high heat. Add the sliced beef and cook for 3-4 minutes until browned and cooked through. Remove the beef from the skillet and set aside.
4. Cook the Vegetables: In the same skillet, add the remaining tablespoon of vegetable oil. Add the minced garlic and grated ginger and cook for 1-2 minutes until fragrant. Add the sliced red bell pepper and cook for 3-4 minutes until tender.
5. Combine Sauce Ingredients: In a small bowl, whisk together the soy sauce, hoisin sauce, oyster sauce, cornstarch, and water until smooth.
6. Combine Everything: Return the cooked beef and blanched broccoli to the skillet. Pour the sauce over the beef and vegetables. Cook, stirring frequently, for 2-3 minutes until the sauce thickens and coats the beef and vegetables.
7. Add Green Onions: Stir in the sliced green onions and sesame oil.
8. Serve: Serve the beef and broccoli stir-fry over cooked jasmine rice or brown rice. Garnish with sesame seeds if desired.

Nutritional Information (per serving):

CALORIES: 350	PROTEIN: 25G	CARBOHYDRATES: 30G	FIBER: 5G	SUGARS: 6G	FAT: 15G	SATURATED FAT: 3G
SODIUM: 800MG	POTASSIUM: 700MG	VITAMIN A: 35% DV	VITAMIN C: 150% DV	CALCIUM: 8% DV	IRON: 20% DV

CHICKPEA AND SPINACH CURRY

BALANCED STIR-FRIES AND CURRIES

PREP TIME
15 MINUTES

COOK TIME
20 MINUTES

DIFFICULTY

SE4VES
4

INGREDIENTS

- 2 tablespoons vegetable oil
- 1 onion, diced
- 3 cloves garlic, minced
- 1 tablespoon fresh ginger, grated
- 1 tablespoon curry powder
- 1 teaspoon ground cumin
- 1 teaspoon ground coriander
- 1/2 teaspoon turmeric
- 1/4 teaspoon cayenne pepper (optional)
- 2 cans (15 oz each) chickpeas, drained and rinsed
- 1 can (14.5 oz) diced tomatoes
- 1 can (14 oz) coconut milk
- 4 cups fresh spinach, chopped
- Salt and pepper to taste
- Juice of 1 lime
- Fresh cilantro, chopped for garnish
- Cooked basmati rice, for serving

INSTRUCTIONS

1. Sauté Aromatics: In a large skillet or pot, heat the vegetable oil over medium heat. Add the diced onion and cook for 3-4 minutes until softened.
2. Add the minced garlic and grated ginger and cook for another 1-2 minutes until fragrant.
3. Add Spices: Stir in the curry powder, ground cumin, ground coriander, turmeric, and cayenne pepper (if using). Cook for 1-2 minutes until the spices are fragrant.
4. Add Chickpeas and Tomatoes: Add the chickpeas and diced tomatoes (with their juice) to the skillet. Stir to combine and cook for 3-4 minutes.
5. Add Coconut Milk: Pour in the coconut milk and bring the mixture to a simmer. Cook for 10-15 minutes until the sauce has thickened slightly.
6. Add Spinach: Stir in the chopped spinach and cook for 2-3 minutes until wilted.
7. Season: Add salt and pepper to taste. Stir in the lime juice.
8. Serve: Serve the chickpea and spinach curry over cooked basmati rice. Garnish with chopped fresh cilantro.

Nutritional Information (per serving):

CALORIES: 400	PROTEIN: 12G	CARBOHYDRATES: 45G	FIBER: 10G	SUGARS: 6G	FAT: 20G	SATURATED FAT: 12G
SODIUM: 600MG	POTASSIUM: 900MG	VITAMIN A: 60% DV	VITAMIN C: 40% DV	CALCIUM: 15% DV	IRON: 30% DV	

SHRIMP AND SNOW PEA STIR-FRY

BALANCED STIR-FRIES AND CURRIES

PREP TIME
15 MINUTES

COOK TIME
10 MINUTES

★☆☆☆☆
DIFFICULTY

SE4VES
4

INGREDIENTS

- 1 pound large shrimp, peeled and deveined
- 2 tablespoons vegetable oil
- 3 cloves garlic, minced
- 1 tablespoon fresh ginger, grated
- 1 red bell pepper, sliced
- 1 cup snow peas
- 1 carrot, julienned
- 3 green onions, sliced
- 1/4 cup low-sodium soy sauce
- 2 tablespoons oyster sauce
- 1 tablespoon rice vinegar
- 1 tablespoon honey
- 1 teaspoon sesame oil
- 1 tablespoon cornstarch mixed with 2 tablespoons water (slurry)
- Sesame seeds (optional)
- Cooked jasmine rice or brown rice, for serving

INSTRUCTIONS

1. Prep All Ingredients: Have all your ingredients prepped and ready to go before starting to cook, as stir-frying goes quickly.
2. Heat the Oil: In a large skillet or wok, heat the vegetable oil over medium-high heat.
3. Cook the Shrimp: Add the shrimp to the skillet and cook for 2-3 minutes, until pink and opaque. Remove the shrimp from the skillet and set aside.
4. Cook the Vegetables: In the same skillet, add the minced garlic and grated ginger. Cook for 1-2 minutes, until fragrant. Add the red bell pepper, snow peas, carrot, and green onions. Stir-fry for 3-4 minutes, until the vegetables are tender-crisp.
5. Make the Sauce: In a small bowl, whisk together the soy sauce, oyster sauce, rice vinegar, honey, and sesame oil.
6. Combine Everything: Return the cooked shrimp to the skillet. Pour the sauce over the shrimp and vegetables. Cook for 1-2 minutes, until the sauce is heated through.
7. Thicken the Sauce: Stir in the cornstarch slurry and cook for another 1-2 minutes, until the sauce thickens and coats the shrimp and vegetables.
8. Serve: Serve the shrimp and snow pea stir-fry over cooked jasmine rice or brown rice. Garnish with sesame seeds if desired.

Nutritional Information (per serving):

CALORIES: 300	PROTEIN: 25G	CARBOHYDRATES: 30G	FIBER: 5G	SUGARS: 8G	FAT: 10G	SATURATED FAT: 1.5G
SODIUM: 800MG	POTASSIUM: 600MG	VITAMIN A: 60% DV	VITAMIN C: 100% DV	CALCIUM: 10% DV	IRON: 20% DV	

Pasta and Grain Dishes with a Healthy Spin

Pasta and grain dishes are staples in many diets, but they can often be high in refined carbohydrates and low in nutrients. By incorporating whole grains, lean proteins, and plenty of vegetables, you can create delicious and balanced meals that are both satisfying and nutritious. This section introduces you to the benefits of healthy pasta and grain dishes, provides tips for making them nutritious and flavorful, and offers a variety of recipes to get you started.

Benefits of Healthy Pasta and Grain Dishes

1. **Balanced Nutrition**: By using whole grains and adding a variety of vegetables and proteins, these dishes can provide a balanced mix of carbohydrates, protein, and healthy fats.
2. **Versatility**: Pasta and grains are incredibly versatile and can be combined with a wide range of ingredients to create different flavor profiles and textures.
3. **Fiber-Rich**: Whole grains are high in dietary fiber, which aids digestion and helps keep you feeling full longer.
4. **Nutrient-Dense**: Adding vegetables and lean proteins increases the nutrient density of these dishes, providing essential vitamins and minerals.
5. **Satisfying**: These dishes are hearty and satisfying, making them perfect for family meals or meal prep.

Tips for Making Nutritious and Flavorful Pasta and Grain Dishes

1. **Choose Whole Grains**: Opt for whole grain pasta, brown rice, quinoa, farro, or barley to increase fiber and nutrient content.
2. **Incorporate Lean Proteins**: Add lean proteins such as chicken, turkey, tofu, legumes, or seafood to make the dish more balanced and filling.
3. **Load Up on Vegetables**: Include a variety of colorful vegetables to add flavor, texture, and nutrients. Fresh, roasted, or sautéed vegetables all work well.
4. **Use Healthy Fats**: Use olive oil, avocado, nuts, and seeds to add healthy fats to your dishes.
5. **Season Well**: Use fresh herbs, spices, and flavorful sauces to enhance the taste without adding excess calories or sodium.
6. **Portion Control**: Be mindful of portion sizes, especially with pasta, to maintain a balanced meal.

QUINOA AND VEGGIE STUFFED PEPPERS

PREP TIME
15 MINUTES

COOK TIME
40 MINUTES

DIFFICULTY

SE4VES
4

INGREDIENTS

- 4 large bell peppers, tops cut off and seeds removed
- 1 cup quinoa, rinsed and drained
- 2 cups vegetable broth
- 1 tablespoon olive oil
- 1 onion, diced
- 2 cloves garlic, minced
- 1 zucchini, diced
- 1 cup cherry tomatoes, halved
- 1 cup black beans, drained and rinsed
- 1 teaspoon ground cumin
- 1 teaspoon smoked paprika
- 1/2 teaspoon dried oregano
- Salt and pepper to taste
- 1/4 cup fresh cilantro, chopped
- 1/4 cup crumbled feta cheese (optional)

INSTRUCTIONS

1. Preheat Oven: Preheat your oven to 375°F (190°C). Line a baking dish with parchment paper or lightly grease it.
2. Cook Quinoa: In a medium saucepan, combine the quinoa and vegetable broth. Bring to a boil, then reduce the heat to low, cover, and simmer for about 15 minutes, or until the quinoa is tender and the liquid is absorbed. Fluff with a fork and set aside.
3. Sauté Vegetables: In a large skillet, heat the olive oil over medium heat. Add the diced onion and cook until softened, about 5 minutes. Add the minced garlic and cook for another 1-2 minutes until fragrant.
4. Add the diced zucchini, cherry tomatoes, and black beans to the skillet. Cook for about 5-7 minutes, until the vegetables are tender.
5. Season: Stir in the ground cumin, smoked paprika, dried oregano, salt, and pepper. Cook for another 1-2 minutes until well combined.
6. Combine with Quinoa: Remove the skillet from heat and stir in the cooked quinoa and chopped cilantro.
7. Stuff Peppers: Stuff each bell pepper with the quinoa and veggie mixture, pressing down lightly to pack the filling.
8. Bake: Place the stuffed peppers in the prepared baking dish. Cover with foil and bake in the preheated oven for 30 minutes. Remove the foil and bake for an additional 10 minutes, or until the peppers are tender and the tops are slightly browned.
9. Garnish and Serve: If using, sprinkle the crumbled feta cheese over the stuffed peppers before serving. Serve hot.

Nutritional Information (per serving):

CALORIES: 300	PROTEIN: 10G	CARBOHYDRATES: 50G	FIBER: 10G	SUGARS: 8G	FAT: 8G	SATURATED FAT: 2G
SODIUM: 600MG	POTASSIUM: 800MG	VITAMIN A: 60% DV	VITAMIN C: 200% DV	CALCIUM: 10% DV	IRON: 20% DV	

WHOLE WHEAT SPAGHETTI WITH TURKEY MEATBALLS

PASTA AND GRAIN DISHES WITH A HEALTHY SPIN

PREP TIME
20 MINUTES

COOK TIME
30 MINUTES

★★☆☆☆
DIFFICULTY

SE4VES
4

INGREDIENTS

Turkey Meatballs:
- 1 pound ground turkey
- 1/4 cup whole wheat breadcrumbs
- 1/4 cup grated Parmesan cheese
- 1 egg, beaten
- 2 cloves garlic, minced
- 1 teaspoon dried oregano
- 1 teaspoon dried basil
- 1/2 teaspoon salt
- 1/4 teaspoon black pepper
- 2 tablespoons olive oil (for frying)

Spaghetti and Sauce:
- 8 ounces whole wheat spaghetti
- 1 tablespoon olive oil
- 1 onion, diced
- 3 cloves garlic, minced
- 1 can (28 oz) crushed tomatoes
- 1 teaspoon dried oregano
- 1 teaspoon dried basil
- 1/2 teaspoon red pepper flakes (optional)
- Salt and pepper to taste
- Fresh basil, chopped for garnish
- Grated Parmesan cheese for garnish

INSTRUCTIONS

1. **Preheat Oven**: Preheat your oven to 375°F (190°C).

2. **Prepare the Meatballs:**
   - In a large bowl, combine the ground turkey, whole wheat breadcrumbs, grated Parmesan cheese, beaten egg, minced garlic, dried oregano, dried basil, salt, and black pepper.
   - Mix until well combined.
   - Shape the mixture into meatballs, about 1 inch in diameter.

3. **Cook the Meatballs:**
   - In a large skillet, heat 2 tablespoons of olive oil over medium heat.
   - Add the meatballs and cook until browned on all sides, about 5-7 minutes.
   - Transfer the browned meatballs to a baking sheet and bake in the preheated oven for 15 minutes, or until cooked through.

4. **Cook the Spaghetti:**
   - While the meatballs are baking, cook the whole wheat spaghetti according to package instructions. Drain and set aside.

5. **Prepare the Sauce:**
   - In the same skillet used for the meatballs, heat 1 tablespoon of olive oil over medium heat.
   - Add the diced onion and cook until softened, about 5 minutes.
   - Add the minced garlic and cook for another 1-2 minutes until fragrant.
   - Stir in the crushed tomatoes, dried oregano, dried basil, red pepper flakes (if using), salt, and pepper.
   - Simmer the sauce for about 10 minutes, until it thickens slightly.

6. **Combine and Serve:**
   - Add the cooked meatballs to the sauce and simmer for another 5 minutes.
   - Serve the turkey meatballs and sauce over the cooked whole wheat spaghetti.
   - Garnish with chopped fresh basil and grated Parmesan cheese.

Nutritional Information (per serving):

CALORIES: 450	PROTEIN: 30G	CARBOHYDRATES: 50G	FIBER: 8G	SUGARS: 8G	FAT: 15G	SATURATED FAT: 4G
SODIUM: 800MG	POTASSIUM: 900MG	VITAMIN A: 15% DV	VITAMIN C: 30% DV	CALCIUM: 20% DV	IRON: 25% DV	

Energy Bars and Bites

Energy bars and bites are a convenient and nutritious option for those looking to boost their energy levels throughout the day. They are perfect for on-the-go snacking, pre- or post-workout fuel, or as a healthy treat. By making your own energy bars and bites at home, you can control the ingredients, ensuring they are packed with nutrients and free from unnecessary additives. This section introduces you to the benefits of homemade energy bars and bites, provides tips for making them, and offers a variety of recipes to get you started.

Benefits of Homemade Energy Bars and Bites

1. **Nutrient-Dense**: Homemade energy bars and bites can be packed with wholesome ingredients like nuts, seeds, dried fruits, and whole grains, providing essential vitamins, minerals, and healthy fats.
2. **Convenient**: These snacks are perfect for busy lifestyles. They can be made in advance, stored easily, and taken with you wherever you go.
3. **Customizable**: You can tailor the ingredients to suit your taste preferences and dietary needs, such as gluten-free, vegan, or low-sugar options.
4. **Cost-Effective**: Making your own energy bars and bites at home is often more affordable than purchasing pre-packaged options from the store.
5. **Controlled Ingredients**: By making them at home, you can avoid artificial additives, preservatives, and excessive sugars that are commonly found in store-bought snacks.

Tips for Making Energy Bars and Bites

1. **Choose a Binding Agent**: Ingredients like nut butters, honey, maple syrup, or dates help bind the bars or bites together.
2. **Add Protein**: Include protein-rich ingredients such as nuts, seeds, protein powder, or Greek yogurt to make the snacks more filling.
3. **Incorporate Healthy Fats**: Use ingredients like nuts, seeds, and coconut oil to provide sustained energy.
4. **Include Fiber**: Add whole grains, oats, chia seeds, or flaxseeds to boost the fiber content and promote digestive health.
5. **Balance Flavors**: Combine sweet, salty, and crunchy elements to create a satisfying snack.
6. **Proper Storage**: Store energy bars and bites in an airtight container in the refrigerator to keep them fresh and extend their shelf life.

ALMOND BUTTER PROTEIN BARS

ENERGY BARS AND BITES

PREP TIME
15 MINUTES

COOK TIME
NONE (CHILL TIME: 1 HOUR)

DIFFICULTY

SE4VES
12 BARS

INGREDIENTS

- 1 cup almond butter
- 1/2 cup honey or maple syrup
- 1 teaspoon vanilla extract
- 2 cups rolled oats
- 1/2 cup protein powder (vanilla or unflavored)
- 1/4 cup chia seeds
- 1/4 cup mini chocolate chips (optional)
- 1/4 cup chopped almonds

INSTRUCTIONS

1. Prepare the Wet Ingredients: In a large microwave-safe bowl, combine the almond butter and honey (or maple syrup). Microwave for 30-40 seconds until warm and slightly runny. Stir in the vanilla extract.
2. Mix Dry Ingredients: In a separate bowl, mix the rolled oats, protein powder, chia seeds, mini chocolate chips (if using), and chopped almonds.
3. Combine Ingredients: Pour the dry ingredients into the wet ingredients. Stir until everything is well combined and forms a thick dough.
4. Press into Pan: Line an 8x8-inch baking pan with parchment paper. Press the mixture firmly into the pan, spreading it out evenly.
5. Chill: Place the pan in the refrigerator and chill for at least 1 hour until the bars are firm.
6. Cut into Bars: Once chilled, remove the mixture from the pan and cut it into 12 bars.
7. Store: Store the bars in an airtight container in the refrigerator for up to 1 week.

Nutritional Information (per serving):

CALORIES: 250	PROTEIN: 10G	CARBOHYDRATES: 25G	FIBER: 5G	SUGARS: 12G	FAT: 12G	SATURATED FAT: 1.5G
SODIUM: 50MG	POTASSIUM: 200MG	VITAMIN A: 0% DV	VITAMIN C: 0% DV	CALCIUM: 10% DV	IRON: 10% DV	

COCONUT DATE ENERGY BITES

ENERGY BARS AND BITES

PREP TIME
15 MINUTES

COOK TIME
NONE (CHILL TIME: 30 MINUTES

DIFFICULTY

SE4VES
20 BITES

INGREDIENTS

- 1 1/2 cups pitted Medjool dates
- 1 cup shredded unsweetened coconut (plus extra for rolling)
- 1/2 cup almonds
- 1/2 cup cashews
- 2 tablespoons chia seeds
- 2 tablespoons cocoa powder
- 1 teaspoon vanilla extract
- 1/4 teaspoon salt
- 2 tablespoons coconut oil, melted

INSTRUCTIONS

1. Prepare Ingredients: Place the pitted dates in a food processor and pulse until they form a sticky paste.
2. Add Nuts and Seeds: Add the almonds, cashews, chia seeds, and shredded coconut to the food processor. Pulse until the mixture is well combined and the nuts are finely chopped.
3. Add Flavorings: Add the cocoa powder, vanilla extract, salt, and melted coconut oil. Pulse until everything is fully combined and the mixture forms a cohesive dough.
4. Form Bites: Using your hands, scoop out about a tablespoon of the mixture and roll it into a ball. Repeat with the remaining mixture.
5. Coat with Coconut: Roll each ball in the extra shredded coconut to coat.
6. Chill: Place the energy bites on a baking sheet and chill in the refrigerator for at least 30 minutes until firm.
7. Store: Store the energy bites in an airtight container in the refrigerator for up to 2 weeks.

Nutritional Information (per serving):

CALORIES: 110	PROTEIN: 2G	CARBOHYDRATES: 14G	FIBER: 3G	SUGARS: 10G	FAT: 6G	SATURATED FAT: 3G
SODIUM: 20MG	POTASSIUM: 200MG	VITAMIN A: 0% DV	VITAMIN C: 0% DV	CALCIUM: 2% DV	IRON: 4% DV	

CHOCOLATE PEANUT BUTTER OAT BARS

 **ENERGY BARS AND BITES**

PREP TIME
15 MINUTES

COOK TIME
NONE (CHILL TIME: 60 MINUTES

 **DIFFICULTY**

SE4VES
12 BARS

INGREDIENTS

- 1 cup peanut butter
- 1/2 cup honey or maple syrup
- 1 teaspoon vanilla extract
- 2 cups rolled oats
- 1/2 cup mini chocolate chips
- 1/4 cup ground flaxseed
- 1/4 cup unsweetened cocoa powder
- 1/4 teaspoon salt

INSTRUCTIONS

1. Prepare the Wet Ingredients: In a large microwave-safe bowl, combine the peanut butter and honey (or maple syrup). Microwave for 30-40 seconds until warm and slightly runny. Stir in the vanilla extract.
2. Mix Dry Ingredients: In a separate bowl, mix the rolled oats, mini chocolate chips, ground flaxseed, cocoa powder, and salt.
3. Combine Ingredients: Pour the dry ingredients into the wet ingredients. Stir until everything is well combined and forms a thick dough.
4. Press into Pan: Line an 8x8-inch baking pan with parchment paper. Press the mixture firmly into the pan, spreading it out evenly.
5. Chill: Place the pan in the refrigerator and chill for at least 1 hour until the bars are firm.
6. Cut into Bars: Once chilled, remove the mixture from the pan and cut it into 12 bars.
7. Store: Store the bars in an airtight container in the refrigerator for up to 1 week.

Nutritional Information (per serving):

CALORIES: 250	PROTEIN: 7G	CARBOHYDRATES: 30G	FIBER: 5G	SUGARS: 15G	FAT: 12G	SATURATED FAT: 3G
SODIUM: 150MG	POTASSIUM: 200MG	VITAMIN A: 0% DV	VITAMIN C: 0% DV		CALCIUM: 4% DV	IRON: 8% DV

APRICOT ALMOND ENERGY BITES

ENERGY BARS AND BITES

PREP TIME
15 MINUTES

COOK TIME
NONE (CHILL TIME: 30 MINUTES

DIFFICULTY

SE4VES
20 BITES

INGREDIENTS

- 1 cup dried apricots
- 1 cup raw almonds
- 1/2 cup unsweetened shredded coconut
- 2 tablespoons chia seeds
- 2 tablespoons honey or maple syrup
- 1 teaspoon vanilla extract
- 1/4 teaspoon salt
- 2 tablespoons water (as needed)

INSTRUCTIONS

1. Prepare Ingredients: Place the dried apricots in a food processor and pulse until they form a sticky paste.
2. Add Nuts and Seeds: Add the raw almonds, shredded coconut, and chia seeds to the food processor. Pulse until the mixture is well combined and the almonds are finely chopped.
3. Add Flavorings: Add the honey or maple syrup, vanilla extract, and salt. Pulse until everything is fully combined and the mixture forms a cohesive dough. If the mixture is too dry, add water a tablespoon at a time until the desired consistency is reached.
4. Form Bites: Using your hands, scoop out about a tablespoon of the mixture and roll it into a ball. Repeat with the remaining mixture.
5. Chill: Place the energy bites on a baking sheet and chill in the refrigerator for at least 30 minutes until firm.
6. Store: Store the energy bites in an airtight container in the refrigerator for up to 2 weeks.

Nutritional Information (per serving):

CALORIES: 100	PROTEIN: 2G	CARBOHYDRATES: 15G	FIBER: 3G	SUGARS: 10G	FAT: 5G	SATURATED FAT: 1G
SODIUM: 20MG	POTASSIUM: 150MG	VITAMIN A: 20% DV	VITAMIN C: 0% DV	CALCIUM: 2% DV	IRON: 4% DV	

MATCHA GREEN TEA ENERGY BITES

PREP TIME
15 MINUTES

COOK TIME
NONE (CHILL TIME: 30 MINUTES

DIFFICULTY

SE4VES
20 BITES

INGREDIENTS

- 1 cup pitted Medjool dates
- 1 cup raw cashews
- 1/2 cup shredded unsweetened coconut
- 2 tablespoons chia seeds
- 1 tablespoon matcha green tea powder
- 1 teaspoon vanilla extract
- 1/4 teaspoon salt
- 2 tablespoons coconut oil, melted
- 1-2 tablespoons water (as needed)

INSTRUCTIONS

1. Prepare Ingredients: Place the pitted dates in a food processor and pulse until they form a sticky paste.
2. Add Nuts and Seeds: Add the raw cashews, shredded coconut, chia seeds, and matcha green tea powder to the food processor. Pulse until the mixture is well combined and the cashews are finely chopped.
3. Add Flavorings: Add the vanilla extract, salt, and melted coconut oil. Pulse until everything is fully combined and the mixture forms a cohesive dough. If the mixture is too dry, add water a tablespoon at a time until the desired consistency is reached.
4. Form Bites: Using your hands, scoop out about a tablespoon of the mixture and roll it into a ball. Repeat with the remaining mixture.
5. Chill: Place the energy bites on a baking sheet and chill in the refrigerator for at least 30 minutes until firm.
6. Store: Store the energy bites in an airtight container in the refrigerator for up to 2 weeks.

Nutritional Information (per serving):

CALORIES: 110	PROTEIN: 2G	CARBOHYDRATES: 15G	FIBER: 3G	SUGARS: 10G	FAT: 5G	SATURATED FAT: 2.5G
SODIUM: 20MG	POTASSIUM: 150MG	VITAMIN A: 0% DV	VITAMIN C: 0% DV	CALCIUM: 2% DV	IRON: 4% DV	

Veggie-Packed Dips and Spreads

Veggie-packed dips and spreads are a fantastic way to incorporate more vegetables into your diet in a delicious and versatile manner. These dips and spreads can be served as appetizers, snacks, or even as part of a meal. They are perfect for dipping fresh veggies, spreading on sandwiches, or adding to grain bowls. This section introduces you to the benefits of veggie-packed dips and spreads, provides tips for making them healthy and flavorful, and offers a variety of recipes to get you started.

Benefits of Veggie-Packed Dips and Spreads

1. **Nutrient-Rich**: These dips and spreads are loaded with vitamins, minerals, and fiber from a variety of vegetables.
2. **Versatile**: They can be used in many ways, such as dips for veggies or chips, spreads for sandwiches, or toppings for grain bowls and salads.
3. **Flavorful**: By using fresh herbs, spices, and various vegetables, you can create a wide range of delicious flavors.
4. **Healthy**: They are a healthier alternative to many store-bought dips and spreads that often contain unhealthy fats, preservatives, and additives.
5. **Easy to Make**: Most veggie-packed dips and spreads can be made quickly and easily with a food processor or blender.

Tips for Making Healthy and Flavorful Veggie-Packed Dips and Spreads

1. **Use Fresh Ingredients**: Fresh vegetables, herbs, and spices will enhance the flavor and nutritional value of your dips and spreads.
2. **Incorporate Healthy Fats**: Use ingredients like olive oil, avocado, or nuts to add healthy fats and a creamy texture.
3. **Season Well**: Don't be afraid to use plenty of herbs, spices, and seasonings to add depth and flavor.
4. **Balance Textures**: Combine smooth and chunky textures for a more interesting dip or spread.
5. **Adjust Consistency**: If your dip or spread is too thick, add a bit of water, broth, or a squeeze of lemon juice to reach your desired consistency.

ROASTED RED PEPPER HUMMUS

PREP TIME
10 MINUTES

COOK TIME
20 MINUTES

DIFFICULTY

SE4VES
8

INGREDIENTS

- 2 large red bell peppers
- 1 can (15 oz) chickpeas, drained and rinsed
- 1/4 cup tahini
- 3 tablespoons lemon juice
- 2 cloves garlic, minced
- 1/2 teaspoon ground cumin
- 1/2 teaspoon smoked paprika
- 1/4 teaspoon cayenne pepper (optional)
- 1/4 cup olive oil
- Salt to taste
- Fresh parsley, chopped for garnish

INSTRUCTIONS

1. Roast the Red Peppers: Preheat your oven to 450°F (230°C). Place the red bell peppers on a baking sheet and roast for 20 minutes, turning them occasionally, until the skins are charred and blistered.
2. Cool and Peel Peppers: Remove the peppers from the oven and place them in a bowl. Cover with plastic wrap and let them cool for about 10 minutes. Once cooled, peel off the skins, remove the stems and seeds, and chop the peppers.
3. Blend Ingredients: In a food processor, combine the roasted red peppers, chickpeas, tahini, lemon juice, minced garlic, ground cumin, smoked paprika, and cayenne pepper (if using). Process until smooth.
4. Add Olive Oil: With the food processor running, slowly drizzle in the olive oil until the hummus is creamy and well combined. Taste and season with salt as needed.
5. Serve: Transfer the hummus to a serving bowl. Garnish with chopped fresh parsley and a drizzle of olive oil if desired. Serve with pita bread, crackers, or fresh vegetables.

Nutritional Information (per serving):

CALORIES: 120	PROTEIN: 3G	CARBOHYDRATES: 10G	FIBER: 3G	SUGARS: 1G	FAT: 8G	SATURATED FAT: 1G
SODIUM: 120MG	POTASSIUM: 180MG	VITAMIN A: 25% DV	VITAMIN C: 80% DV		CALCIUM: 2% DV	IRON: 6% DV

SPINACH AND ARTICHOKE DIP

PREP TIME
15 MINUTES

COOK TIME
20 MINUTES

DIFFICULTY

SE4VES
8

INGREDIENTS

- 1 tablespoon olive oil
- 1 onion, finely diced
- 3 cloves garlic, minced
- 1 can (14 oz) artichoke hearts, drained and chopped
- 4 cups fresh spinach, chopped
- 1/2 cup Greek yogurt
- 1/2 cup sour cream
- 1/2 cup cream cheese, softened
- 1/2 cup grated Parmesan cheese
- 1/2 cup shredded mozzarella cheese
- 1 teaspoon lemon juice
- 1/4 teaspoon ground nutmeg
- Salt and pepper to taste
- Fresh parsley, chopped for garnish

INSTRUCTIONS

1. Preheat Oven: Preheat your oven to 375°F (190°C).
2. Sauté Onion and Garlic: In a large skillet, heat the olive oil over medium heat. Add the finely diced onion and cook until softened, about 5 minutes. Add the minced garlic and cook for another 1-2 minutes until fragrant.
3. Add Spinach and Artichokes: Add the chopped artichoke hearts and spinach to the skillet. Cook until the spinach is wilted, about 3-4 minutes.
4. Combine with Creamy Ingredients: In a large bowl, mix together the Greek yogurt, sour cream, and cream cheese until smooth. Add the cooked spinach and artichoke mixture, grated Parmesan cheese, shredded mozzarella cheese, lemon juice, ground nutmeg, salt, and pepper. Stir until well combined.
5. Bake: Transfer the mixture to a baking dish and spread it out evenly. Bake in the preheated oven for 20 minutes, or until the dip is hot and bubbly.
6. Serve: Garnish with chopped fresh parsley and serve hot with pita bread, crackers, or fresh vegetables.

Nutritional Information (per serving):

CALORIES: 150	PROTEIN: 6G	CARBOHYDRATES: 8G	FIBER: 3G	SUGARS: 3G	FAT: 10G	SATURATED FAT: 5G
SODIUM: 350MG	POTASSIUM: 300MG	VITAMIN A: 60% DV	VITAMIN C: 10% DV	CALCIUM: 15% DV	IRON: 6% DV	

AVOCADO AND BLACK BEAN DIP

 **VEGGIE-PACKED DIPS AND SPREADS**

PREP TIME
15 MINUTES

COOK TIME
0 MINUTES

★☆☆☆☆
DIFFICULTY

SE4VES
8

INGREDIENTS

- 2 large ripe avocados, peeled and pitted
- 1 can (15 oz) black beans, drained and rinsed
- 1 cup cherry tomatoes, diced
- 1/4 cup red onion, finely diced
- 1 jalapeño, seeded and finely chopped
- 1/4 cup fresh cilantro, chopped
- 2 tablespoons lime juice
- 1 teaspoon ground cumin
- 1/2 teaspoon smoked paprika
- Salt and pepper to taste

INSTRUCTIONS

1. Mash Avocados: In a large bowl, mash the avocados until smooth.
2. Add Black Beans: Add the drained and rinsed black beans to the bowl and mix gently.
3. Combine Vegetables: Add the diced cherry tomatoes, finely diced red onion, chopped jalapeño, and fresh cilantro to the bowl. Stir to combine.
4. Season: Add the lime juice, ground cumin, smoked paprika, salt, and pepper. Mix well until all ingredients are evenly combined.
5. Serve: Transfer the dip to a serving bowl. Serve immediately with tortilla chips, pita chips, or fresh vegetables.

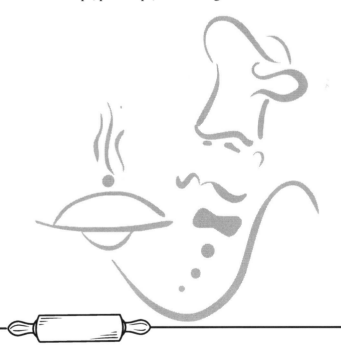

Nutritional Information (per serving):

CALORIES: 140	PROTEIN: 3G	CARBOHYDRATES: 15G	FIBER: 7G	SUGARS: 1G	FAT: 8G	SATURATED FAT: 1G
SODIUM: 150MG	POTASSIUM: 450MG	VITAMIN A: 8% DV	VITAMIN C: 20% DV		CALCIUM: 2% DV	IRON: 6% DV

CARROT AND GINGER DIP

PREP TIME
15 MINUTES

COOK TIME
20 MINUTES

DIFFICULTY

SE4VES
8

INGREDIENTS

- 4 large carrots, peeled and chopped
- 2 tablespoons olive oil
- 1 onion, diced
- 3 cloves garlic, minced
- 1 tablespoon fresh ginger, grated
- 1/4 cup tahini
- 2 tablespoons lemon juice
- 1 teaspoon ground cumin
- 1/2 teaspoon ground coriander
- Salt and pepper to taste
- Fresh parsley, chopped for garnish

INSTRUCTIONS

1. Cook Carrots: In a medium saucepan, bring water to a boil. Add the chopped carrots and cook until tender, about 10-12 minutes. Drain and set aside.
2. Sauté Onion and Garlic: In a large skillet, heat the olive oil over medium heat. Add the diced onion and cook until softened, about 5 minutes. Add the minced garlic and grated ginger and cook for another 1-2 minutes until fragrant.
3. Blend Ingredients: In a food processor, combine the cooked carrots, sautéed onion, garlic, and ginger, tahini, lemon juice, ground cumin, ground coriander, salt, and pepper. Process until smooth and well combined.
4. Adjust Seasoning: Taste the dip and adjust the seasoning with more salt, pepper, or lemon juice if needed.
5. Serve: Transfer the dip to a serving bowl. Garnish with chopped fresh parsley and serve with pita bread, crackers, or fresh vegetables.

Nutritional Information (per serving):

CALORIES: 100	PROTEIN: 2G	CARBOHYDRATES: 12G	FIBER: 3G	SUGARS: 5G	FAT: 6G	SATURATED FAT: 1G
SODIUM: 150MG	POTASSIUM: 300MG	VITAMIN A: 200% DV	VITAMIN C: 10% DV	CALCIUM: 4% DV	IRON: 4% DV	

EDAMAME AND MISO DIP

PREP TIME
10 MINUTES

COOK TIME
5 MINUTES

★☆☆☆☆
DIFFICULTY

SE4VES
8

INGREDIENTS

- 2 cups shelled edamame (fresh or frozen)
- 2 tablespoons white miso paste
- 2 tablespoons tahini
- 1 clove garlic, minced
- 1 tablespoon fresh ginger, grated
- 3 tablespoons lemon juice
- 1 tablespoon soy sauce (low sodium)
- 2 tablespoons olive oil
- 1/4 cup water (more as needed)
- 1/4 teaspoon salt
- Fresh chives, chopped for garnish
- Sesame seeds for garnish

INSTRUCTIONS

1. Cook Edamame: If using frozen edamame, cook according to package instructions. Drain and set aside.
2. Blend Ingredients: In a food processor, combine the cooked edamame, white miso paste, tahini, minced garlic, grated ginger, lemon juice, soy sauce, and olive oil. Process until smooth.
3. Adjust Consistency: Add water, one tablespoon at a time, until the dip reaches your desired consistency. You may need to add more or less water depending on your preference.
4. Season: Taste and adjust the seasoning with salt if needed.
5. Serve: Transfer the dip to a serving bowl. Garnish with chopped fresh chives and sesame seeds. Serve with rice crackers, fresh vegetables, or pita bread.

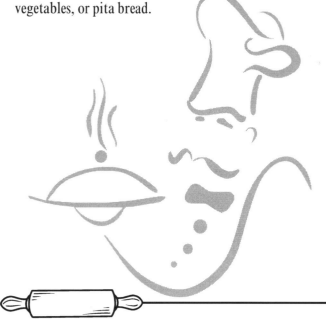

Nutritional Information (per serving):

CALORIES: 110	PROTEIN: 5G	CARBOHYDRATES: 8G	FIBER: 3G	SUGARS: 1G	FAT: 7G	SATURATED FAT: 1G
SODIUM: 250MG	POTASSIUM: 250MG	VITAMIN A: 2% DV	VITAMIN C: 8% DV	CALCIUM: 4% DV		IRON: 8% DV

Nutritious Chips and Crackers

Nutritious chips and crackers are a fantastic way to enjoy crunchy, satisfying snacks without the unhealthy fats and additives often found in store-bought versions. These homemade alternatives can be packed with whole grains, seeds, and vegetables, making them a healthier choice for snacking. This section introduces you to the benefits of making your own chips and crackers, provides tips for achieving the perfect crunch, and offers a variety of recipes to get you started.

Benefits of Nutritious Chips and Crackers

1. **Healthier Ingredients**: Homemade chips and crackers allow you to control the ingredients, ensuring they are made with whole grains, seeds, and vegetables.
2. **Lower in Unhealthy Fats**: By baking instead of frying, you can significantly reduce the amount of unhealthy fats in your snacks.
3. **Customizable**: You can tailor the flavors and ingredients to suit your taste preferences and dietary needs, such as gluten-free or vegan options.
4. **Nutrient-Dense**: Incorporating seeds, nuts, and whole grains boosts the nutritional value, providing fiber, protein, and essential vitamins and minerals.
5. **No Additives**: Making your own snacks means avoiding preservatives, artificial flavors, and excessive sodium often found in store-bought varieties.

Tips for Making Nutritious Chips and Crackers

1. **Use Whole Grains and Seeds**: Incorporate ingredients like whole wheat flour, quinoa, chia seeds, and flaxseeds to boost fiber and nutrient content.
2. **Bake, Don't Fry**: Baking chips and crackers ensures they are lower in unhealthy fats and calories.
3. **Season Well**: Use herbs, spices, and natural seasonings to add flavor without relying on excess salt.
4. **Cut Evenly**: For even baking, make sure your chips and crackers are cut to a uniform thickness.
5. **Cool Completely**: Allow your chips and crackers to cool completely before storing to maintain their crunch.

BAKED SWEET POTATO CHIPS

 **NUTRITIOUS CHIPS AND CRACKERS**

PREP TIME
10 MINUTES

COOK TIME
20-25 MINUTES

★☆☆☆☆
DIFFICULTY

SE4VES
4

INGREDIENTS

- 2 large sweet potatoes, washed and thinly sliced
- 2 tablespoons olive oil
- 1 teaspoon sea salt
- 1/2 teaspoon smoked paprika (optional)
- 1/2 teaspoon garlic powder (optional)
- Fresh rosemary or thyme for garnish (optional)

INSTRUCTIONS

1. Preheat Oven: Preheat your oven to 400°F (200°C). Line two baking sheets with parchment paper.
2. Slice Sweet Potatoes: Using a mandoline or a sharp knife, thinly slice the sweet potatoes into even rounds, about 1/8 inch thick.
3. Season: In a large bowl, toss the sweet potato slices with olive oil, sea salt, smoked paprika, and garlic powder until evenly coated.
4. Arrange on Baking Sheets: Spread the sweet potato slices in a single layer on the prepared baking sheets. Make sure the slices do not overlap to ensure even baking.
5. Bake: Bake in the preheated oven for 20-25 minutes, or until the chips are crispy and golden brown, flipping the slices halfway through the baking time. Keep an eye on them to prevent burning.
6. Cool: Remove the chips from the oven and let them cool on the baking sheets for a few minutes. They will continue to crisp up as they cool.
7. Serve: Transfer the sweet potato chips to a serving bowl. Garnish with fresh rosemary or thyme if desired. Serve immediately or store in an airtight container for up to 3 days.

Nutritional Information (per serving):

CALORIES: 120	PROTEIN: 2G	CARBOHYDRATES: 18G	FIBER: 3G	SUGARS: 4G	FAT: 5G	SATURATED FAT: 0.5G
SODIUM: 300MG	POTASSIUM: 350MG	VITAMIN A: 200% DV	VITAMIN C: 4% DV		CALCIUM: 4% DV	IRON: 4% DV

FLAXSEED AND SESAME CRACKERS

NUTRITIOUS CHIPS AND CRACKERS

PREP TIME
15 MINUTES

COOK TIME
20-25 MINUTES

★☆☆☆☆
DIFFICULTY

SE4VES
6

INGREDIENTS

- 1 cup whole flaxseeds
- 1/2 cup sesame seeds
- 1 cup water
- 1/2 teaspoon sea salt (plus extra for sprinkling)
- 1/2 teaspoon garlic powder (optional)
- 1/2 teaspoon onion powder (optional)

INSTRUCTIONS

1. Preheat Oven: Preheat your oven to 350°F (175°C). Line a baking sheet with parchment paper.
2. Mix Ingredients: In a large bowl, combine the flaxseeds, sesame seeds, water, sea salt, garlic powder, and onion powder. Stir until well mixed and let sit for 10-15 minutes until the mixture thickens and becomes gel-like.
3. Spread Mixture: Spread the seed mixture evenly onto the prepared baking sheet, pressing down to ensure it is an even thickness. The mixture should be about 1/8 inch thick.
4. Score the Crackers: Using a knife or pizza cutter, score the mixture into cracker-sized squares. This will make it easier to break apart once baked.
5. Bake: Bake in the preheated oven for 20-25 minutes, or until the crackers are golden brown and crisp. If the edges brown faster, you can remove the outer crackers and continue baking the center ones.
6. Cool: Remove from the oven and let cool completely on the baking sheet.
7. Break Apart: Once cooled, break the crackers along the scored lines.
8. Store: Store in an airtight container at room temperature for up to 1 week.

Nutritional Information (per serving):

CALORIES: 150	PROTEIN: 6G	CARBOHYDRATES: 7G	FIBER: 6G	SUGARS: 0G	FAT: 11G	SATURATED FAT: 1.5G
SODIUM: 150MG	POTASSIUM: 150MG	VITAMIN A: 0% DV	VITAMIN C: 0% DV	CALCIUM: 15% DV	IRON: 10% DV	

KALE CHIPS WITH SEA SALT

PREP TIME
10 MINUTES

COOK TIME
20 MINUTES

★☆☆☆☆

DIFFICULTY

SE4VES
4

INGREDIENTS

- 1 bunch of kale
- 1 tablespoon olive oil
- 1/2 teaspoon sea salt

INSTRUCTIONS

1. Preheat Oven: Preheat your oven to 300°F (150°C). Line a baking sheet with parchment paper.
2. Prepare Kale: Wash and thoroughly dry the kale leaves. Remove the tough stems and tear the leaves into bite-sized pieces.
3. Massage with Oil: In a large bowl, drizzle the kale with olive oil. Massage the leaves with your hands to ensure they are evenly coated with oil.
4. Season: Sprinkle the sea salt over the kale and toss to distribute evenly.
5. Arrange on Baking Sheet: Spread the kale pieces in a single layer on the prepared baking sheet, ensuring they do not overlap.
6. Bake: Bake in the preheated oven for 15-20 minutes, or until the kale is crispy and slightly browned at the edges. Check frequently to prevent burning.
7. Cool and Serve: Remove from the oven and let cool on the baking sheet for a few minutes. Serve immediately or store in an airtight container for up to 2 days.

Nutritional Information (per serving):

CALORIES: 50	PROTEIN: 2G	CARBOHYDRATES: 7G	FIBER: 2G	SUGARS: 0G	FAT: 2.5G	SATURATED FAT: 0.5G
SODIUM: 150MG	POTASSIUM: 300MG	VITAMIN A: 100% DV	VITAMIN C: 80% DV	CALCIUM: 10% DV	IRON: 5% DV	

QUINOA AND CHIA SEED CRACKERS

NUTRITIOUS CHIPS AND CRACKERS

PREP TIME
15 MINUTES

COOK TIME
30 MINUTES

DIFFICULTY

SE4VES
6

INGREDIENTS

- 1 cup cooked quinoa
- 1/2 cup chia seeds
- 1/2 cup water
- 1/2 cup rolled oats, ground into flour
- 2 tablespoons olive oil
- 1/2 teaspoon sea salt (plus extra for sprinkling)
- 1/2 teaspoon garlic powder (optional)
- 1/2 teaspoon onion powder (optional)

INSTRUCTIONS

1. Preheat Oven: Preheat your oven to 350°F (175°C). Line a baking sheet with parchment paper.
2. Mix Ingredients: In a large bowl, combine the cooked quinoa, chia seeds, and water. Let the mixture sit for 10-15 minutes until it thickens and becomes gel-like.
3. Add Dry Ingredients: Add the ground oats, olive oil, sea salt, garlic powder, and onion powder to the quinoa mixture. Stir until well combined.
4. Spread Mixture: Spread the mixture evenly onto the prepared baking sheet, pressing down to ensure it is an even thickness. The mixture should be about 1/8 inch thick.
5. Score the Crackers: Using a knife or pizza cutter, score the mixture into cracker-sized squares. This will make it easier to break apart once baked.
6. Bake: Bake in the preheated oven for 25-30 minutes, or until the crackers are golden brown and crisp. If the edges brown faster, you can remove the outer crackers and continue baking the center ones.
7. Cool: Remove from the oven and let cool completely on the baking sheet.
8. Break Apart: Once cooled, break the crackers along the scored lines.
9. Store: Store in an airtight container at room temperature for up to 1 week.

Nutritional Information (per serving):

CALORIES: 120	PROTEIN: 4G	CARBOHYDRATES: 14G	FIBER: 5G	SUGARS: 0G	FAT: 6G	SATURATED FAT: 0.5G
SODIUM: 150MG	POTASSIUM: 150MG	VITAMIN A: 0% DV	VITAMIN C: 0% DV	CALCIUM: 8% DV	IRON: 6% DV	

Fresh and Dried Fruit Combinations

Fresh and dried fruit combinations are an excellent way to enjoy the natural sweetness of fruit while benefiting from their high nutritional content. These combinations can serve as quick snacks, delicious additions to meals, or healthy dessert alternatives. This section introduces you to the benefits of incorporating fresh and dried fruits into your diet, provides tips for creating delicious combinations, and offers a variety of recipes to get you started.

Benefits of Fresh and Dried Fruit Combinations

1. **Nutrient-Rich**: Both fresh and dried fruits are packed with essential vitamins, minerals, antioxidants, and fiber.
2. **Convenient**: Dried fruits are easy to store and carry, making them a convenient snack option, while fresh fruits provide a hydrating and refreshing element.
3. **Natural Sweetness**: These combinations can satisfy sweet cravings in a healthy way, reducing the need for processed sugars.
4. **Versatile**: Fresh and dried fruits can be combined in numerous ways to create a variety of flavors and textures.
5. **Balanced Energy**: The natural sugars in fruits provide quick energy, while the fiber helps maintain steady blood sugar levels.

Tips for Creating Delicious Fresh and Dried Fruit Combinations

1. **Balance Flavors**: Combine sweet, tart, and tangy fruits to create a well-rounded flavor profile.
2. **Mix Textures**: Pair the chewy texture of dried fruits with the crispness of fresh fruits for an enjoyable eating experience.
3. **Add Nuts and Seeds**: Incorporate nuts and seeds to add protein, healthy fats, and crunch to your fruit combinations.
4. **Use Seasonal Fresh Fruits**: Take advantage of seasonal fresh fruits for the best flavor and nutritional value.
5. **Mind Portion Sizes**: Dried fruits are more calorie-dense than fresh fruits, so be mindful of portion sizes to maintain a balanced diet.

APPLE AND CINNAMON FRUIT LEATHER

PREP TIME
15 MINUTES

COOK TIME
6-8 HOURS (DRYING TIME)

DIFFICULTY

SE4VES
10

INGREDIENTS

- 4 large apples, peeled, cored, and chopped
- 1/2 cup water
- 1 tablespoon lemon juice
- 1 teaspoon ground cinnamon
- 1-2 tablespoons honey or maple syrup (optional, for added sweetness)

INSTRUCTIONS

1. Preheat Oven: Preheat your oven to the lowest temperature setting, usually around 140-170°F (60-75°C), or use a food dehydrator if you have one.
2. Cook Apples: In a medium saucepan, combine the chopped apples, water, and lemon juice. Cook over medium heat until the apples are soft and tender, about 10-15 minutes.
3. Blend: Transfer the cooked apples to a blender or food processor. Add the ground cinnamon and honey or maple syrup (if using). Blend until smooth and puree.
4. Prepare Baking Sheet: Line a baking sheet with parchment paper or a silicone baking mat.
5. Spread Puree: Pour the apple puree onto the prepared baking sheet. Use a spatula to spread it out evenly into a thin layer, about 1/8 inch thick.
6. Dry: Place the baking sheet in the oven and dry the puree for 6-8 hours, or until the fruit leather is no longer sticky and peels away easily from the parchment paper. If using a food dehydrator, follow the manufacturer's instructions.
7. Cool and Cut: Allow the fruit leather to cool completely. Once cooled, peel it off the parchment paper and cut it into strips or shapes using scissors or a sharp knife.
8. Store: Roll up the fruit leather strips in parchment paper and store them in an airtight container for up to 2 weeks.

Nutritional Information (per serving):

CALORIES: 45	PROTEIN: 0G	CARBOHYDRATES: 12G	FIBER: 2G	SUGARS: 9G	FAT: 0G	SATURATED FAT: 0G
SODIUM: 0MG	POTASSIUM: 90MG	VITAMIN A: 1% DV	VITAMIN C: 4% DV	CALCIUM: 1% DV	IRON: 1% DV	

Naturally Sweetened Treats

Indulging in desserts doesn't have to mean compromising on health. Naturally sweetened treats are a fantastic way to enjoy sweet flavors without relying on refined sugars and artificial sweeteners. By using ingredients like fruits, honey, maple syrup, and other natural sweeteners, you can create delicious desserts that are both satisfying and nutritious. This section introduces you to the benefits of naturally sweetened treats, provides tips for making them, and offers a variety of recipes to get you started.

Benefits of Naturally Sweetened Treats

1. **Lower in Refined Sugars**: These treats avoid refined sugars, which can cause spikes in blood sugar levels and are linked to various health issues.
2. **Nutrient-Rich**: Natural sweeteners often come with additional nutrients and antioxidants, unlike refined sugars.
3. **Better Digestion**: Naturally sweetened desserts can be easier on the digestive system, reducing the likelihood of sugar crashes and digestive discomfort.
4. **Improved Flavor**: Natural sweeteners provide a rich and complex flavor profile that enhances the taste of desserts.
5. **Healthier Ingredients**: Using whole, unprocessed ingredients contributes to a healthier overall diet.

Tips for Making Naturally Sweetened Treats

1. **Choose Your Sweetener Wisely**: Use sweeteners like honey, maple syrup, dates, bananas, and applesauce for their natural sweetness and additional nutrients.
2. **Balance Flavors**: Complement the natural sweetness with spices like cinnamon, nutmeg, and vanilla extract to enhance flavor.
3. **Use Whole Grains**: Incorporate whole grain flours like whole wheat, oat flour, or almond flour to add fiber and nutrients.
4. **Add Fruits and Nuts**: Incorporate fruits and nuts to boost the nutritional content and add texture.
5. **Portion Control**: Even naturally sweetened desserts should be enjoyed in moderation. Be mindful of portion sizes to maintain a balanced diet.

BANANA OATMEAL COOKIES

NATURALLY SWEETENED TREATS

PREP TIME
10 MINUTES

COOK TIME
15 MINUTES

DIFFICULTY

SE4VES
24 COOKIES

INGREDIENTS

- 2 large ripe bananas, mashed
- 1/2 cup unsweetened applesauce
- 1/4 cup honey or maple syrup
- 1 teaspoon vanilla extract
- 1 teaspoon ground cinnamon
- 1/2 teaspoon baking soda
- 1/4 teaspoon salt
- 1 1/2 cups rolled oats
- 1/2 cup whole wheat flour
- 1/2 cup raisins or chocolate chips (optional)
- 1/4 cup chopped nuts (optional)

INSTRUCTIONS

1. Preheat Oven: Preheat your oven to 350°F (175°C). Line a baking sheet with parchment paper or a silicone baking mat.
2. Mix Wet Ingredients: In a large bowl, combine the mashed bananas, unsweetened applesauce, honey or maple syrup, and vanilla extract. Mix until well combined.
3. Add Dry Ingredients: Add the ground cinnamon, baking soda, and salt to the wet mixture. Stir until evenly distributed.
4. Incorporate Oats and Flour: Stir in the rolled oats and whole wheat flour until the mixture is well combined. If using, fold in the raisins or chocolate chips and chopped nuts.
5. Drop Cookies onto Baking Sheet: Using a tablespoon or cookie scoop, drop spoonfuls of the dough onto the prepared baking sheet, spacing them about 2 inches apart.
6. Bake: Bake in the preheated oven for 12-15 minutes, or until the edges are golden brown and the cookies are set.
7. Cool: Remove from the oven and let the cookies cool on the baking sheet for 5 minutes, then transfer them to a wire rack to cool completely.
8. Store: Store the cookies in an airtight container at room temperature for up to 5 days.

Nutritional Information (per serving):

CALORIES: 70	PROTEIN: 1.5G	CARBOHYDRATES: 14G	FIBER: 2G	SUGARS: 5G	FAT: 1G	SATURATED FAT: 0.2G
SODIUM: 40MG	POTASSIUM: 90MG	VITAMIN A: 0% DV	VITAMIN C: 2% DV	CALCIUM: 1% DV	IRON: 3% DV	

ALMOND BUTTER BROWNIES

PREP TIME
10 MINUTES

COOK TIME
25 MINUTES

DIFFICULTY

SE4VES
12

INGREDIENTS

- 1 cup almond butter
- 1/2 cup honey or maple syrup
- 2 large eggs
- 1/4 cup unsweetened cocoa powder
- 1/4 cup almond flour
- 1 teaspoon vanilla extract
- 1/2 teaspoon baking soda
- 1/4 teaspoon salt
- 1/2 cup dark chocolate chips (optional)

INSTRUCTIONS

1. Preheat Oven: Preheat your oven to 350°F (175°C). Line an 8x8-inch baking pan with parchment paper or lightly grease it.
2. Mix Wet Ingredients: In a large bowl, combine the almond butter, honey or maple syrup, eggs, and vanilla extract. Mix until smooth.
3. Add Dry Ingredients: Add the unsweetened cocoa powder, almond flour, baking soda, and salt to the wet mixture. Stir until well combined. If using, fold in the dark chocolate chips.
4. Pour into Pan: Pour the batter into the prepared baking pan and spread it out evenly.
5. Bake: Bake in the preheated oven for 20-25 minutes, or until a toothpick inserted into the center comes out clean or with a few moist crumbs.
6. Cool: Remove from the oven and let the brownies cool completely in the pan.
7. Cut and Serve: Once cooled, lift the brownies out of the pan using the parchment paper and cut into 12 squares. Serve immediately or store in an airtight container.

Nutritional Information (per serving):

CALORIES: 190	PROTEIN: 5G	CARBOHYDRATES: 18G	FIBER: 3G	SUGARS: 12G	FAT: 12G	SATURATED FAT: 2G
SODIUM: 110MG	POTASSIUM: 150MG	VITAMIN A: 0% DV	VITAMIN C: 0% DV		CALCIUM: 6% DV	IRON: 6% DV

APPLE CINNAMON MUFFINS

PREP TIME
15 MINUTES

COOK TIME
25 MINUTES

DIFFICULTY

SE4VES
12

INGREDIENTS

- 1 1/2 cups whole wheat flour
- 1 teaspoon baking powder
- 1/2 teaspoon baking soda
- 1/2 teaspoon salt
- 1 teaspoon ground cinnamon
- 1/4 teaspoon ground nutmeg
- 1/2 cup unsweetened applesauce
- 1/2 cup honey or maple syrup
- 2 large eggs
- 1/4 cup olive oil or melted coconut oil
- 1 teaspoon vanilla extract
- 1 cup grated apple (about 2 medium apples)
- 1/2 cup chopped walnuts or pecans (optional)

INSTRUCTIONS

1. Preheat Oven: Preheat your oven to 350°F (175°C). Line a 12-cup muffin tin with paper liners or lightly grease it.
2. Mix Dry Ingredients: In a large bowl, whisk together the whole wheat flour, baking powder, baking soda, salt, ground cinnamon, and ground nutmeg.
3. Mix Wet Ingredients: In another bowl, combine the unsweetened applesauce, honey or maple syrup, eggs, oil, and vanilla extract. Mix until smooth.
4. Combine Wet and Dry Ingredients: Pour the wet ingredients into the dry ingredients and stir until just combined. Be careful not to overmix.
5. Fold in Apples and Nuts: Gently fold in the grated apple and chopped walnuts or pecans (if using).
6. Fill Muffin Tin: Divide the batter evenly among the 12 muffin cups, filling each about 3/4 full.
7. Bake: Bake in the preheated oven for 20-25 minutes, or until a toothpick inserted into the center of a muffin comes out clean.
8. Cool: Remove from the oven and let the muffins cool in the tin for 5 minutes, then transfer to a wire rack to cool completely.
9. Serve: Serve the muffins warm or at room temperature. Store in an airtight container for up to 3 days.

Nutritional Information (per serving):

CALORIES: 160	PROTEIN: 3G	CARBOHYDRATES: 26G	FIBER: 3G	SUGARS: 15G	FAT: 6G	SATURATED FAT: 1G
SODIUM: 180MG	POTASSIUM: 90MG	VITAMIN A: 2% DV	VITAMIN C: 2% DV		CALCIUM: 4% DV	IRON: 6% DV

CARROT CAKE BITES

PREP TIME
15 MINUTES

COOK TIME
NONE (CHILL TIME: 30 MINUTES)

DIFFICULTY

SE4VES
20 BITES

INGREDIENTS

- 1 cup grated carrots (about 2 medium carrots)
- 1 cup pitted Medjool dates
- 1 cup rolled oats
- 1/2 cup unsweetened shredded coconut
- 1/2 cup almond flour
- 1/4 cup chopped walnuts or pecans
- 1 teaspoon ground cinnamon
- 1/4 teaspoon ground nutmeg
- 1/4 teaspoon ground ginger
- 1/4 teaspoon salt
- 1 teaspoon vanilla extract
- 2 tablespoons honey or maple syrup (optional)
- 2 tablespoons water (as needed)

INSTRUCTIONS

1. Prepare Ingredients: Place the grated carrots and pitted dates in a food processor. Pulse until finely chopped and well combined.
2. Add Dry Ingredients: Add the rolled oats, shredded coconut, almond flour, chopped walnuts or pecans, ground cinnamon, ground nutmeg, ground ginger, and salt to the food processor. Pulse until the mixture is well combined and forms a dough-like consistency.
3. Add Wet Ingredients: Add the vanilla extract and honey or maple syrup (if using) to the mixture. Pulse until everything is well incorporated. If the mixture is too dry, add water a tablespoon at a time until the desired consistency is reached.
4. Form Bites: Using your hands, scoop out about a tablespoon of the mixture and roll it into a ball. Repeat with the remaining mixture.
5. Chill: Place the carrot cake bites on a baking sheet and chill in the refrigerator for at least 30 minutes until firm.
6. Serve: Serve the bites immediately or store in an airtight container in the refrigerator for up to 1 week.

Nutritional Information (per serving):

CALORIES: 80	PROTEIN: 2G	CARBOHYDRATES: 12G	FIBER: 3G	SUGARS: 7G	FAT: 3G	SATURATED FAT: 1G
SODIUM: 30MG	POTASSIUM: 150MG	VITAMIN A: 30% DV	VITAMIN C: 2% DV	CALCIUM: 2% DV		IRON: 4% DV

DARK CHOCOLATE AVOCADO MOUSSE

NATURALLY SWEETENED TREATS

 PREP TIME
10 MINUTES

 COOK TIME
0 MINUTES

★☆☆☆☆
DIFFICULTY

 SE4VES
4

INGREDIENTS

- 2 ripe avocados, peeled and pitted
- 1/2 cup unsweetened cocoa powder
- 1/4 cup honey or maple syrup
- 1/4 cup almond milk (or any plant-based milk)
- 1 teaspoon vanilla extract
- 1/4 teaspoon salt
- 1/4 cup dark chocolate chips, melted (optional for richer flavor)

INSTRUCTIONS

1. Prepare Avocados: Place the peeled and pitted avocados in a food processor or blender.
2. Add Ingredients: Add the unsweetened cocoa powder, honey or maple syrup, almond milk, vanilla extract, and salt to the food processor.
3. Blend Until Smooth: Blend until the mixture is smooth and creamy. If using, add the melted dark chocolate chips and blend until well combined.
4. Taste and Adjust: Taste the mousse and adjust the sweetness or cocoa powder to your liking.
5. Chill: Spoon the mousse into serving bowls or glasses. Refrigerate for at least 30 minutes to allow the flavors to meld and the mousse to firm up.
6. Serve: Serve chilled, garnished with fresh berries, a dollop of whipped cream, or a sprinkle of cocoa powder if desired.

Nutritional Information (per serving):

CALORIES: 200	PROTEIN: 3G	CARBOHYDRATES: 29G	FIBER: 7G	SUGARS: 18G	FAT: 11G	SATURATED FAT: 2G
SODIUM: 150MG	POTASSIUM: 500MG	VITAMIN A: 4% DV	VITAMIN C: 15% DV	CALCIUM: 4% DV	IRON: 10% DV	

Protein-Packed Desserts

Protein-packed desserts are a great way to satisfy your sweet tooth while supporting muscle maintenance and overall health. These desserts incorporate high-protein ingredients such as Greek yogurt, protein powder, nuts, seeds, and legumes, making them a nutritious and filling option for any time of day. This section introduces you to the benefits of protein-packed desserts, provides tips for incorporating protein into your desserts, and offers a variety of recipes to get you started.

Benefits of Protein-Packed Desserts

1. **Muscle Maintenance**: Protein is essential for muscle repair and growth, making these desserts ideal for post-workout snacks or anytime you need a protein boost.
2. **Satiety**: Protein helps you feel fuller for longer, reducing the likelihood of overeating and helping with weight management.
3. **Balanced Nutrition**: By adding protein to your desserts, you create a more balanced treat that includes not just carbohydrates and fats, but also essential amino acids.
4. **Versatility**: Protein-packed desserts can be enjoyed as snacks, post-workout recovery, or even as a healthy option for breakfast or dessert.
5. **Healthy Ingredients**: Using whole food protein sources, such as Greek yogurt, nuts, and seeds, adds additional nutrients like healthy fats, fiber, and vitamins.

Tips for Incorporating Protein into Desserts

1. **Use Protein Powder**: Add protein powder to your baked goods, smoothies, and no-bake treats to increase the protein content.
2. **Incorporate Greek Yogurt**: Greek yogurt is a versatile ingredient that can be used in parfaits, smoothies, and as a substitute for sour cream or cream cheese in recipes.
3. **Add Nuts and Seeds**: Nuts and seeds not only boost protein but also add healthy fats and texture to your desserts.
4. **Utilize Legumes**: Beans and lentils can be used in creative ways, such as in black bean brownies or chickpea cookie dough, to add protein and fiber.
5. **Experiment with Tofu**: Silken tofu can be blended into smoothies, puddings, and cheesecakes for a creamy texture and added protein.

PEANUT BUTTER PROTEIN BALLS

PROTEIN-PACKED DESSERTS

PREP TIME
15 MINUTES

COOK TIME
NONE (CHILL TIME: 30 MINUTES)

★☆☆☆☆
DIFFICULTY

SE4VES
20 BALLS

INGREDIENTS

- 1 cup old-fashioned rolled oats
- 1/2 cup peanut butter (natural, no added sugar)
- 1/2 cup protein powder (vanilla or chocolate)
- 1/4 cup honey or maple syrup
- 1/4 cup ground flaxseed
- 1/4 cup mini chocolate chips (optional)
- 1 teaspoon vanilla extract
- 2-3 tablespoons almond milk (or any plant-based milk)

INSTRUCTIONS

1. Combine Dry Ingredients: In a large bowl, mix together the rolled oats, protein powder, and ground flaxseed.
2. Add Wet Ingredients: Add the peanut butter, honey or maple syrup, vanilla extract, and mini chocolate chips (if using). Stir until well combined.
3. Adjust Consistency: Gradually add almond milk, one tablespoon at a time, until the mixture is moist enough to hold together but not too sticky.
4. Form Balls: Using your hands, scoop out about a tablespoon of the mixture and roll it into a ball. Repeat with the remaining mixture.
5. Chill: Place the protein balls on a baking sheet and chill in the refrigerator for at least 30 minutes to firm up.
6. Store: Store the peanut butter protein balls in an airtight container in the refrigerator for up to 1 week, or freeze for up to 1 month.

Nutritional Information (per serving):

CALORIES: 100	PROTEIN: 5G	CARBOHYDRATES: 10G	FIBER: 2G	SUGARS: 5G	FAT: 5G	SATURATED FAT: 1G
SODIUM: 50MG	POTASSIUM: 120MG	VITAMIN A: 0% DV		VITAMIN C: 0% DV	CALCIUM: 2% DV	IRON: 4% DV

GREEK YOGURT BERRY PARFAIT

PREP TIME 10 MINUTES	COOK TIME 0 MINUTES	★☆☆☆☆ DIFFICULTY	SE4VES 4

INGREDIENTS

- 2 cups Greek yogurt (plain or vanilla)
- 1 cup mixed berries (such as strawberries, blueberries, raspberries, and blackberries)
- 1/4 cup honey or maple syrup
- 1 teaspoon vanilla extract (if using plain yogurt)
- 1/2 cup granola
- Fresh mint leaves for garnish (optional)

INSTRUCTIONS

1. Prepare Yogurt: In a medium bowl, mix the Greek yogurt with honey or maple syrup and vanilla extract (if using plain yogurt). Stir until well combined.
2. Layer Ingredients: In four serving glasses or bowls, layer the parfaits as follows:
   - Start with a spoonful of yogurt mixture at the bottom.
   - Add a layer of mixed berries.
   - Add another layer of yogurt.
   - Sprinkle a layer of granola.
   - Repeat the layers until the glasses are filled, ending with a layer of berries and a sprinkle of granola on top.
3. Garnish: Garnish with fresh mint leaves if desired.
4. Serve Immediately: Serve the parfaits immediately for the best texture, or refrigerate for up to 2 hours if preparing in advance.

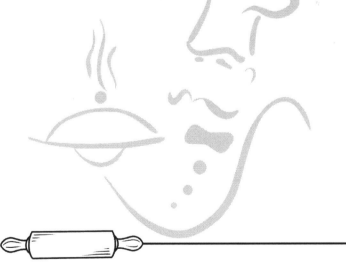

Nutritional Information (per serving):

CALORIES: 200	PROTEIN: 10G	CARBOHYDRATES: 30G	FIBER: 4G	SUGARS: 20G	FAT: 5G	SATURATED FAT: 2G
SODIUM: 60MG	POTASSIUM: 300MG	VITAMIN A: 2% DV	VITAMIN C: 30% DV		CALCIUM: 15% DV	IRON: 4% DV

Low-Calorie Baked Goods

Low-calorie baked goods are perfect for those who want to enjoy delicious treats while maintaining a balanced diet. By using healthier ingredients and mindful baking techniques, you can create desserts that are lower in calories but still satisfy your sweet tooth. This section introduces you to the benefits of low-calorie baked goods, provides tips for making them, and offers a variety of recipes to get you started.

Benefits of Low-Calorie Baked Goods

1. **Weight Management**: Lower calorie treats help you enjoy your favorite desserts without consuming excessive calories, aiding in weight management.
2. **Healthier Ingredients**: Using whole grains, natural sweeteners, and reduced-fat ingredients can increase the nutritional value of your baked goods.
3. **Balanced Diet**: Incorporating low-calorie desserts into your diet allows you to enjoy treats while still adhering to a healthy eating plan.
4. **Reduced Sugar and Fat**: By cutting back on sugar and fat, you can create baked goods that are healthier but still delicious.
5. **Portion Control**: Low-calorie recipes often focus on smaller portions, helping you enjoy your desserts mindfully.

Tips for Making Low-Calorie Baked Goods

1. **Use Whole Grains**: Substitute white flour with whole wheat flour, oat flour, or almond flour to increase fiber and nutrients.
2. **Sweeten Naturally**: Use natural sweeteners like honey, maple syrup, or mashed bananas instead of refined sugar.
3. **Reduce Fat**: Replace some of the fat with healthier options like applesauce, Greek yogurt, or mashed avocado.
4. **Incorporate Fruits and Vegetables**: Adding fruits and vegetables like apples, carrots, zucchini, and berries can boost the nutritional content and moisture of your baked goods.
5. **Watch Portions**: Be mindful of portion sizes to keep calorie intake in check while still enjoying your treats.

SKINNY BLUEBERRY MUFFINS

PREP TIME
15 MINUTES

COOK TIME
25 MINUTES

DIFFICULTY

SE4VES
12

INGREDIENTS

- 1 1/2 cups whole wheat flour
- 1/2 cup rolled oats
- 1 teaspoon baking powder
- 1/2 teaspoon baking soda
- 1/4 teaspoon salt
- 1 teaspoon ground cinnamon
- 2 large eggs
- 1/2 cup unsweetened applesauce
- 1/2 cup honey or maple syrup
- 1/4 cup Greek yogurt (non-fat or low-fat)
- 1 teaspoon vanilla extract
- 1 cup fresh or frozen blueberries

INSTRUCTIONS

1. Preheat Oven: Preheat your oven to 350°F (175°C). Line a 12-cup muffin tin with paper liners or lightly grease it.
2. Mix Dry Ingredients: In a large bowl, whisk together the whole wheat flour, rolled oats, baking powder, baking soda, salt, and ground cinnamon.
3. Mix Wet Ingredients: In another bowl, whisk together the eggs, unsweetened applesauce, honey or maple syrup, Greek yogurt, and vanilla extract until well combined.
4. Combine Wet and Dry Ingredients: Pour the wet ingredients into the dry ingredients and stir until just combined. Be careful not to overmix.
5. Fold in Blueberries: Gently fold in the blueberries.
6. Fill Muffin Tin: Divide the batter evenly among the 12 muffin cups, filling each about 3/4 full.
7. Bake: Bake in the preheated oven for 20-25 minutes, or until a toothpick inserted into the center of a muffin comes out clean.
8. Cool: Remove from the oven and let the muffins cool in the tin for 5 minutes, then transfer to a wire rack to cool completely.
9. Serve: Serve the muffins warm or at room temperature. Store in an airtight container for up to 3 days.

Nutritional Information (per serving):

CALORIES: 120	PROTEIN: 4G	CARBOHYDRATES: 23G	FIBER: 4G	SUGARS: 10G	FAT: 2G	SATURATED FAT: 0.5G
SODIUM: 130MG	POTASSIUM: 100MG	VITAMIN A: 2% DV	VITAMIN C: 5% DV		CALCIUM: 4% DV	IRON: 6% DV

LOW-FAT CHOCOLATE CHIP COOKIES

PREP TIME
10 MINUTES

COOK TIME
10 MINUTES

★☆☆☆☆
DIFFICULTY

SE4VES
24 COOKIES

INGREDIENTS

- 1 1/2 cups whole wheat flour
- 1/2 teaspoon baking soda
- 1/4 teaspoon salt
- 1/4 cup unsweetened applesauce
- 1/4 cup Greek yogurt (non-fat or low-fat)
- 1/4 cup honey or maple syrup
- 1/4 cup brown sugar
- 1 large egg
- 1 teaspoon vanilla extract
- 1/2 cup mini dark chocolate chips

INSTRUCTIONS

1. Preheat Oven: Preheat your oven to 350°F (175°C). Line two baking sheets with parchment paper or silicone baking mats.
2. Mix Dry Ingredients: In a medium bowl, whisk together the whole wheat flour, baking soda, and salt.
3. Mix Wet Ingredients: In a large bowl, combine the unsweetened applesauce, Greek yogurt, honey or maple syrup, and brown sugar. Mix until smooth. Add the egg and vanilla extract, and continue to mix until well combined.
4. Combine Wet and Dry Ingredients: Gradually add the dry ingredients to the wet ingredients, mixing until just combined. Be careful not to overmix.
5. Fold in Chocolate Chips: Gently fold in the mini dark chocolate chips.
6. Form Cookies: Using a tablespoon or cookie scoop, drop spoonfuls of dough onto the prepared baking sheets, spacing them about 2 inches apart.
7. Bake: Bake in the preheated oven for 10-12 minutes, or until the edges are lightly browned. The centers will still be soft.
8. Cool: Remove from the oven and let the cookies cool on the baking sheets for 5 minutes, then transfer to a wire rack to cool completely.
9. Serve: Serve the cookies at room temperature. Store in an airtight container for up to 1 week.

Nutritional Information (per serving):

CALORIES: 70	PROTEIN: 1.5G	CARBOHYDRATES: 13G	FIBER: 1G	SUGARS: 8G	FAT: 1.5G	SATURATED FAT: 0.5G
SODIUM: 60MG	POTASSIUM: 40MG	VITAMIN A: 0% DV	VITAMIN C: 0% DV	CALCIUM: 2% DV	IRON: 4% DV	

Dairy-Free and Gluten-Free Options

Dairy-free and gluten-free options cater to those with dietary restrictions or preferences, ensuring that everyone can enjoy delicious desserts without compromising on taste or nutrition. These desserts use alternative ingredients to replace dairy and gluten, making them suitable for people with lactose intolerance, dairy allergies, celiac disease, or gluten sensitivity. This section introduces you to the benefits of dairy-free and gluten-free desserts, provides tips for making them, and offers a variety of recipes to get you started.

Benefits of Dairy-Free and Gluten-Free Desserts

1. **Inclusive Eating**: These desserts allow people with dairy and gluten sensitivities to enjoy sweet treats without discomfort.
2. **Nutrient-Dense Ingredients**: Using whole food alternatives like almond flour, coconut milk, and other plant-based ingredients can enhance the nutritional profile of your desserts.
3. **Reduced Inflammation**: Many people find that eliminating dairy and gluten from their diet helps reduce inflammation and improve digestive health.
4. **Improved Digestion**: Dairy-free and gluten-free desserts can be easier to digest for those with sensitive stomachs.
5. **Variety and Flavor**: Exploring dairy-free and gluten-free options introduces a variety of new ingredients and flavors to your dessert repertoire.

Tips for Making Dairy-Free and Gluten-Free Desserts

1. **Use Gluten-Free Flours**: Substitute traditional wheat flour with almond flour, coconut flour, oat flour (certified gluten-free), or a gluten-free all-purpose flour blend.
2. **Choose Plant-Based Milks**: Use almond milk, coconut milk, soy milk, or other plant-based milks instead of dairy milk.
3. **Binders and Leavening Agents**: Use ingredients like flax eggs (flaxseed meal mixed with water), chia eggs, or baking powder/soda to help with binding and leavening.
4. **Natural Sweeteners**: Opt for natural sweeteners like honey, maple syrup, dates, or coconut sugar instead of refined sugars.
5. **Experiment with Textures**: Combine different gluten-free flours and starches to achieve the desired texture in your baked goods.

COCONUT FLOUR CHOCOLATE CAKE

DAIRY-FREE AND GLUTEN-FREE OPTIONS

PREP TIME
15 MINUTES

COOK TIME
30 MINUTES

DIFFICULTY

SE4VES
8

INGREDIENTS

- 1/2 cup coconut flour
- 1/2 cup unsweetened cocoa powder
- 1 teaspoon baking powder
- 1/4 teaspoon salt
- 6 large eggs
- 1/2 cup coconut oil, melted
- 1/2 cup honey or maple syrup
- 1 tablespoon vanilla extract
- 1/2 cup almond milk (or any plant-based milk)

INSTRUCTIONS

1. Preheat Oven: Preheat your oven to 350°F (175°C). Grease an 8-inch round cake pan and line the bottom with parchment paper.
2. Mix Dry Ingredients: In a large bowl, sift together the coconut flour, unsweetened cocoa powder, baking powder, and salt.
3. Combine Wet Ingredients: In another bowl, whisk together the eggs, melted coconut oil, honey or maple syrup, vanilla extract, and almond milk until well combined.
4. Mix Dry and Wet Ingredients: Gradually add the wet ingredients to the dry ingredients, stirring until a smooth batter forms. The batter will be thick due to the coconut flour.
5. Pour Batter into Pan: Pour the batter into the prepared cake pan and spread it out evenly.
6. Bake: Bake in the preheated oven for 25-30 minutes, or until a toothpick inserted into the center of the cake comes out clean.
7. Cool: Remove the cake from the oven and let it cool in the pan for 10 minutes. Then, transfer the cake to a wire rack to cool completely.
8. Serve: Once cooled, slice and serve the cake. Optionally, you can dust it with powdered sugar or serve it with fresh berries.

Nutritional Information (per serving):

CALORIES: 220	PROTEIN: 5G	CARBOHYDRATES: 22G	FIBER: 6G	SUGARS: 14G	FAT: 12G	SATURATED FAT: 8G
SODIUM: 200MG	POTASSIUM: 100MG	VITAMIN A: 4% DV	VITAMIN C: 0% DV	CALCIUM: 6% DV	IRON: 10% DV	

BATCH COOKING BASICS

Mastering Batch Cooking

Batch cooking is a fantastic strategy for saving time, reducing stress, and ensuring you always have healthy meals on hand. By preparing large quantities of food at once and storing them for later use, you can streamline your meal preparation and make it easier to stick to a healthy eating plan. This section will guide you through the basics of batch cooking, provide tips for mastering the process, and explain the benefits of incorporating batch cooking into your routine.

Benefits of Batch Cooking

1. **Time-Saving**: Cooking in large quantities reduces the amount of time you spend in the kitchen during the week.
2. **Cost-Effective**: Buying ingredients in bulk and reducing food waste can help lower your grocery bills.
3. **Healthier Eating**: Having pre-prepared meals on hand makes it easier to avoid unhealthy fast food or takeout options.
4. **Less Stress**: Knowing you have meals ready to go can reduce the stress of daily meal planning and preparation.
5. **Flexibility**: Batch cooking allows you to have a variety of meals available, making it easy to mix and match throughout the week.

Tips for Mastering Batch Cooking

1. **Plan Ahead**: Decide on your menu and create a shopping list before you start cooking. Choose recipes that share common ingredients to simplify your prep work.
2. **Invest in Storage**: Make sure you have enough storage containers, such as glass or BPA-free plastic containers, freezer bags, and mason jars.
3. **Prep Ingredients First**: Chop vegetables, cook grains, and measure out spices before you start cooking to streamline the process.
4. **Cook in Stages**: Use your oven, stove, and slow cooker simultaneously to cook multiple dishes at once.
5. **Label and Date**: Label each container with the name of the dish and the date it was prepared to keep track of freshness.
6. **Use Versatile Ingredients**: Cook ingredients that can be used in multiple dishes, such as grilled chicken, roasted vegetables, and cooked grains.
7. **Freeze for Later**: Freeze portions of meals that you won't eat within a few days to extend their shelf life.

CHICKEN AND VEGETABLE STIR-FRY

MASTERING BATCH COOKING

PREP TIME
15 MINUTES

COOK TIME
15 MINUTES

★☆☆☆☆
DIFFICULTY

SE4VES
6

INGREDIENTS

- 1.5 pounds boneless, skinless chicken breasts, sliced into thin strips
- 3 tablespoons soy sauce (low-sodium)
- 2 tablespoons hoisin sauce
- 1 tablespoon rice vinegar
- 1 tablespoon sesame oil
- 1 tablespoon olive oil
- 2 cloves garlic, minced
- 1 tablespoon fresh ginger, grated
- 1 red bell pepper, sliced
- 1 yellow bell pepper, sliced
- 1 large carrot, julienned
- 1 cup broccoli florets
- 1 cup snap peas
- 4 green onions, sliced
- 2 tablespoons sesame seeds (optional)
- Cooked brown rice or quinoa, for serving

INSTRUCTIONS

1. Prepare the Marinade: In a medium bowl, combine the soy sauce, hoisin sauce, rice vinegar, and sesame oil. Add the chicken strips and toss to coat. Let marinate for at least 10 minutes.
2. Heat the Pan: In a large skillet or wok, heat the olive oil over medium-high heat. Add the minced garlic and grated ginger, and sauté for 1-2 minutes until fragrant.
3. Cook the Chicken: Add the marinated chicken strips to the skillet. Cook for 5-7 minutes until the chicken is cooked through and no longer pink. Remove the chicken from the skillet and set aside.
4. Cook the Vegetables: In the same skillet, add the red bell pepper, yellow bell pepper, carrot, broccoli, and snap peas. Stir-fry for 5-7 minutes until the vegetables are tender-crisp.
5. Combine Chicken and Vegetables: Return the cooked chicken to the skillet with the vegetables. Toss to combine and heat through for an additional 2 minutes.
6. Serve: Serve the chicken and vegetable stir-fry over cooked brown rice or quinoa. Garnish with sliced green onions and sesame seeds if desired.

Nutritional Information (per serving):

CALORIES: 280	PROTEIN: 30G	CARBOHYDRATES: 15G	FIBER: 3G	SUGARS: 5G	FAT: 10G	SATURATED FAT: 2G
SODIUM: 450MG	POTASSIUM: 700MG	VITAMIN A: 90% DV	VITAMIN C: 150% DV		CALCIUM: 6% DV	IRON: 10% DV

SHEET-PAN ROASTED VEGETABLES

MASTERING BATCH COOKING

PREP TIME
15 MINUTES

COOK TIME
30 MINUTES

DIFFICULTY

SE4VES
6

INGREDIENTS

- 1 large sweet potato, peeled and diced
- 2 large carrots, peeled and sliced
- 1 red bell pepper, diced
- 1 yellow bell pepper, diced
- 1 red onion, cut into wedges
- 1 zucchini, sliced
- 1 cup broccoli florets
- 1 cup cauliflower florets
- 3 tablespoons olive oil
- 1 teaspoon garlic powder
- 1 teaspoon dried thyme
- 1 teaspoon dried rosemary
- Salt and pepper to taste
- 1 tablespoon balsamic vinegar (optional)

INSTRUCTIONS

1. Preheat Oven: Preheat your oven to 425°F (220°C). Line a large baking sheet with parchment paper or a silicone baking mat.
2. Prepare Vegetables: In a large bowl, combine the sweet potato, carrots, red bell pepper, yellow bell pepper, red onion, zucchini, broccoli, and cauliflower.
3. Season Vegetables: Drizzle the olive oil over the vegetables. Sprinkle with garlic powder, dried thyme, dried rosemary, salt, and pepper. Toss until all the vegetables are evenly coated with oil and seasonings.
4. Arrange on Baking Sheet: Spread the vegetables in a single layer on the prepared baking sheet. Make sure they are spread out to ensure even roasting.
5. Roast Vegetables: Roast in the preheated oven for 25-30 minutes, or until the vegetables are tender and slightly caramelized, stirring halfway through cooking.
6. Optional Balsamic Glaze: If desired, drizzle the roasted vegetables with balsamic vinegar immediately after removing them from the oven. Toss to coat.
7. Serve: Serve the roasted vegetables immediately, or let them cool and store in an airtight container in the refrigerator for up to 5 days. They can be reheated or enjoyed cold.

Nutritional Information (per serving):

CALORIES: 120	PROTEIN: 2G	CARBOHYDRATES: 18G	FIBER: 3G	SUGARS: 6G	FAT: 6G	SATURATED FAT: 1G
SODIUM: 150MG	POTASSIUM: 400MG	VITAMIN A: 200% DV	VITAMIN C: 100% DV		CALCIUM: 4% DV	IRON: 6% DV

Versatile Base Recipes (Rice, Quinoa, Beans, etc.)

Versatile base recipes are the cornerstone of batch cooking, providing a foundation for countless meal combinations. By preparing these staples in bulk, you can save time and ensure you have nutritious ingredients ready to go for a variety of dishes. This section introduces you to the benefits of versatile base recipes, offers tips for cooking and storing them, and provides a variety of recipes to get you started.

Benefits of Versatile Base Recipes

1. **Time-Saving**: Cooking staples like rice, quinoa, and beans in bulk reduces the time needed for meal preparation during the week.
2. **Cost-Effective**: Buying and cooking these ingredients in bulk can save money and reduce food waste.
3. **Nutritional Value**: Whole grains and legumes are rich in essential nutrients, providing a healthy foundation for your meals.
4. **Versatility**: These base recipes can be used in a wide range of dishes, from salads and stir-fries to soups and casseroles.
5. **Convenience**: Having cooked grains and beans on hand makes it easy to put together quick and nutritious meals.

Tips for Cooking and Storing Versatile Base Recipes

1. **Rinse Grains and Legumes**: Rinse rice, quinoa, and beans thoroughly before cooking to remove excess starch and any debris.
2. **Use Broth or Stock**: Cooking grains in vegetable or chicken broth instead of water adds flavor and depth to your base recipes.
3. **Season Lightly**: Season your base recipes with a pinch of salt or other mild seasonings, allowing them to be easily adapted to various dishes.
4. **Cool Properly**: After cooking, allow grains and beans to cool completely before storing to prevent excess moisture and sogginess.
5. **Store Efficiently**: Divide cooked grains and beans into portion-sized containers or freezer bags for easy access and longer shelf life. Label and date them for better organization.

PERFECTLY COOKED QUINOA

PREP TIME
5 MINUTES

COOK TIME
15 MINUTES

DIFFICULTY

SE4VES
4

INGREDIENTS

- 1 cup quinoa, rinsed
- 2 cups water or vegetable broth
- 1/4 teaspoon salt

INSTRUCTIONS

1. Rinse Quinoa: Place the quinoa in a fine-mesh strainer and rinse under cold water for about 30 seconds. This removes the natural coating, called saponin, which can make quinoa taste bitter.
2. Boil Water: In a medium saucepan, bring the water or vegetable broth to a boil.
3. Add Quinoa: Stir in the rinsed quinoa and salt. Reduce the heat to low, cover, and simmer for about 15 minutes, or until the water is absorbed and the quinoa is tender.
4. Fluff and Cool: Remove the saucepan from heat and let it sit, covered, for 5 minutes. Fluff the quinoa with a fork. Let it cool completely before storing.
5. Store: Divide the cooked quinoa into portion-sized containers and store in the refrigerator for up to 5 days or freeze for up to 3 months.

Nutritional Information (per serving):

CALORIES: 110	PROTEIN: 4G	CARBOHYDRATES: 19G	FIBER: 3G	SUGARS: 0G	FAT: 2G	SATURATED FAT: 0G
SODIUM: 150MG	POTASSIUM: 150MG	VITAMIN A: 0% DV	VITAMIN C: 0% DV	CALCIUM: 2% DV	IRON: 8% DV	

BROWN RICE PILAF

VERSATILE BASE RECIPES (RICE, QUINOA, BEANS, ETC.)

PREP TIME
10 MINUTES

COOK TIME
45 MINUTES

DIFFICULTY

SE4VES
6

INGREDIENTS

- 1 1/2 cups brown rice
- 2 tablespoons olive oil
- 1 small onion, finely chopped
- 2 cloves garlic, minced
- 1 carrot, peeled and diced
- 1 celery stalk, diced
- 1 red bell pepper, diced
- 3 cups low-sodium chicken or vegetable broth
- 1 teaspoon salt
- 1/2 teaspoon black pepper
- 1/2 teaspoon dried thyme
- 1/4 teaspoon dried rosemary
- 1/4 cup chopped fresh parsley (optional)
- 1/4 cup slivered almonds, toasted (optional)

INSTRUCTIONS

1. Rinse Rice: Place the brown rice in a fine-mesh strainer and rinse under cold water until the water runs clear. This helps remove excess starch and prevents the rice from becoming sticky.
2. Sauté Vegetables: In a large saucepan, heat the olive oil over medium heat. Add the chopped onion and sauté for 3-4 minutes until translucent. Add the minced garlic, carrot, celery, and red bell pepper. Cook for an additional 5 minutes until the vegetables are tender.
3. Toast Rice: Add the rinsed brown rice to the saucepan with the vegetables. Stir to coat the rice with the oil and vegetables, cooking for 2-3 minutes until the rice is lightly toasted.
4. Add Broth and Seasonings: Pour in the chicken or vegetable broth, and add the salt, black pepper, dried thyme, and dried rosemary. Stir to combine.
5. Simmer: Bring the mixture to a boil, then reduce the heat to low. Cover the saucepan and let the rice simmer for about 45 minutes, or until the liquid is absorbed and the rice is tender.
6. Fluff and Serve: Remove the saucepan from heat and let it sit, covered, for 5 minutes. Fluff the rice with a fork. Stir in the chopped fresh parsley and toasted slivered almonds if desired.
7. Store: Divide the rice pilaf into portion-sized containers and store in the refrigerator for up to 5 days or freeze for up to 3 months.

Nutritional Information (per serving):

CALORIES: 210	PROTEIN: 4G	CARBOHYDRATES: 36G	FIBER: 3G	SUGARS: 2G	FAT: 6G	SATURATED FAT: 1G
SODIUM: 300MG	POTASSIUM: 200MG	VITAMIN A: 40% DV	VITAMIN C: 40% DV	CALCIUM: 4% DV	IRON: 8% DV	

SEASONED BLACK BEANS

VERSATILE BASE RECIPES (RICE, QUINOA, BEANS, ETC.)

PREP TIME
10 MINUTES

COOK TIME
30 MINUTES

DIFFICULTY

SE4VES
6

INGREDIENTS

- 1 tablespoon olive oil
- 1 small onion, finely chopped
- 2 cloves garlic, minced
- 1 red bell pepper, diced
- 1 teaspoon ground cumin
- 1 teaspoon smoked paprika
- 1/2 teaspoon dried oregano
- 1/4 teaspoon cayenne pepper (optional)
- 2 cans (15 oz each) black beans, drained and rinsed
- 1 cup vegetable broth or water
- Salt and pepper to taste
- 1 tablespoon lime juice
- 2 tablespoons chopped fresh cilantro (optional)

INSTRUCTIONS

1. Sauté Vegetables: In a large saucepan, heat the olive oil over medium heat. Add the chopped onion and sauté for 3-4 minutes until translucent. Add the minced garlic and diced red bell pepper. Cook for an additional 5 minutes until the vegetables are tender.
2. Add Spices: Stir in the ground cumin, smoked paprika, dried oregano, and cayenne pepper (if using). Cook for 1-2 minutes until the spices are fragrant.
3. Add Beans and Broth: Add the drained and rinsed black beans to the saucepan. Pour in the vegetable broth or water. Stir to combine.
4. Simmer: Bring the mixture to a boil, then reduce the heat to low. Let it simmer for about 20 minutes, stirring occasionally, until the beans are heated through and the flavors have melded together.
5. Season: Season with salt and pepper to taste. Stir in the lime juice.
6. Garnish and Serve: Remove from heat and stir in the chopped fresh cilantro if desired. Serve the seasoned black beans as a side dish, in burritos, or over rice.
7. Store: Divide the seasoned black beans into portion-sized containers and store in the refrigerator for up to 5 days or freeze for up to 3 months.

Nutritional Information (per serving):

CALORIES: 150	PROTEIN: 7G	CARBOHYDRATES: 25G	FIBER: 7G	SUGARS: 2G	FAT: 3G	SATURATED FAT: 0.5G
SODIUM: 300MG	POTASSIUM: 500MG	VITAMIN A: 20% DV	VITAMIN C: 30% DV		CALCIUM: 4% DV	IRON: 10% DV

Creative Ways to Use Leftovers

Using leftovers creatively not only reduces food waste but also saves time and money while keeping your meals exciting and varied. This section will guide you through innovative ways to transform your leftovers into delicious new dishes, provide tips for storing and repurposing leftovers, and offer a variety of recipes to get you started.

Benefits of Using Leftovers Creatively

1. **Reduces Food Waste**: Repurposing leftovers helps minimize the amount of food that gets thrown away.
2. **Saves Time**: Using pre-cooked ingredients means less time spent preparing and cooking meals.
3. **Saves Money**: Making the most of your food reduces grocery bills and helps you get more value from your purchases.
4. **Adds Variety**: Transforming leftovers into new dishes keeps your meals interesting and prevents food fatigue.
5. **Enhances Nutrition**: Combining different leftovers can create balanced, nutrient-dense meals.

Tips for Storing and Repurposing Leftovers

1. **Store Properly**: Use airtight containers to keep leftovers fresh and prevent them from drying out or absorbing odors from the fridge.
2. **Label and Date**: Label containers with the contents and date to keep track of freshness and avoid food waste.
3. **Plan Ahead**: When cooking, intentionally make extra portions that can be easily transformed into new dishes.
4. **Freeze for Later**: If you don't plan to use leftovers within a few days, freeze them for future use.
5. **Be Creative**: Think beyond just reheating leftovers. Use them as ingredients in soups, salads, casseroles, and more.

LEFTOVER TURKEY AND VEGGIE SOUP

PREP TIME
10 MINUTES

COOK TIME
30 MINUTES

DIFFICULTY

SE4VES
6

INGREDIENTS

- 2 cups cooked turkey, shredded or chopped
- 1 tablespoon olive oil
- 1 onion, chopped
- 2 cloves garlic, minced
- 3 carrots, peeled and sliced
- 2 celery stalks, sliced
- 1 red bell pepper, diced
- 1 cup green beans, trimmed and cut into 1-inch pieces
- 6 cups low-sodium chicken or vegetable broth
- 1 can (14.5 oz) diced tomatoes
- 1 teaspoon dried thyme
- 1 teaspoon dried oregano
- Salt and pepper to taste
- 1/4 cup chopped fresh parsley (optional)

INSTRUCTIONS

1. Sauté Vegetables: In a large pot, heat the olive oil over medium heat. Add the chopped onion and sauté for 3-4 minutes until translucent. Add the minced garlic and cook for an additional 1 minute until fragrant.
2. Add Vegetables: Add the carrots, celery, red bell pepper, and green beans to the pot. Cook for 5-7 minutes until the vegetables begin to soften.
3. Add Broth and Tomatoes: Pour in the chicken or vegetable broth and the can of diced tomatoes. Stir to combine.
4. Add Seasonings: Add the dried thyme, dried oregano, salt, and pepper. Bring the soup to a boil, then reduce the heat to low and simmer for 15-20 minutes until the vegetables are tender.
5. Add Turkey: Stir in the cooked turkey and continue to simmer for an additional 5 minutes until the turkey is heated through.
6. Serve: Ladle the soup into bowls and garnish with chopped fresh parsley if desired. Serve hot.

Nutritional Information (per serving):

CALORIES: 200	PROTEIN: 20G	CARBOHYDRATES: 15G	FIBER: 3G	SUGARS: 6G	FAT: 7G	SATURATED FAT: 1.5G
SODIUM: 450MG	POTASSIUM: 600MG	VITAMIN A: 100% DV	VITAMIN C: 60% DV		CALCIUM: 8% DV	IRON: 10% DV

QUINOA AND VEGGIE STUFFED PEPPERS

 **CREATIVE WAYS TO USE LEFTOVERS**

PREP TIME
15 MINUTES

COOK TIME
40 MINUTES

★☆☆☆☆
DIFFICULTY

SE4VES
6

INGREDIENTS

- 6 large bell peppers (any color)
- 1 cup cooked quinoa
- 1 can (15 oz) black beans, drained and rinsed
- 1 cup corn kernels (fresh, frozen, or canned)
- 1 cup diced tomatoes (canned or fresh)
- 1 small onion, finely chopped
- 2 cloves garlic, minced
- 1 teaspoon ground cumin
- 1 teaspoon chili powder
- 1/2 teaspoon smoked paprika
- 1/2 teaspoon salt
- 1/4 teaspoon black pepper
- 1 cup shredded cheese (optional, for topping)
- 2 tablespoons olive oil
- Fresh cilantro, chopped for garnish (optional)
- Lime wedges, for serving (optional)

INSTRUCTIONS

1. Preheat Oven: Preheat your oven to 375°F (190°C).
2. Prepare Peppers: Cut the tops off the bell peppers and remove the seeds and membranes. Lightly brush the outside of the peppers with 1 tablespoon of olive oil.
3. Sauté Onion and Garlic: In a large skillet, heat the remaining 1 tablespoon of olive oil over medium heat. Add the chopped onion and sauté for 3-4 minutes until translucent. Add the minced garlic and cook for an additional 1 minute until fragrant.
4. Combine Filling Ingredients: In a large bowl, combine the cooked quinoa, black beans, corn, diced tomatoes, sautéed onion and garlic, ground cumin, chili powder, smoked paprika, salt, and black pepper. Mix until well combined.
5. Stuff Peppers: Stuff each bell pepper with the quinoa and veggie mixture, pressing down gently to fill completely.
6. Bake: Place the stuffed peppers in a baking dish. Cover the dish with aluminum foil and bake in the preheated oven for 30 minutes. If using cheese, remove the foil, sprinkle the cheese on top of the peppers, and bake uncovered for an additional 10 minutes until the cheese is melted and bubbly.
7. Serve: Garnish with chopped fresh cilantro and serve with lime wedges if desired.

Nutritional Information (per serving):

CALORIES: 210	PROTEIN: 8G	CARBOHYDRATES: 32G	FIBER: 7G	SUGARS: 6G	FAT: 6G	SATURATED FAT: 1G
SODIUM: 380MG	POTASSIUM: 500MG	VITAMIN A: 70% DV	VITAMIN C: 200% DV	CALCIUM: 6% DV	IRON: 15% DV	

Freezer-Friendly Meals

Freezer-friendly meals are a lifesaver for busy days when you don't have time to cook from scratch. Preparing meals in advance and freezing them ensures you always have a healthy, homemade option ready to go. This section will guide you through the benefits of freezer-friendly meals, offer tips for effective freezing and reheating, and provide a variety of recipes to get you started.

Benefits of Freezer-Friendly Meals

1. **Convenience**: Having meals ready in the freezer means you can have a healthy, home-cooked meal in minutes.
2. **Time-Saving**: Cooking in bulk and freezing meals saves time on busy days.
3. **Reduced Food Waste**: Freezing leftovers or extra portions prevents food from going to waste.
4. **Cost-Effective**: Buying ingredients in bulk and preparing meals ahead can save money.
5. **Stress Reduction**: Knowing you have meals ready can reduce the stress of daily meal planning and cooking.

Tips for Effective Freezing and Reheating

1. **Cool Before Freezing**: Let cooked food cool completely before freezing to prevent ice crystals and freezer burn.
2. **Use Proper Containers**: Use airtight containers, freezer bags, or vacuum-sealed bags to keep food fresh and prevent freezer burn.
3. **Label and Date**: Always label containers with the name of the dish and the date it was frozen to keep track of freshness.
4. **Portion Control**: Freeze meals in individual or family-sized portions for easy reheating.
5. **Thaw Safely**: Thaw frozen meals in the refrigerator overnight or use the defrost function on your microwave. Avoid leaving food out at room temperature to thaw.

BEEF AND VEGETABLE CHILI

FREEZER-FRIENDLY MEALS

PREP TIME
15 MINUTES

COOK TIME
60 MINUTES

DIFFICULTY

SE4VES
8

INGREDIENTS

- 1 tablespoon olive oil
- 1 large onion, chopped
- 3 cloves garlic, minced
- 1 pound ground beef (lean)
- 2 bell peppers (any color), diced
- 2 large carrots, peeled and diced
- 2 celery stalks, diced
- 1 zucchini, diced
- 1 can (28 oz) diced tomatoes
- 1 can (15 oz) kidney beans, drained and rinsed
- 1 can (15 oz) black beans, drained and rinsed
- 1 can (15 oz) corn kernels, drained
- 2 cups low-sodium beef broth
- 2 tablespoons tomato paste
- 2 tablespoons chili powder
- 1 tablespoon ground cumin
- 1 teaspoon smoked paprika
- 1 teaspoon dried oregano
- Salt and pepper to taste
- Optional toppings: shredded cheese, sour cream, chopped fresh cilantro, sliced green onions

INSTRUCTIONS

1. Sauté Vegetables: In a large pot or Dutch oven, heat the olive oil over medium heat. Add the chopped onion and sauté for 3-4 minutes until translucent. Add the minced garlic and cook for an additional 1 minute until fragrant.
2. Cook Beef: Add the ground beef to the pot. Cook until browned, breaking it up with a spoon as it cooks, about 5-7 minutes. Drain any excess fat if necessary.
3. Add Vegetables: Stir in the diced bell peppers, carrots, celery, and zucchini. Cook for another 5 minutes until the vegetables start to soften.
4. Add Beans and Tomatoes: Stir in the diced tomatoes, kidney beans, black beans, and corn.
5. Season and Simmer: Add the beef broth, tomato paste, chili powder, ground cumin, smoked paprika, dried oregano, salt, and pepper. Stir well to combine. Bring the mixture to a boil, then reduce the heat to low. Cover and let it simmer for 45 minutes, stirring occasionally.
6. Adjust Seasoning: Taste and adjust the seasoning with more salt and pepper if needed.
7. Cool and Store: Allow the chili to cool completely. Portion it into airtight containers or freezer bags. Label with the name and date before placing in the freezer.

Freezing and Reheating Instructions:
- Freezing: Freeze the chili in portion-sized containers for up to 3 months.
- Reheating: Thaw overnight in the refrigerator. Reheat in a pot over medium heat until warmed through, or microwave on high, stirring occasionally, until hot.

Nutritional Information (per serving):

CALORIES: 280	PROTEIN: 20G	CARBOHYDRATES: 30G	FIBER: 7G	SUGARS: 7G	FAT: 10G	SATURATED FAT: 3G
SODIUM: 480MG	POTASSIUM: 900MG	VITAMIN A: 100% DV	VITAMIN C: 60% DV		CALCIUM: 8% DV	IRON: 25% DV

SPINACH AND CHEESE LASAGNA ROLL-UPS

FREEZER-FRIENDLY MEALS

PREP TIME
25 MINUTES

COOK TIME
30 MINUTES

★☆☆☆☆
DIFFICULTY

SE4VES
6

INGREDIENTS

- 12 lasagna noodles
- 1 tablespoon olive oil
- 2 cloves garlic, minced
- 1 (10 oz) package frozen spinach, thawed and drained
- 1 cup ricotta cheese
- 1 cup shredded mozzarella cheese, divided
- 1/2 cup grated Parmesan cheese
- 1 egg, beaten
- 1 teaspoon dried basil
- 1 teaspoon dried oregano
- Salt and pepper to taste
- 2 cups marinara sauce

INSTRUCTIONS

1. Preheat Oven: Preheat your oven to 375°F (190°C). Lightly grease a 9x13-inch baking dish.
2. Cook Noodles: Cook the lasagna noodles according to package instructions. Drain and lay them flat on a clean kitchen towel to cool and dry.
3. Prepare Filling: In a large skillet, heat the olive oil over medium heat. Add the minced garlic and sauté for 1-2 minutes until fragrant. Add the thawed and drained spinach and cook for another 2-3 minutes, stirring occasionally. Remove from heat and let cool slightly.
4. Mix Cheeses: In a large bowl, combine the ricotta cheese, 1/2 cup shredded mozzarella cheese, grated Parmesan cheese, beaten egg, dried basil, dried oregano, salt, and pepper. Stir in the cooked spinach and garlic mixture.
5. Assemble Roll-Ups: Spread a thin layer of marinara sauce on the bottom of the prepared baking dish. Lay a lasagna noodle flat on a clean surface. Spread about 2-3 tablespoons of the spinach and cheese mixture evenly over the noodle. Roll up the noodle and place it seam-side down in the baking dish. Repeat with the remaining noodles and filling.
6. Top with Sauce and Cheese: Pour the remaining marinara sauce over the lasagna roll-ups. Sprinkle the top with the remaining 1/2 cup of shredded mozzarella cheese.
7. Bake: Cover the baking dish with aluminum foil and bake in the preheated oven for 20 minutes. Remove the foil and bake for an additional 10 minutes, or until the cheese is melted and bubbly.
8. Serve: Let the lasagna roll-ups cool for a few minutes before serving. Garnish with chopped fresh basil or parsley if desired.

Freezing and Reheating Instructions:

- Freezing: After assembling the roll-ups and topping with sauce and cheese, cover the baking dish tightly with plastic wrap and aluminum foil. Label with the name and date. Freeze for up to 3 months.
- Reheating: Thaw overnight in the refrigerator. Remove the plastic wrap and cover with aluminum foil. Bake in a preheated 375°F (190°C) oven for 30-35 minutes, or until heated through.

Nutritional Information (per serving):

CALORIES: 350	PROTEIN: 18G	CARBOHYDRATES: 40G	FIBER: 5G	SUGARS: 8G	FAT: 14G	SATURATED FAT: 6G
SODIUM: 600MG	POTASSIUM: 500MG	VITAMIN A: 120% DV	VITAMIN C: 20% DV		CALCIUM: 35% DV	IRON: 15% DV

CHICKEN AND SWEET POTATO STEW

FREEZER-FRIENDLY MEALS

PREP TIME
15 MINUTES

COOK TIME
45 MINUTES

★☆☆☆☆
DIFFICULTY

SE4VES
6

INGREDIENTS

- 1 tablespoon olive oil
- 1 large onion, chopped
- 3 cloves garlic, minced
- 1 pound boneless, skinless chicken thighs, cut into bite-sized pieces
- 2 large sweet potatoes, peeled and diced
- 3 carrots, peeled and sliced
- 2 celery stalks, sliced
- 1 red bell pepper, diced
- 4 cups low-sodium chicken broth
- 1 can (14.5 oz) diced tomatoes
- 1 teaspoon dried thyme
- 1 teaspoon dried oregano
- 1/2 teaspoon ground cumin
- 1/2 teaspoon smoked paprika
- Salt and pepper to taste
- 1 cup frozen peas
- 2 tablespoons chopped fresh parsley (optional)

INSTRUCTIONS

1. Heat Oil: In a large pot or Dutch oven, heat the olive oil over medium heat. Add the chopped onion and sauté for 3-4 minutes until translucent. Add the minced garlic and cook for an additional 1 minute until fragrant.
2. Cook Chicken: Add the chicken pieces to the pot. Cook until browned on all sides, about 5-7 minutes.
3. Add Vegetables: Stir in the sweet potatoes, carrots, celery, and red bell pepper. Cook for another 5 minutes until the vegetables start to soften.
4. Add Broth and Seasonings: Pour in the chicken broth and diced tomatoes. Stir in the dried thyme, dried oregano, ground cumin, smoked paprika, salt, and pepper. Bring the mixture to a boil, then reduce the heat to low. Cover and let it simmer for 30 minutes, stirring occasionally.
5. Add Peas: Stir in the frozen peas and cook for an additional 5 minutes until the peas are heated through.
6. Serve: Ladle the stew into bowls and garnish with chopped fresh parsley if desired. Serve hot.

Freezing and Reheating Instructions:

- Freezing: Allow the stew to cool completely. Portion it into airtight containers or freezer bags. Label with the name and date before placing in the freezer. Freeze for up to 3 months.
- Reheating: Thaw overnight in the refrigerator. Reheat in a pot over medium heat until warmed through, or microwave on high, stirring occasionally, until hot.

Nutritional Information (per serving):

CALORIES: 280	PROTEIN: 20G	CARBOHYDRATES: 30G	FIBER: 5G	SUGARS: 10G	FAT: 9G	SATURATED FAT: 2G
SODIUM: 400MG	POTASSIUM: 800MG	VITAMIN A: 220% DV	VITAMIN C: 50% DV	CALCIUM: 8% DV	IRON: 15% DV	

Vegetarian and Vegan Meal Prep

V egetarian and vegan meal prep focuses on creating delicious, plant-based meals that are both nutritious and satisfying. By preparing meals in advance, you can ensure you have a variety of healthy, meat-free options ready to enjoy throughout the week. This section introduces the benefits of vegetarian and vegan meal prep, provides tips for successful meal planning, and offers a variety of recipes to get you started.

Benefits of Vegetarian and Vegan Meal Prep

1. **Nutrient-Dense**: Plant-based meals are rich in vitamins, minerals, antioxidants, and fiber, contributing to overall health and well-being.
2. **Environmental Impact**: Reducing meat consumption can help lower your carbon footprint and support environmental sustainability.
3. **Cost-Effective**: Plant-based ingredients are often less expensive than meat and dairy products, helping you save money on groceries.
4. **Health Benefits**: Diets rich in fruits, vegetables, whole grains, and legumes have been linked to a reduced risk of chronic diseases such as heart disease, diabetes, and certain cancers.
5. **Variety and Flavor**: Vegetarian and vegan diets encourage the use of a wide variety of ingredients and flavors, making meals more exciting and diverse.

Tips for Successful Vegetarian and Vegan Meal Prep

1. **Plan Your Meals**: Create a weekly meal plan that includes a variety of protein sources, vegetables, grains, and healthy fats. This ensures balanced nutrition and prevents meal fatigue.
2. **Batch Cooking**: Cook large batches of staples like grains, beans, and roasted vegetables to use in multiple meals throughout the week.
3. **Versatile Ingredients**: Choose ingredients that can be used in various dishes, such as chickpeas, lentils, quinoa, and sweet potatoes.
4. **Storage Solutions**: Invest in high-quality storage containers to keep your prepped meals fresh and easily accessible.
5. **Flavor Enhancers**: Use herbs, spices, sauces, and dressings to add flavor and variety to your meals.

VEGAN CHICKPEA CURRY

VEGETARIAN AND VEGAN MEAL PREP

PREP TIME
10 MINUTES

COOK TIME
30 MINUTES

DIFFICULTY

SE4VES
4

INGREDIENTS

- 1 tablespoon coconut oil
- 1 large onion, chopped
- 3 cloves garlic, minced
- 1 tablespoon fresh ginger, grated
- 2 teaspoons ground cumin
- 2 teaspoons ground coriander
- 1 teaspoon ground turmeric
- 1/2 teaspoon cayenne pepper (optional)
- 1 can (14.5 oz) diced tomatoes
- 1 can (14.5 oz) coconut milk
- 2 cans (15 oz each) chickpeas, drained and rinsed
- 1 cup vegetable broth
- 1 large sweet potato, peeled and diced
- 2 cups spinach, chopped
- Salt and pepper to taste
- Fresh cilantro, chopped (for garnish)

INSTRUCTIONS

1. Heat Oil: In a large pot or Dutch oven, heat the coconut oil over medium heat. Add the chopped onion and sauté for 3-4 minutes until translucent. Add the minced garlic and grated ginger, and cook for an additional 1-2 minutes until fragrant.
2. Add Spices: Stir in the ground cumin, ground coriander, ground turmeric, and cayenne pepper (if using). Cook for 1-2 minutes until the spices are well combined and fragrant.
3. Add Tomatoes and Coconut Milk: Pour in the diced tomatoes and coconut milk. Stir to combine.
4. Add Chickpeas and Sweet Potato: Add the chickpeas, vegetable broth, and diced sweet potato. Bring the mixture to a boil, then reduce the heat to low and let it simmer for 20-25 minutes, or until the sweet potato is tender.
5. Add Spinach: Stir in the chopped spinach and cook for an additional 2-3 minutes until wilted.
6. Season: Season with salt and pepper to taste.
7. Serve: Serve the chickpea curry over rice or with naan bread. Garnish with chopped fresh cilantro.

Nutritional Information (per serving):

CALORIES: 300	PROTEIN: 10G	CARBOHYDRATES: 45G	FIBER: 12G	SUGARS: 8G	FAT: 10G	SATURATED FAT: 6G
SODIUM: 450MG	POTASSIUM: 800MG	VITAMIN A: 150% DV	VITAMIN C: 35% DV	CALCIUM: 10% DV	IRON: 25% DV	

QUINOA AND BLACK BEAN STUFFED BELL PEPPERS

VEGETARIAN AND VEGAN MEAL PREP

| PREP TIME 15 MINUTES | COOK TIME 30 MINUTES | ★☆☆☆☆ DIFFICULTY | SE4VES 6 |

INGREDIENTS

- 6 large bell peppers (any color)
- 1 cup quinoa, rinsed and cooked according to package instructions
- 1 can (15 oz) black beans, drained and rinsed
- 1 cup corn kernels (fresh, frozen, or canned)
- 1 can (14.5 oz) diced tomatoes, drained
- 1 small onion, finely chopped
- 2 cloves garlic, minced
- 1 teaspoon ground cumin
- 1 teaspoon chili powder
- 1/2 teaspoon smoked paprika
- Salt and pepper to taste
- 1 cup shredded vegan cheese (optional)
- Fresh cilantro, chopped (for garnish)
- Lime wedges (for serving)

INSTRUCTIONS

1. Preheat Oven: Preheat your oven to 375°F (190°C). Lightly grease a 9x13-inch baking dish.
2. Prepare Bell Peppers: Cut the tops off the bell peppers and remove the seeds and membranes. Lightly brush the outside of the peppers with a bit of oil if desired.
3. Cook Quinoa: Rinse 1 cup of quinoa under cold water. Cook according to package instructions.
4. Sauté Onion and Garlic: In a large skillet, heat a tablespoon of oil over medium heat. Add the chopped onion and sauté for 3-4 minutes until translucent. Add the minced garlic and cook for an additional 1 minute until fragrant.
5. Mix Filling: In a large bowl, combine the cooked quinoa, black beans, corn kernels, diced tomatoes, sautéed onion and garlic, ground cumin, chili powder, smoked paprika, salt, and pepper. Mix until well combined.
6. Stuff Bell Peppers: Stuff each bell pepper with the quinoa and black bean mixture, pressing down gently to fill completely.
7. Top with Cheese (Optional): If using, sprinkle shredded vegan cheese on top of each stuffed pepper.
8. Bake: Place the stuffed peppers in the prepared baking dish. Cover the dish with aluminum foil and bake in the preheated oven for 25 minutes. Remove the foil and bake for an additional 5 minutes, or until the cheese is melted and bubbly.
9. Serve: Garnish with chopped fresh cilantro and serve with lime wedges if desired.

Nutritional Information (per serving):

CALORIES: 220	PROTEIN: 8G	CARBOHYDRATES: 35G	FIBER: 8G	SUGARS: 6G	FAT: 5G	SATURATED FAT: 1G
SODIUM: 350MG	POTASSIUM: 700MG	VITAMIN A: 90% DV	VITAMIN C: 200% DV	CALCIUM: 10% DV	IRON: 15% DV	

SWEET POTATO AND BLACK BEAN TACOS

VEGETARIAN AND VEGAN MEAL PREP

PREP TIME
15 MINUTES

COOK TIME
25 MINUTES

★☆☆☆☆
DIFFICULTY

SE4VES
6

INGREDIENTS

- 2 large sweet potatoes, peeled and diced
- 2 tablespoons olive oil
- 1 teaspoon ground cumin
- 1 teaspoon chili powder
- 1/2 teaspoon smoked paprika
- 1/2 teaspoon garlic powder
- Salt and pepper to taste
- 1 can (15 oz) black beans, drained and rinsed
- 12 small corn tortillas
- 1 avocado, sliced
- 1 cup shredded red cabbage
- 1/2 cup fresh cilantro, chopped
- 1/4 cup lime juice
- 1/4 cup vegan sour cream (optional)

INSTRUCTIONS

1. Preheat Oven: Preheat your oven to 425°F (220°C). Line a baking sheet with parchment paper.
2. Prepare Sweet Potatoes: In a large bowl, toss the diced sweet potatoes with olive oil, ground cumin, chili powder, smoked paprika, garlic powder, salt, and pepper until evenly coated.
3. Roast Sweet Potatoes: Spread the sweet potatoes in a single layer on the prepared baking sheet. Roast in the preheated oven for 20-25 minutes, or until tender and slightly caramelized, stirring halfway through cooking.
4. Heat Black Beans: While the sweet potatoes are roasting, heat the black beans in a small saucepan over medium heat until warmed through. Season with a pinch of salt and pepper if desired.
5. Warm Tortillas: Warm the corn tortillas in a dry skillet over medium heat for about 30 seconds on each side, or until pliable.
6. Assemble Tacos: Divide the roasted sweet potatoes and black beans evenly among the warmed tortillas. Top with sliced avocado, shredded red cabbage, and chopped fresh cilantro.
7. Add Toppings: Drizzle with lime juice and add a dollop of vegan sour cream if desired.
8. Serve: Serve the tacos immediately, garnished with additional lime wedges if desired.

Nutritional Information (per serving):

CALORIES: 250	PROTEIN: 6G	CARBOHYDRATES: 40G	FIBER: 10G	SUGARS: 5G	FAT: 9G	SATURATED FAT: 1G
SODIUM: 200MG	POTASSIUM: 600MG	VITAMIN A: 200% DV	VITAMIN C: 30% DV		CALCIUM: 10% DV	IRON: 15% DV

LENTIL AND VEGETABLE SHEPHERD'S PIE

VEGETARIAN AND VEGAN MEAL PREP

PREP TIME
20 MINUTES

COOK TIME
45 MINUTES

★★★☆☆
DIFFICULTY

SE4VES
6

INGREDIENTS

- 1 cup green or brown lentils, rinsed
- 2 1/2 cups vegetable broth
- 1 tablespoon olive oil
- 1 large onion, chopped
- 2 cloves garlic, minced
- 2 carrots, peeled and diced
- 2 celery stalks, diced
- 1 cup frozen peas
- 1 cup frozen corn
- 2 tablespoons tomato paste
- 1 teaspoon dried thyme
- 1 teaspoon dried rosemary
- Salt and pepper to taste
- 4 cups mashed potatoes (prepared using dairy-free milk and butter if vegan)

INSTRUCTIONS

1. Cook Lentils: In a medium saucepan, combine the lentils and vegetable broth. Bring to a boil, then reduce the heat and simmer for 25-30 minutes, or until the lentils are tender and the liquid is absorbed. Set aside.
2. Preheat Oven: Preheat your oven to 375°F (190°C).
3. Sauté Vegetables: In a large skillet, heat the olive oil over medium heat. Add the chopped onion and sauté for 3-4 minutes until translucent. Add the minced garlic, carrots, and celery. Cook for an additional 5-7 minutes until the vegetables are tender.
4. Add Tomato Paste and Seasonings: Stir in the tomato paste, dried thyme, dried rosemary, salt, and pepper. Cook for another 2 minutes until well combined.
5. Combine Lentils and Vegetables: Add the cooked lentils to the skillet with the sautéed vegetables. Stir in the frozen peas and corn. Cook for an additional 2-3 minutes until everything is heated through and well combined.
6. Assemble Shepherd's Pie: Transfer the lentil and vegetable mixture to a 9x13-inch baking dish. Spread it out evenly. Top with the mashed potatoes, spreading them out to cover the lentil mixture completely.
7. Bake: Bake in the preheated oven for 20 minutes, or until the mashed potatoes are golden brown and the filling is bubbling.
8. Serve: Let the shepherd's pie cool for a few minutes before serving. Garnish with chopped fresh parsley if desired.

Nutritional Information (per serving):

CALORIES: 320	PROTEIN: 12G	CARBOHYDRATES: 55G	FIBER: 15G	SUGARS: 8G	FAT: 7G	SATURATED FAT: 1G
SODIUM: 450MG	POTASSIUM: 1200MG	VITAMIN A: 120% DV	VITAMIN C: 30% DV		CALCIUM: 8% DV	IRON: 20% DV

VEGAN BUDDHA BOWL WITH TAHINI DRESSING

PREP TIME
20 MINUTES

COOK TIME
25 MINUTES

★★☆☆☆
DIFFICULTY

SE4VES
4

INGREDIENTS

For the Buddha Bowl:
- 1 cup quinoa, rinsed
- 2 cups water
- 1 tablespoon olive oil
- 1 large sweet potato, peeled and diced
- 1 can (15 oz) chickpeas, drained and rinsed
- 1 teaspoon ground cumin
- 1 teaspoon smoked paprika
- Salt and pepper to taste
- 2 cups fresh spinach, chopped
- 1 avocado, sliced
- 1 cup shredded carrots
- 1 cup purple cabbage, thinly sliced

For the Tahini Dressing:
- 1/4 cup tahini
- 2 tablespoons lemon juice
- 2 tablespoons water (more as needed)
- 1 tablespoon maple syrup
- 1 clove garlic, minced
- Salt and pepper to taste

INSTRUCTIONS

1. Cook Quinoa: In a medium saucepan, bring the water to a boil. Add the quinoa, reduce the heat to low, cover, and simmer for about 15 minutes or until the water is absorbed and the quinoa is tender. Remove from heat and let it sit, covered, for 5 minutes. Fluff with a fork.

2. Prepare Sweet Potatoes and Chickpeas: Preheat your oven to 400°F (200°C). On a baking sheet, toss the diced sweet potatoes and chickpeas with olive oil, ground cumin, smoked paprika, salt, and pepper. Spread in a single layer and roast for 20-25 minutes, or until the sweet potatoes are tender and the chickpeas are slightly crispy.

3. Make the Tahini Dressing: In a small bowl, whisk together the tahini, lemon juice, water, maple syrup, minced garlic, salt, and pepper. Add more water as needed to reach your desired consistency.

4. Assemble the Buddha Bowls: Divide the cooked quinoa among four bowls. Top each with roasted sweet potatoes and chickpeas, fresh spinach, sliced avocado, shredded carrots, and sliced purple cabbage.

5. Drizzle and Serve: Drizzle the tahini dressing over each bowl. Serve immediately, garnished with additional lemon wedges or fresh herbs if desired.

Nutritional Information (per serving):

CALORIES: 450	PROTEIN: 12G	CARBOHYDRATES: 58G	FIBER: 15G	SUGARS: 10G	FAT: 18G	SATURATED FAT: 2.5G
SODIUM: 320MG	POTASSIUM: 1200MG	VITAMIN A: 210% DV	VITAMIN C: 70% DV	CALCIUM: 15% DV	IRON: 25% DV	

Gluten-Free and Dairy-Free Recipes

Gluten-free and dairy-free recipes cater to those with dietary restrictions or preferences, ensuring that everyone can enjoy delicious and nutritious meals without compromising on taste or health. This section introduces the benefits of gluten-free and dairy-free eating, provides tips for successful meal planning and preparation, and offers a variety of recipes to get you started.

Benefits of Gluten-Free and Dairy-Free Eating

1. **Inclusive Eating**: These recipes accommodate people with celiac disease, gluten sensitivity, lactose intolerance, or dairy allergies.
2. **Improved Digestion**: Many people experience improved digestion and reduced bloating when they eliminate gluten and dairy from their diet.
3. **Reduced Inflammation**: A gluten-free and dairy-free diet can help reduce inflammation, which may alleviate symptoms of chronic conditions such as arthritis.
4. **Nutrient-Rich**: By focusing on whole foods like fruits, vegetables, nuts, seeds, and lean proteins, these recipes are often more nutrient-dense.
5. **Weight Management**: Some people find it easier to manage their weight when they eliminate gluten and dairy, as they often reduce their intake of processed foods.

Tips for Successful Gluten-Free and Dairy-Free Meal Prep

1. **Read Labels Carefully**: Ensure all ingredients are certified gluten-free and dairy-free to avoid cross-contamination and hidden sources of gluten and dairy.
2. **Stock Your Pantry**: Keep your pantry stocked with gluten-free grains (quinoa, rice, millet), dairy-free milk alternatives (almond, coconut, soy), and gluten-free flours (almond, coconut, rice).
3. **Plan Ahead**: Plan your meals for the week, including breakfast, lunch, dinner, and snacks, to ensure you have all necessary ingredients and reduce the temptation to eat out.
4. **Batch Cooking**: Prepare large batches of gluten-free and dairy-free staples like grains, legumes, and roasted vegetables to use throughout the week.
5. **Flavor Enhancers**: Use herbs, spices, and homemade dressings or sauces to add flavor and variety to your meals.

GLUTEN-FREE QUINOA SALAD WITH LEMON VINAIGRETTE

PREP TIME
15 MINUTES

COOK TIME
15 MINUTES

DIFFICULTY

SE4VES
4

INGREDIENTS

- 1 cup quinoa, rinsed
- 2 cups water or vegetable broth
- 1 cup cherry tomatoes, halved
- 1 cucumber, diced
- 1 red bell pepper, diced
- 1/4 cup red onion, finely chopped
- 1/4 cup fresh parsley, chopped
- 1/4 cup fresh mint, chopped

For the Lemon Vinaigrette:
- 1/4 cup olive oil
- 1/4 cup fresh lemon juice
- 1 teaspoon Dijon mustard
- 1 garlic clove, minced
- Salt and pepper to taste

INSTRUCTIONS

1. Cook Quinoa: In a medium saucepan, bring the water or vegetable broth to a boil. Add the quinoa, reduce heat to low, cover, and simmer for about 15 minutes, or until the water is absorbed and the quinoa is tender. Remove from heat and let it sit, covered, for 5 minutes. Fluff with a fork and let cool.
2. Prepare Vegetables: While the quinoa is cooking, prepare the cherry tomatoes, cucumber, red bell pepper, red onion, parsley, and mint.
3. Make the Vinaigrette: In a small bowl, whisk together the olive oil, lemon juice, Dijon mustard, minced garlic, salt, and pepper.
4. Combine Salad: In a large bowl, combine the cooked quinoa, cherry tomatoes, cucumber, red bell pepper, red onion, parsley, and mint. Pour the lemon vinaigrette over the salad and toss to coat evenly.
5. Serve: Serve the quinoa salad chilled or at room temperature. Store any leftovers in an airtight container in the refrigerator for up to 3 days.

Nutritional Information (per serving):

CALORIES: 220	PROTEIN: 6G	CARBOHYDRATES: 26G	FIBER: 5G	SUGARS: 4G	FAT: 10G	SATURATED FAT: 1.5G
SODIUM: 150MG	POTASSIUM: 450MG	VITAMIN A: 20% DV	VITAMIN C: 60% DV		CALCIUM: 4% DV	IRON: 15% DV

DAIRY-FREE CAULIFLOWER ALFREDO

PREP TIME
15 MINUTES

COOK TIME
20 MINUTES

★☆☆☆☆

DIFFICULTY

SE4VES
4

INGREDIENTS

- 1 medium head of cauliflower, cut into florets
- 2 tablespoons olive oil
- 3 cloves garlic, minced
- 1 cup unsweetened almond milk (or any dairy-free milk)
- 1/4 cup nutritional yeast
- 1 tablespoon lemon juice
- 1/2 teaspoon salt
- 1/4 teaspoon black pepper
- 1/4 teaspoon nutmeg
- 1/4 cup fresh parsley, chopped (optional, for garnish)
- 12 ounces gluten-free pasta (such as fettuccine or spaghetti)

INSTRUCTIONS

1. Cook Cauliflower: In a large pot, bring water to a boil. Add the cauliflower florets and cook for about 10 minutes, or until tender. Drain and set aside.
2. Cook Pasta: While the cauliflower is cooking, prepare the gluten-free pasta according to package instructions. Drain and set aside.
3. Sauté Garlic: In a large skillet, heat the olive oil over medium heat. Add the minced garlic and sauté for 1-2 minutes until fragrant.
4. Blend Alfredo Sauce: In a blender, combine the cooked cauliflower, sautéed garlic, almond milk, nutritional yeast, lemon juice, salt, black pepper, and nutmeg. Blend until smooth and creamy.
5. Heat Sauce: Pour the cauliflower Alfredo sauce back into the skillet. Heat over medium-low heat, stirring occasionally, until warmed through. If the sauce is too thick, add a little more almond milk to reach the desired consistency.
6. Combine with Pasta: Add the cooked pasta to the skillet with the Alfredo sauce. Toss to coat the pasta evenly with the sauce.
7. Serve: Divide the pasta among four plates. Garnish with chopped fresh parsley if desired. Serve immediately

Nutritional Information (per serving):

CALORIES: 320	PROTEIN: 10G	CARBOHYDRATES: 55G	FIBER: 7G	SUGARS: 5G	FAT: 8G	SATURATED FAT: 1G
SODIUM: 300MG	POTASSIUM: 600MG	VITAMIN A: 2% DV	VITAMIN C: 70% DV		CALCIUM: 15% DV	IRON: 15% DV

GLUTEN-FREE STUFFED MUSHROOMS

PREP TIME
15 MINUTES

COOK TIME
20 MINUTES

★☆☆☆☆
DIFFICULTY

SE4VES
6

INGREDIENTS

- 16 large white or cremini mushrooms, stems removed and finely chopped
- 2 tablespoons olive oil
- 1 small onion, finely chopped
- 2 cloves garlic, minced
- 1/2 red bell pepper, finely chopped
- 1 cup gluten-free breadcrumbs
- 1/4 cup nutritional yeast
- 1 teaspoon dried Italian seasoning
- 1/4 teaspoon salt
- 1/4 teaspoon black pepper
- 2 tablespoons fresh parsley, chopped (optional, for garnish)

INSTRUCTIONS

1. Preheat Oven: Preheat your oven to 375°F (190°C). Lightly grease a baking sheet or line it with parchment paper.
2. Prepare Mushrooms: Clean the mushrooms and remove the stems. Finely chop the stems and set aside. Arrange the mushroom caps on the prepared baking sheet.
3. Sauté Vegetables: In a large skillet, heat the olive oil over medium heat. Add the chopped mushroom stems, onion, garlic, and red bell pepper. Sauté for 5-7 minutes, or until the vegetables are tender and the moisture from the mushrooms has evaporated.
4. Prepare Filling: In a large bowl, combine the sautéed vegetables, gluten-free breadcrumbs, nutritional yeast, dried Italian seasoning, salt, and black pepper. Mix well to combine.
5. Stuff Mushrooms: Spoon the filling into each mushroom cap, pressing down gently to pack the filling in.
6. Bake: Bake in the preheated oven for 15-20 minutes, or until the mushrooms are tender and the filling is golden brown.
7. Serve: Garnish with chopped fresh parsley if desired. Serve warm as an appetizer or side dish.

Nutritional Information (per serving):

CALORIES: 120	PROTEIN: 4G	CARBOHYDRATES: 12G	FIBER: 2G	SUGARS: 2G	FAT: 7G	SATURATED FAT: 1G
SODIUM: 200MG	POTASSIUM: 300MG	VITAMIN A: 10% DV	VITAMIN C: 20% DV	CALCIUM: 2% DV	IRON: 6% DV	

DAIRY-FREE COCONUT YOGURT PARFAIT

PREP TIME
10 MINUTES

COOK TIME
0 MINUTES

★☆☆☆☆
DIFFICULTY

SE4VES
4

INGREDIENTS

- 2 cups dairy-free coconut yogurt
- 1 cup granola (ensure gluten-free if needed)
- 1 cup mixed berries (such as strawberries, blueberries, and raspberries)
- 1 tablespoon chia seeds
- 2 tablespoons maple syrup or agave nectar
- 1 teaspoon vanilla extract
- Fresh mint leaves (optional, for garnish)

INSTRUCTIONS

1. Prepare Yogurt Mixture: In a medium bowl, combine the dairy-free coconut yogurt, chia seeds, maple syrup or agave nectar, and vanilla extract. Mix well.
2. Layer Ingredients: In four serving glasses or bowls, layer the parfaits as follows:
- Start with a few spoonfuls of the yogurt mixture at the bottom.
- Add a layer of mixed berries.
- Sprinkle a layer of granola.
- Repeat the layers until the glasses are filled, ending with a layer of berries and a sprinkle of granola on top.
3. Garnish: Garnish with fresh mint leaves if desired.
4. Serve Immediately: Serve the parfaits immediately for the best texture, or refrigerate for up to 2 hours before serving.

Nutritional Information (per serving):

CALORIES: 250	PROTEIN: 4G	CARBOHYDRATES: 38G	FIBER: 6G	SUGARS: 16G	FAT: 10G	SATURATED FAT: 6G
SODIUM: 60MG	POTASSIUM: 300MG	VITAMIN A: 2% DV	VITAMIN C: 30% DV	CALCIUM: 6% DV	IRON: 10% DV	

GLUTEN-FREE VEGETABLE STIR-FRY

PREP TIME
15 MINUTES

COOK TIME
15 MINUTES

★☆☆☆☆
DIFFICULTY

SE4VES
4

INGREDIENTS

- 2 tablespoons sesame oil or olive oil
- 1 onion, thinly sliced
- 2 cloves garlic, minced
- 1-inch piece fresh ginger, grated
- 1 red bell pepper, thinly sliced
- 1 yellow bell pepper, thinly sliced
- 1 large carrot, julienned
- 1 zucchini, thinly sliced
- 1 cup broccoli florets
- 1 cup snap peas
- 3 tablespoons gluten-free soy sauce or tamari
- 1 tablespoon rice vinegar
- 1 tablespoon maple syrup or honey
- 1 teaspoon cornstarch mixed with 2 tablespoons water (optional, for thickening)
- 2 green onions, sliced
- Sesame seeds (optional, for garnish)
- Cooked rice or quinoa, for serving

INSTRUCTIONS

1. Prepare Sauce: In a small bowl, whisk together the gluten-free soy sauce or tamari, rice vinegar, and maple syrup or honey. Set aside.
2. Heat Oil: In a large skillet or wok, heat the sesame oil or olive oil over medium-high heat.
3. Sauté Aromatics: Add the sliced onion, minced garlic, and grated ginger to the skillet. Sauté for 2-3 minutes until fragrant and the onion is translucent.
4. Add Vegetables: Add the sliced red and yellow bell peppers, julienned carrot, sliced zucchini, broccoli florets, and snap peas to the skillet. Stir-fry for 5-7 minutes until the vegetables are tender-crisp.
5. Add Sauce: Pour the prepared sauce over the vegetables. Stir to coat the vegetables evenly. If you prefer a thicker sauce, add the cornstarch mixture and stir until the sauce has thickened, about 1-2 minutes.
6. Finish and Serve: Stir in the sliced green onions. Remove from heat. Serve the vegetable stir-fry over cooked rice or quinoa. Garnish with sesame seeds if desired.

Nutritional Information (per serving):

CALORIES: 180	PROTEIN: 5G	CARBOHYDRATES: 25G	FIBER: 6G	SUGARS: 9G	FAT: 7G	SATURATED FAT: 1G
SODIUM: 480MG	POTASSIUM: 600MG	VITAMIN A: 100% DV	VITAMIN C: 150% DV		CALCIUM: 6% DV	IRON: 10% DV

Low-Carb and Keto-Friendly Options

Low-carb and keto-friendly recipes are designed to minimize carbohydrate intake while maximizing healthy fats and proteins. These meals are ideal for those following a ketogenic diet or anyone looking to reduce their carb consumption for health or weight management reasons. This section introduces the benefits of low-carb and keto-friendly eating, provides tips for successful meal planning and preparation, and offers a variety of recipes to get you started.

Benefits of Low-Carb and Keto-Friendly Eating

1. **Weight Management**: Reducing carbohydrate intake can help with weight loss and management by promoting fat burning and reducing hunger.
2. **Blood Sugar Control**: Low-carb and keto diets can help stabilize blood sugar levels, which is beneficial for people with diabetes or insulin resistance.
3. **Increased Energy**: Many people experience improved energy levels and mental clarity when they switch to a low-carb or keto diet.
4. **Reduced Inflammation**: A diet low in refined carbs and sugars can help reduce inflammation, potentially alleviating symptoms of chronic conditions like arthritis.
5. **Heart Health**: Healthy fats and proteins from sources like avocados, nuts, seeds, and fatty fish can support cardiovascular health.

Tips for Successful Low-Carb and Keto Meal Prep

1. **Focus on Whole Foods**: Prioritize whole, unprocessed foods like vegetables, meats, fish, nuts, seeds, and healthy fats.
2. **Plan Your Meals**: Create a weekly meal plan that includes a variety of proteins, healthy fats, and low-carb vegetables.
3. **Batch Cooking**: Prepare large batches of keto-friendly staples like grilled chicken, roasted vegetables, and cauliflower rice to use throughout the week.
4. **Smart Swaps**: Use low-carb substitutes for high-carb foods, such as zucchini noodles instead of pasta, cauliflower rice instead of regular rice, and lettuce wraps instead of bread.
5. **Flavor Enhancers**: Use herbs, spices, and healthy fats like olive oil, coconut oil, and avocado to add flavor and variety to your meals.

KETO ZUCCHINI NOODLES WITH PESTO

LOW-CARB AND KETO-FRIENDLY OPTIONS

PREP TIME
15 MINUTES

COOK TIME
10 MINUTES

DIFFICULTY

SE4VES
4

INGREDIENTS

- 4 medium zucchinis, spiralized into noodles
- 1 cup fresh basil leaves
- 1/4 cup pine nuts
- 2 cloves garlic
- 1/2 cup olive oil
- 1/4 cup grated Parmesan cheese (optional for dairy-free, use nutritional yeast)
- Salt and pepper to taste
- Cherry tomatoes, halved (optional, for garnish)
- Grilled chicken or shrimp (optional, for added protein)

INSTRUCTIONS

1. Prepare Pesto: In a food processor, combine the fresh basil leaves, pine nuts, garlic, and Parmesan cheese or nutritional yeast. Pulse until finely chopped. With the processor running, slowly drizzle in the olive oil until the pesto is smooth and creamy. Season with salt and pepper to taste.
2. Cook Zucchini Noodles: In a large skillet, heat a tablespoon of olive oil over medium heat. Add the spiralized zucchini noodles and sauté for 3-4 minutes, or until they are just tender.
3. Combine: Remove the skillet from heat and toss the zucchini noodles with the prepared pesto until they are evenly coated.
4. Serve: Divide the pesto zucchini noodles among four plates. Garnish with halved cherry tomatoes and grilled chicken or shrimp if desired. Serve immediately.

Nutritional Information (per serving):

CALORIES: 220	PROTEIN: 4G	CARBOHYDRATES: 6G	FIBER: 2G	SUGARS: 4G	FAT: 20G	SATURATED FAT: 3G
SODIUM: 150MG	POTASSIUM: 500MG	VITAMIN A: 15% DV	VITAMIN C: 30% DV	CALCIUM: 10% DV	IRON: 8% DV	

LOW-CARB CAULIFLOWER FRIED RICE

LOW-CARB AND KETO-FRIENDLY OPTIONS

PREP TIME
15 MINUTES

COOK TIME
15 MINUTES

★☆☆☆☆
DIFFICULTY

SE4VES
4

INGREDIENTS

- 1 large head of cauliflower, riced (about 4 cups)
- 2 tablespoons sesame oil
- 1 small onion, finely chopped
- 2 cloves garlic, minced
- 1 cup frozen peas and carrots, thawed
- 1 red bell pepper, diced
- 3 green onions, sliced (whites and greens separated)
- 3 large eggs, lightly beaten
- 3 tablespoons gluten-free soy sauce or tamari
- 1 teaspoon grated fresh ginger
- Salt and pepper to taste
- Optional toppings: sliced green onions, sesame seeds, sriracha sauce

INSTRUCTIONS

1. Prepare Cauliflower Rice: Remove the leaves and core from the cauliflower. Cut into florets and place them in a food processor. Pulse until the cauliflower resembles rice. Alternatively, you can use pre-riced cauliflower from the store.
2. Cook Vegetables: In a large skillet or wok, heat 1 tablespoon of sesame oil over medium-high heat. Add the finely chopped onion and cook for 2-3 minutes until translucent. Add the minced garlic and cook for another 30 seconds until fragrant.
3. Add Cauliflower Rice: Add the riced cauliflower to the skillet. Cook for 5-7 minutes, stirring occasionally, until the cauliflower is tender but not mushy.
4. Cook Peas and Carrots: In the same skillet, push the cauliflower rice to one side. Add the remaining 1 tablespoon of sesame oil to the empty side of the skillet. Add the peas, carrots, diced red bell pepper, and the white parts of the green onions. Cook for 3-4 minutes, stirring occasionally.
5. Scramble Eggs: Push the vegetables to one side of the skillet. Pour the beaten eggs into the empty side of the skillet. Scramble the eggs until fully cooked, then mix them into the vegetables and cauliflower rice.
6. Season: Add the gluten-free soy sauce or tamari, grated fresh ginger, and salt and pepper to taste. Stir well to combine all the ingredients and heat through.
7. Serve: Remove from heat and garnish with the green parts of the green onions. Serve immediately, topped with optional toppings like sesame seeds or sriracha sauce if desired.

Nutritional Information (per serving):

CALORIES: 180	PROTEIN: 8G	CARBOHYDRATES: 12G	FIBER: 5G	SUGARS: 4G	FAT: 12G	SATURATED FAT: 2G
SODIUM: 600MG	POTASSIUM: 600MG	VITAMIN A: 50% DV	VITAMIN C: 120% DV	CALCIUM: 6% DV	IRON: 8% DV

KETO AVOCADO AND BACON SALAD

PREP TIME
15 MINUTES

COOK TIME
10 MINUTES

DIFFICULTY

SE4VES
4

INGREDIENTS

- 6 slices of bacon
- 2 large avocados, diced
- 1 head of romaine lettuce, chopped
- 1 cup cherry tomatoes, halved
- 1/4 red onion, thinly sliced
- 1/4 cup crumbled feta cheese (optional)
- 2 tablespoons olive oil
- 1 tablespoon apple cider vinegar
- 1 teaspoon Dijon mustard
- Salt and pepper to taste

INSTRUCTIONS

1. Cook Bacon: In a large skillet, cook the bacon over medium heat until crispy. Remove from the skillet and place on a paper towel-lined plate to drain. Once cooled, crumble the bacon into bite-sized pieces.
2. Prepare Vegetables: In a large bowl, combine the chopped romaine lettuce, diced avocados, halved cherry tomatoes, and sliced red onion.
3. Make Dressing: In a small bowl, whisk together the olive oil, apple cider vinegar, Dijon mustard, salt, and pepper.
4. Assemble Salad: Pour the dressing over the salad and toss to coat evenly. Add the crumbled bacon and feta cheese (if using) and gently toss again to combine.
5. Serve: Divide the salad among

Nutritional Information (per serving):

CALORIES: 320	PROTEIN: 7G	CARBOHYDRATES: 10G	FIBER: 7G	SUGARS: 2G	FAT: 28G	SATURATED FAT: 6G
SODIUM: 600MG	POTASSIUM: 900MG	VITAMIN A: 100% DV	VITAMIN C: 30% DV		CALCIUM: 10% DV	IRON: 8% DV

LOW-CARB CHICKEN AND BROCCOLI CASSEROLE

LOW-CARB AND KETO-FRIENDLY OPTIONS

PREP TIME
20 MINUTES

COOK TIME
30 MINUTES

★★☆☆☆
DIFFICULTY

SE4VES
6

INGREDIENTS

- 1 tablespoon olive oil
- 1 small onion, chopped
- 3 cloves garlic, minced
- 1 pound boneless, skinless chicken breasts, cooked and shredded
- 4 cups broccoli florets
- 1 cup shredded cheddar cheese (optional for dairy-free, use dairy-free cheese)
- 1 cup unsweetened almond milk (or any dairy-free milk)
- 1/2 cup mayonnaise (ensure gluten-free if needed)
- 1/4 cup grated Parmesan cheese (optional for dairy-free, use nutritional yeast)
- 1 teaspoon dried thyme
- 1 teaspoon dried oregano
- 1/2 teaspoon salt
- 1/4 teaspoon black pepper
- 1/4 teaspoon paprika
- 1/4 teaspoon ground mustard
- 1/4 teaspoon ground nutmeg (optional)
- Fresh parsley, chopped (for garnish)

INSTRUCTIONS

1. Preheat Oven: Preheat your oven to 375°F (190°C). Grease a 9x13-inch baking dish.
2. Cook Onion and Garlic: In a large skillet, heat the olive oil over medium heat. Add the chopped onion and cook for 3-4 minutes until translucent. Add the minced garlic and cook for an additional 1 minute until fragrant.
3. Blanch Broccoli: Bring a pot of water to a boil and blanch the broccoli florets for 2-3 minutes until they are bright green and tender-crisp. Drain and set aside.
4. Prepare Sauce: In a large bowl, whisk together the almond milk, mayonnaise, Parmesan cheese or nutritional yeast, dried thyme, dried oregano, salt, black pepper, paprika, ground mustard, and ground nutmeg.
5. Combine Ingredients: Add the shredded chicken, cooked onion and garlic, and blanched broccoli to the bowl with the sauce. Stir until everything is well combined.
6. Transfer to Baking Dish: Transfer the mixture to the prepared baking dish. Spread it out evenly.
7. Top with Cheese: Sprinkle the shredded cheddar cheese over the top if using.
8. Bake: Bake in the preheated oven for 25-30 minutes, or until the casserole is bubbly and the cheese is melted and golden brown.
9. Garnish and Serve: Remove from the oven and let it cool for a few minutes. Garnish with chopped fresh parsley before serving.

Nutritional Information (per serving):

CALORIES: 350	PROTEIN: 28G	CARBOHYDRATES: 10G	FIBER: 3G	SUGARS: 2G	FAT: 22G	SATURATED FAT: 6G
SODIUM: 500MG	POTASSIUM: 600MG	VITAMIN A: 20% DV	VITAMIN C: 70% DV	CALCIUM: 20% DV	IRON: 10% DV	

KETO EGG MUFFINS WITH SPINACH AND CHEESE

LOW-CARB AND KETO-FRIENDLY OPTIONS

PREP TIME
10 MINUTES

COOK TIME
20 MINUTES

★★☆☆☆
DIFFICULTY

SE4VES
6

INGREDIENTS

- 8 large eggs
- 1/4 cup heavy cream (or coconut milk for dairy-free)
- 1 cup fresh spinach, chopped
- 1/2 cup shredded cheddar cheese (optional for dairy-free, use dairy-free cheese)
- 1/4 cup red bell pepper, finely diced
- 1/4 cup onion, finely chopped
- 1/4 teaspoon salt
- 1/4 teaspoon black pepper
- 1/4 teaspoon garlic powder
- 1/4 teaspoon smoked paprika
- Cooking spray or olive oil (for greasing the muffin tin)

INSTRUCTIONS

1. Preheat Oven: Preheat your oven to 375°F (190°C). Grease a 12-cup muffin tin with cooking spray or olive oil.
2. Whisk Eggs: In a large bowl, whisk together the eggs and heavy cream (or coconut milk) until well combined.
3. Add Vegetables and Cheese: Stir in the chopped spinach, shredded cheddar cheese, diced red bell pepper, and chopped onion.
4. Season: Add the salt, black pepper, garlic powder, and smoked paprika to the egg mixture. Stir until all ingredients are evenly distributed.
5. Fill Muffin Tin: Pour the egg mixture evenly into the prepared muffin tin, filling each cup about 3/4 full.
6. Bake: Bake in the preheated oven for 18-20 minutes, or until the egg muffins are set and lightly golden on top.
7. Cool and Serve: Let the muffins cool in the tin for a few minutes before removing. Serve warm or at room temperature.

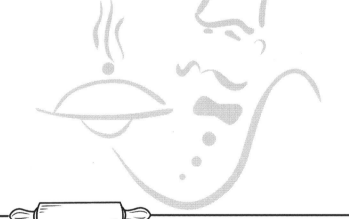

Nutritional Information (per serving):

CALORIES: 150	PROTEIN: 10G	CARBOHYDRATES: 2G	FIBER: 1G	SUGARS: 1G	FAT: 11G	SATURATED FAT: 5G
SODIUM: 250MG	POTASSIUM: 200MG	VITAMIN A: 25% DV	VITAMIN C: 15% DV	CALCIUM: 10% DV	IRON: 6% DV	

Recipes for Muscle Building and Weight Loss

Recipes designed for muscle building and weight loss focus on high-protein, nutrient-dense ingredients that support muscle growth and repair while aiding in fat loss. These recipes help maintain a calorie deficit for weight loss while providing the necessary nutrients for muscle maintenance and growth. This section introduces the benefits of muscle-building and weight-loss recipes, offers tips for successful meal planning and preparation, and provides a variety of recipes to get you started.

Benefits of Muscle-Building and Weight-Loss Recipes

1. **High Protein**: These recipes prioritize protein, which is essential for muscle repair and growth, as well as for keeping you full and satisfied.
2. **Nutrient-Dense**: Emphasis on whole foods rich in vitamins, minerals, and antioxidants supports overall health and recovery.
3. **Controlled Calories**: Recipes are designed to be calorie-conscious to help maintain a calorie deficit for weight loss while ensuring adequate nutrition.
4. **Balanced Macronutrients**: Proper balance of proteins, fats, and carbohydrates supports energy levels and muscle synthesis.
5. **Satiating**: High-fiber ingredients and healthy fats help you feel full longer, reducing the temptation to overeat.

Tips for Successful Muscle-Building and Weight-Loss Meal Prep

1. **Prioritize Protein**: Include a source of lean protein in every meal, such as chicken, turkey, fish, eggs, or plant-based proteins like beans and tofu.
2. **Incorporate Healthy Fats**: Use healthy fats like avocados, nuts, seeds, and olive oil to support hormone function and satiety.
3. **Focus on Fiber**: Include plenty of vegetables, fruits, and whole grains to provide fiber, which aids in digestion and helps you feel full.
4. **Control Portions**: Use measuring tools and portion control to avoid overeating and to maintain calorie goals.
5. **Stay Hydrated**: Drink plenty of water throughout the day to support metabolism and overall health.

HIGH-PROTEIN LENTIL SALAD

PREP TIME
15 MINUTES

COOK TIME
25 MINUTES

DIFFICULTY

SE4VES
4

INGREDIENTS

- 1 cup green or brown lentils, rinsed and drained
- 4 cups water or low-sodium vegetable broth
- 1 small red onion, finely chopped
- 1 red bell pepper, diced
- 1 cucumber, diced
- 1/2 cup cherry tomatoes, halved
- 1/4 cup fresh parsley, chopped
- 1/4 cup fresh mint, chopped

For the Dressing:
- 1/4 cup olive oil
- 2 tablespoons lemon juice
- 1 tablespoon apple cider vinegar
- 1 teaspoon Dijon mustard
- 1 garlic clove, minced
- Salt and pepper to taste

INSTRUCTIONS

1. Cook Lentils: In a medium saucepan, bring the water or vegetable broth to a boil. Add the lentils, reduce heat, and simmer for 20-25 minutes until tender. Drain and let cool.
2. Prepare Vegetables: While the lentils are cooking, chop the red onion, red bell pepper, cucumber, cherry tomatoes, parsley, and mint.
3. Make Dressing: In a small bowl, whisk together the olive oil, lemon juice, apple cider vinegar, Dijon mustard, minced garlic, salt, and pepper.
4. Combine Ingredients: In a large bowl, combine the cooked lentils, chopped vegetables, and herbs. Pour the dressing over the salad and toss to coat evenly.
5. Serve: Serve immediately or refrigerate for up to 3 days for flavors to meld.

Nutritional Information (per serving):

CALORIES: 300	PROTEIN: 15G	CARBOHYDRATES: 35G	FIBER: 15G	SUGARS: 6G	FAT: 12G	SATURATED FAT: 2G
SODIUM: 200MG	POTASSIUM: 800MG	VITAMIN A: 25% DV	VITAMIN C: 60% DV	CALCIUM: 6% DV	IRON: 30% DV	

TURKEY AND QUINOA STUFFED PEPPERS

RECIPES FOR MUSCLE BUILDING AND WEIGHT LOSS

PREP TIME
20 MINUTES

COOK TIME
30 MINUTES

DIFFICULTY

SE4VES
4

INGREDIENTS

- 4 large bell peppers (any color)
- 1 tablespoon olive oil
- 1 small onion, finely chopped
- 2 cloves garlic, minced
- 1 pound ground turkey
- 1 cup cooked quinoa
- 1 can (14.5 oz) diced tomatoes, drained
- 1 teaspoon ground cumin
- 1 teaspoon dried oregano
- 1/2 teaspoon smoked paprika
- Salt and pepper to taste
- 1 cup shredded cheese (optional for dairy-free, use dairy-free cheese)
- Fresh parsley, chopped (for garnish)

INSTRUCTIONS

1. Preheat Oven: Preheat your oven to 375°F (190°C). Lightly grease a baking dish large enough to hold the peppers upright.
2. Prepare Bell Peppers: Cut the tops off the bell peppers and remove the seeds and membranes. Lightly brush the outside of the peppers with a bit of oil if desired. Place the peppers upright in the prepared baking dish.
3. Cook Onion and Garlic: In a large skillet, heat the olive oil over medium heat. Add the chopped onion and cook for 3-4 minutes until translucent. Add the minced garlic and cook for an additional 1 minute until fragrant.
4. Cook Turkey: Add the ground turkey to the skillet. Cook until browned, breaking it up with a spoon as it cooks, about 5-7 minutes. Drain any excess fat if necessary.
5. Add Ingredients: Stir in the cooked quinoa, diced tomatoes, ground cumin, dried oregano, smoked paprika, salt, and pepper. Cook for an additional 2-3 minutes until everything is heated through and well combined.
6. Stuff Peppers: Spoon the turkey and quinoa mixture into each bell pepper, pressing down gently to fill completely. Top with shredded cheese if using.
7. Bake: Cover the baking dish with aluminum foil and bake in the preheated oven for 20 minutes. Remove the foil and bake for an additional 10 minutes, or until the cheese is melted and the peppers are tender.
8. Serve: Garnish with chopped fresh parsley before serving.

Nutritional Information (per serving):

CALORIES: 350	PROTEIN: 28G	CARBOHYDRATES: 20G	FIBER: 5G	SUGARS: 6G	FAT: 18G	SATURATED FAT: 5G
SODIUM: 450MG	POTASSIUM: 700MG	VITAMIN A: 60% DV	VITAMIN C: 200% DV	CALCIUM: 15% DV	IRON: 20% DV	

GRILLED CHICKEN AND VEGETABLE SKEWERS

PREP TIME
20 MINUTES

COOK TIME
15 MINUTES

★★☆☆☆
DIFFICULTY

SE4VES
4

INGREDIENTS

- 1 pound boneless, skinless chicken breasts, cut into 1-inch cubes
- 1 red bell pepper, cut into 1-inch pieces
- 1 yellow bell pepper, cut into 1-inch pieces
- 1 zucchini, sliced into thick rounds
- 1 red onion, cut into wedges
- 1 cup cherry tomatoes
- 2 tablespoons olive oil
- 2 tablespoons lemon juice
- 3 cloves garlic, minced
- 1 teaspoon dried oregano
- 1 teaspoon dried thyme
- 1/2 teaspoon salt
- 1/2 teaspoon black pepper
- Fresh parsley, chopped (for garnish)

INSTRUCTIONS

1. Prepare Marinade: In a large bowl, whisk together the olive oil, lemon juice, minced garlic, dried oregano, dried thyme, salt, and black pepper.
2. Marinate Chicken: Add the cubed chicken to the bowl and toss to coat evenly with the marinade. Cover and refrigerate for at least 30 minutes, or up to 2 hours for more flavor.
3. Preheat Grill: Preheat your grill to medium-high heat.
4. Assemble Skewers: Thread the marinated chicken, red bell pepper, yellow bell pepper, zucchini, red onion, and cherry tomatoes onto metal or soaked wooden skewers, alternating pieces of chicken and vegetables.
5. Grill Skewers: Place the skewers on the preheated grill. Grill for 10-15 minutes, turning occasionally, until the chicken is cooked through and the vegetables are tender and slightly charred.
6. Serve: Remove the skewers from the grill and let them rest for a few minutes. Garnish with chopped fresh parsley before serving.

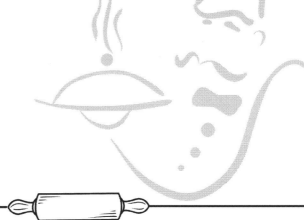

Nutritional Information (per serving):

CALORIES: 300	PROTEIN: 28G	CARBOHYDRATES: 10G	FIBER: 5G	SUGARS: 5G	FAT: 16G	SATURATED FAT: 3G
SODIUM: 450MG	POTASSIUM: 700MG	VITAMIN A: 35% DV	VITAMIN C: 150% DV		CALCIUM: 4% DV	IRON: 10% DV

GREEK YOGURT AND BERRY PROTEIN SMOOTHIE

PREP TIME
5 MINUTES

COOK TIME
0 MINUTES

★☆☆☆☆
DIFFICULTY

SE4VES
2

INGREDIENTS

- 1 cup Greek yogurt (plain, unsweetened)
- 1 cup mixed berries (fresh or frozen)
- 1 scoop vanilla protein powder
- 1 cup unsweetened almond milk (or any dairy-free milk)
- 1 tablespoon chia seeds
- 1 tablespoon honey or maple syrup (optional)
- 1/2 teaspoon vanilla extract
- Ice cubes (optional, for a thicker smoothie)

INSTRUCTIONS

1. Blend Ingredients: In a blender, combine the Greek yogurt, mixed berries, vanilla protein powder, almond milk, chia seeds, honey or maple syrup (if using), and vanilla extract. Blend until smooth and creamy.
2. Adjust Consistency: If the smoothie is too thick, add a bit more almond milk until you reach your desired consistency. If you prefer a thicker smoothie, add a few ice cubes and blend again.
3. Serve: Pour the smoothie into two glasses and serve immediately.

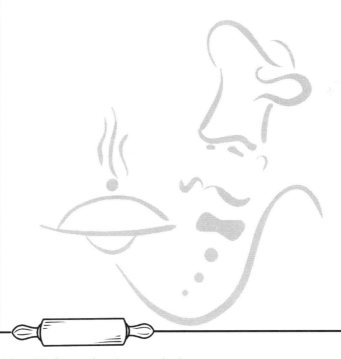

Nutritional Information (per serving):

CALORIES: 250	PROTEIN: 20G	CARBOHYDRATES: 25G	FIBER: 7G	SUGARS: 15G	FAT: 6G	SATURATED FAT: 1G
SODIUM: 100MG	POTASSIUM: 400MG	VITAMIN A: 2% DV	VITAMIN C: 50% DV		CALCIUM: 20% DV	IRON: 6% DV

SPICY BLACK BEAN AND SWEET POTATO HASH

PREP TIME
15 MINUTES

COOK TIME
20 MINUTES

DIFFICULTY

SE4VES
4

INGREDIENTS

- 2 tablespoons olive oil
- 1 large sweet potato, peeled and diced into small cubes
- 1 small onion, finely chopped
- 1 red bell pepper, diced
- 2 cloves garlic, minced
- 1 can (15 oz) black beans, drained and rinsed
- 1 teaspoon ground cumin
- 1/2 teaspoon smoked paprika
- 1/4 teaspoon cayenne pepper (optional, for extra spice)
- Salt and pepper to taste
- 1/4 cup fresh cilantro, chopped
- 1 avocado, sliced (for serving)
- Lime wedges (for serving)

INSTRUCTIONS

1. Heat Oil: In a large skillet, heat the olive oil over medium heat. Add the diced sweet potato and cook for about 10 minutes, stirring occasionally, until the sweet potato is tender and slightly crispy.
2. Add Vegetables: Add the chopped onion and red bell pepper to the skillet. Cook for another 5 minutes, stirring occasionally, until the vegetables are soft.
3. Add Garlic and Spices: Stir in the minced garlic, ground cumin, smoked paprika, cayenne pepper (if using), salt, and pepper. Cook for 1-2 minutes until fragrant.
4. Add Black Beans: Add the drained black beans to the skillet and cook for another 3-4 minutes, stirring occasionally, until the beans are heated through.
5. Garnish and Serve: Remove the skillet from heat. Stir in the chopped fresh cilantro. Serve the hash topped with sliced avocado and lime wedges on the side.

Nutritional Information (per serving):

CALORIES: 280	PROTEIN: 7G	CARBOHYDRATES: 40G	FIBER: 12G	SUGARS: 7G	FAT: 11G	SATURATED FAT: 1.5G
SODIUM: 200MG	POTASSIUM: 900MG	VITAMIN A: 300% DV	VITAMIN C: 60% DV	CALCIUM: 8% DV	IRON: 15% DV	

Sneaky Ways to Add More Veggies

Incorporating more vegetables into your diet can be challenging, especially if you or your family members are not fond of them. However, with a bit of creativity, you can "sneak" veggies into meals in ways that are both delicious and nutritious. This section introduces the benefits of adding more vegetables to your diet, provides tips for incorporating veggies into your meals, and offers a variety of strategies to get you started.

Benefits of Adding More Veggies

1. **Nutrient-Rich**: Vegetables are packed with vitamins, minerals, fiber, and antioxidants that are essential for overall health.
2. **Low in Calories**: Most vegetables are low in calories, making them ideal for weight management and promoting a feeling of fullness.
3. **Improved Digestion**: The high fiber content in vegetables aids digestion and supports gut health.
4. **Disease Prevention**: A diet rich in vegetables is associated with a lower risk of chronic diseases such as heart disease, diabetes, and certain cancers.
5. **Enhanced Flavor and Texture**: Vegetables can add a variety of flavors, textures, and colors to your meals, making them more enjoyable and visually appealing.

Tips for Sneaking Veggies into Your Meals

1. **Blend into Smoothies**: Add spinach, kale, or zucchini to your fruit smoothies. The fruit masks the taste of the vegetables while boosting the nutrient content.
2. **Puree into Sauces**: Blend vegetables like carrots, zucchini, and spinach into tomato sauce or marinara. This is an excellent way to add extra nutrients to pasta dishes without altering the flavor.
3. **Bake into Goods**: Incorporate grated or pureed vegetables such as carrots, zucchini, and pumpkin into baked goods like muffins, breads, and brownies.
4. **Mix into Meat Dishes**: Finely chop or grate vegetables and mix them into meatballs, meatloaf, or burgers. Vegetables like onions, bell peppers, and carrots work well.
5. **Swap Noodles**: Use vegetable noodles such as zucchini noodles (zoodles) or spaghetti squash in place of traditional pasta.
6. **Layer in Casseroles**: Add layers of spinach, mushrooms, or zucchini to casseroles and lasagnas. The vegetables will blend in with the other ingredients.
7. **Top Your Pizza**: Add a variety of vegetables to your pizza toppings. Try bell peppers, mushrooms, spinach, and artichokes for a nutrient boost.
8. **Stuff It**: Use bell peppers, tomatoes, or mushrooms as vessels to stuff with grains, meats, or other vegetables.
9. **Add to Soups and Stews**: Incorporate a variety of vegetables into soups and stews. Vegetables like carrots, celery, and kale work well in most recipes.
10. **Use in Dips and Spreads**: Blend vegetables like roasted red peppers, spinach, or artichokes into dips and spreads for a healthy snack option.

SPINACH AND BERRY SMOOTHIE

SNEAKY WAYS TO ADD MORE VEGGIES

PREP TIME
5 MINUTES

COOK TIME
0 MINUTES

DIFFICULTY

SE4VES
2

INGREDIENTS

- 1 cup fresh spinach leaves
- 1 cup mixed berries (fresh or frozen)
- 1 banana
- 1 cup unsweetened almond milk (or any dairy-free milk)
- 1 tablespoon chia seeds
- 1 tablespoon almond butter (optional)
- 1 teaspoon honey or maple syrup (optional)
- Ice cubes (optional, for a thicker smoothie)

INSTRUCTIONS

1. Combine Ingredients: In a blender, add the fresh spinach leaves, mixed berries, banana, unsweetened almond milk, chia seeds, almond butter (if using), and honey or maple syrup (if using).
2. Blend: Blend until smooth and creamy. If the smoothie is too thick, add a bit more almond milk until you reach your desired consistency. If you prefer a thicker smoothie, add a few ice cubes and blend again.
3. Serve: Pour the smoothie into two glasses and serve immediately.

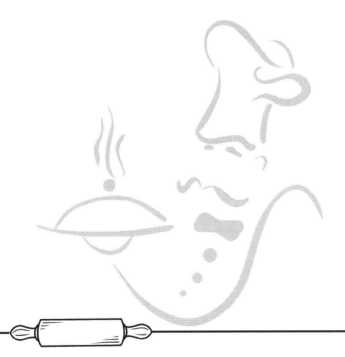

Nutritional Information (per serving):

CALORIES: 180	PROTEIN: 4G	CARBOHYDRATES: 32G	FIBER: 8G	SUGARS: 18G	FAT: 6G	SATURATED FAT: 0.5G
SODIUM: 80MG	POTASSIUM: 550MG	VITAMIN A: 30% DV	VITAMIN C: 100% DV	CALCIUM: 20% DV	IRON: 10% DV	

HIDDEN VEGGIE MARINARA SAUCE

PREP TIME
15 MINUTES

COOK TIME
45 MINUTES

DIFFICULTY

SE4VES
6

INGREDIENTS

- 2 tablespoons olive oil
- 1 large onion, finely chopped
- 3 cloves garlic, minced
- 2 carrots, peeled and finely chopped
- 1 zucchini, finely chopped
- 1 red bell pepper, finely chopped
- 1 can (28 oz) crushed tomatoes
- 1 can (15 oz) tomato sauce
- 1 teaspoon dried oregano
- 1 teaspoon dried basil
- 1/2 teaspoon dried thyme
- 1/2 teaspoon salt
- 1/4 teaspoon black pepper
- 1/4 teaspoon red pepper flakes (optional)
- 1 tablespoon tomato paste
- 1 teaspoon sugar or honey (optional, to balance acidity)
- Fresh basil, chopped (for garnish)

INSTRUCTIONS

1. Heat Oil: In a large pot or Dutch oven, heat the olive oil over medium heat. Add the chopped onion and sauté for 3-4 minutes until translucent. Add the minced garlic and cook for an additional 1 minute until fragrant.
2. Add Vegetables: Add the finely chopped carrots, zucchini, and red bell pepper to the pot. Cook for 7-10 minutes, stirring occasionally, until the vegetables are soft.
3. Add Tomatoes and Spices: Stir in the crushed tomatoes, tomato sauce, dried oregano, dried basil, dried thyme, salt, black pepper, and red pepper flakes (if using). Add the tomato paste and sugar or honey (if using). Stir well to combine.
4. Simmer: Bring the sauce to a simmer. Reduce the heat to low and let it simmer for 30 minutes, stirring occasionally, until the sauce thickens and the flavors meld together.
5. Blend (Optional): For a smoother sauce, use an immersion blender to puree the sauce to your desired consistency. Alternatively, let the sauce cool slightly and blend it in batches in a blender.
6. Serve: Serve the hidden veggie marinara sauce over your favorite pasta, zoodles, or use as a base for pizza. Garnish with chopped fresh basil before serving.

Nutritional Information (per serving):

| CALORIES: 120 | PROTEIN: 2G | CARBOHYDRATES: 15G | FIBER: 4G | SUGARS: 8G | FAT: 5G | SATURATED FAT: 1G |
| SODIUM: 400MG | POTASSIUM: 550MG | VITAMIN A: 80% DV | VITAMIN C: 50% DV | CALCIUM: 6% DV | IRON: 10% DV |

Reducing Sugar and Salt without Sacrificing Flavor

Reducing sugar and salt in your diet is crucial for maintaining good health and preventing chronic diseases. However, it doesn't mean that you have to compromise on flavor. With the right techniques and ingredients, you can create delicious meals that are low in sugar and salt but rich in taste. This section introduces the benefits of reducing sugar and salt, provides tips for enhancing flavor without these ingredients, and offers practical recipes to get you started.

Benefits of Reducing Sugar and Salt

1. **Heart Health**: Lowering salt intake helps reduce blood pressure, which is beneficial for heart health.
2. **Weight Management**: Reducing sugar can help control calorie intake, aiding in weight management.
3. **Diabetes Prevention**: Cutting back on sugar helps maintain stable blood sugar levels, reducing the risk of diabetes.
4. **Kidney Health**: Less salt reduces the strain on kidneys, promoting better kidney health.
5. **Overall Wellness**: Reducing both sugar and salt contributes to overall health and wellness, reducing the risk of various chronic diseases.

Tips for Enhancing Flavor Without Sugar and Salt

1. **Use Herbs and Spices**: Fresh and dried herbs and spices like basil, cilantro, parsley, rosemary, thyme, cumin, paprika, and cinnamon add depth and flavor without the need for extra salt or sugar.
2. **Citrus and Vinegar**: Lemon, lime, and vinegar can brighten up flavors and add a tangy zest to your dishes.
3. **Aromatics**: Garlic, onions, ginger, and shallots can add a robust flavor profile to any meal.
4. **Umami-Rich Ingredients**: Foods like mushrooms, tomatoes, soy sauce (low-sodium), and nutritional yeast are rich in umami, providing a savory depth that reduces the need for salt.
5. **Healthy Fats**: Use healthy fats like olive oil, avocado, and nuts to add richness and enhance the mouthfeel of your dishes.
6. **Natural Sweeteners**: Use fruits, especially dried fruits like dates, raisins, or fresh berries, to add natural sweetness to recipes.
7. **Roasting and Grilling**: These cooking methods can enhance the natural flavors of vegetables and proteins, making them more flavorful without added sugar or salt.

SPICED APPLE AND CARROT MUFFINS

REDUCING SUGAR AND SALT WITHOUT SACRIFICING FLAVOR

PREP TIME
15 MINUTES

COOK TIME
20 MINUTES

DIFFICULTY

SE4VES
12 MUFFINS

INGREDIENTS

- 1 cup whole wheat flour
- 1/2 cup oat flour
- 1 teaspoon baking powder
- 1/2 teaspoon baking soda
- 1/2 teaspoon salt
- 1 teaspoon ground cinnamon
- 1/2 teaspoon ground nutmeg
- 1/4 teaspoon ground cloves
- 1/4 teaspoon ground ginger
- 2 large eggs
- 1/4 cup coconut oil, melted
- 1/4 cup unsweetened applesauce
- 1/4 cup honey or maple syrup
- 1 teaspoon vanilla extract
- 1 cup grated apple (about 1 large apple)
- 1 cup grated carrot (about 2 medium carrots)

INSTRUCTIONS

1. Preheat Oven: Preheat your oven to 350°F (175°C). Line a 12-cup muffin tin with paper liners or grease with cooking spray.
2. Mix Dry Ingredients: In a large bowl, whisk together the whole wheat flour, oat flour, baking powder, baking soda, salt, ground cinnamon, ground nutmeg, ground cloves, and ground ginger.
3. Mix Wet Ingredients: In another bowl, whisk together the eggs, melted coconut oil, unsweetened applesauce, honey or maple syrup, and vanilla extract until well combined.
4. Combine Ingredients: Add the wet ingredients to the dry ingredients and mix until just combined. Fold in the grated apple and grated carrot.
5. Fill Muffin Tin: Divide the batter evenly among the 12 muffin cups, filling each about 3/4 full.
6. Bake: Bake in the preheated oven for 18-20 minutes, or until a toothpick inserted into the center of a muffin comes out clean.
7. Cool and Serve: Allow the muffins to cool in the tin for 5 minutes, then transfer to a wire rack to cool completely. Serve warm or at room temperature.

Nutritional Information (per serving):

CALORIES: 130	PROTEIN: 3G	CARBOHYDRATES: 20G	FIBER: 4G	SUGARS: 8G	FAT: 5G	SATURATED FAT: 3G
SODIUM: 150MG	POTASSIUM: 150MG	VITAMIN A: 35% DV	VITAMIN C: 2% DV		CALCIUM: 3% DV	IRON: 5% DV

Making Healthy Swaps in Your Favorite Recipes

Healthy swaps in recipes can make a significant difference in your overall nutrition without sacrificing flavor or enjoyment. By replacing less nutritious ingredients with healthier alternatives, you can create meals that are lower in calories, fat, sugar, and sodium, while increasing their nutrient density. This section introduces the benefits of making healthy swaps, provides tips for common ingredient substitutions, and offers practical examples to get you started.

Benefits of Making Healthy Swaps

1. **Nutrient Boost**: Swapping in healthier ingredients can increase the vitamin, mineral, and fiber content of your meals.
2. **Lower Calories**: Many healthy swaps help reduce the overall calorie count of a dish, aiding in weight management.
3. **Better Blood Sugar Control**: Replacing refined sugars and grains with whole foods can help stabilize blood sugar levels.
4. **Reduced Saturated Fat and Sodium**: Healthier fats and reduced sodium options can improve heart health.
5. **Enhanced Flavor and Variety**: Experimenting with new ingredients can add exciting flavors and textures to your favorite dishes.

Tips for Healthy Ingredient Swaps

1. **Whole Grains for Refined Grains**: Use whole wheat flour instead of white flour, brown rice instead of white rice, and whole grain pasta instead of regular pasta.
2. **Greek Yogurt for Sour Cream**: Greek yogurt is a high-protein, lower-fat alternative to sour cream in dips, dressings, and baked goods.
3. **Applesauce for Oil or Butter**: Replace some or all of the oil or butter in baked goods with unsweetened applesauce to reduce fat and add moisture.
4. **Mashed Avocado for Butter**: Use mashed avocado as a spread or in place of butter in baking to add healthy fats and a creamy texture.
5. **Zoodles for Pasta**: Replace traditional pasta with spiralized zucchini noodles (zoodles) for a low-carb, nutrient-rich option.
6. **Cauliflower Rice for White Rice**: Use finely chopped or riced cauliflower instead of white rice to cut calories and add fiber.
7. **Nutritional Yeast for Cheese**: Nutritional yeast adds a cheesy flavor to dishes without the calories and fat of dairy cheese.
8. **Nut Flours for Wheat Flour**: Almond flour and coconut flour are great gluten-free, lower-carb alternatives to wheat flour.
9. **Leafy Greens for Tortillas**: Use large leaves of lettuce or collard greens as wraps instead of tortillas to reduce carbs and add nutrients.
10. **Chia Seeds for Eggs**: Use a chia seed mixture (1 tablespoon chia seeds + 3 tablespoons water) as an egg substitute in baking for a vegan and fiber-rich alternative.

CAULIFLOWER CRUST PIZZA

PREP TIME
20 MINUTES

COOK TIME
25 MINUTES

★★★☆☆
DIFFICULTY

SE4VES
4

INGREDIENTS

- 1 medium head of cauliflower, riced (about 4 cups)
- 1/4 cup grated Parmesan cheese (optional for dairy-free, use nutritional yeast)
- 1/4 cup shredded mozzarella cheese (optional for dairy-free, use dairy-free cheese)
- 1 large egg, beaten
- 1 teaspoon dried oregano
- 1/2 teaspoon garlic powder
- 1/2 teaspoon salt
- 1/4 teaspoon black pepper
- 1/2 cup marinara sauce (ensure low-sugar)
- 1 cup shredded mozzarella cheese (optional for dairy-free, use dairy-free cheese)
- Toppings of choice (e.g., sliced bell peppers, mushrooms, spinach, tomatoes)

INSTRUCTIONS

1. Preheat Oven: Preheat your oven to 425°F (220°C). Line a baking sheet with parchment paper.
2. Prepare Cauliflower: Remove the leaves and core from the cauliflower. Cut into florets and place them in a food processor. Pulse until the cauliflower resembles rice. Alternatively, you can use pre-riced cauliflower from the store.
3. Cook Cauliflower: Place the riced cauliflower in a microwave-safe bowl and microwave for 4-5 minutes until soft. Let it cool slightly, then transfer to a clean kitchen towel and squeeze out as much moisture as possible.
4. Make Crust: In a large bowl, combine the cauliflower, grated Parmesan cheese, shredded mozzarella cheese, beaten egg, dried oregano, garlic powder, salt, and black pepper. Mix until well combined.
5. Form Crust: Transfer the cauliflower mixture to the prepared baking sheet. Press it into a round or rectangular crust about 1/4-inch thick.
6. Bake Crust: Bake in the preheated oven for 12-15 minutes until golden brown and firm.
7. Add Toppings: Remove the crust from the oven. Spread the marinara sauce over the crust and sprinkle with shredded mozzarella cheese. Add your desired toppings.
8. Bake Pizza: Return the pizza to the oven and bake for an additional 8-10 minutes until the cheese is melted and bubbly.
9. Serve: Let the pizza cool for a few minutes before slicing and serving.

Nutritional Information (per serving):

CALORIES: 200	PROTEIN: 12G	CARBOHYDRATES: 10G	FIBER: 4G	SUGARS: 4G	FAT: 13G	SATURATED FAT: 6G
SODIUM: 500MG	POTASSIUM: 400MG	VITAMIN A: 10% DV	VITAMIN C: 70% DV		CALCIUM: 20% DV	IRON: 4% DV

Time-Saving Kitchen Hacks

In today's fast-paced world, finding time to prepare healthy meals can be a challenge. However, with some strategic planning and clever kitchen hacks, you can save time and still enjoy nutritious, home-cooked meals. This section introduces the benefits of time-saving kitchen hacks, provides practical tips to streamline your cooking process, and offers examples of recipes that can be prepared quickly and efficiently.

Benefits of Time-Saving Kitchen Hacks

1. **Efficiency**: Reducing time spent on meal prep allows you to balance your schedule better and reduces stress associated with cooking.
2. **Consistency**: When meal prep is quick and easy, you're more likely to stick to a healthy eating plan.
3. **Less Waste**: Efficient kitchen practices help minimize food waste and make the most of your ingredients.
4. **Enjoyment**: Less time in the kitchen means more time to enjoy your meals and engage in other activities.

Tips for Time-Saving in the Kitchen

1. **Meal Prep and Planning**: Plan your meals for the week and prepare ingredients in advance. Batch cook grains, proteins, and vegetables to use throughout the week.
2. **Use Kitchen Gadgets**: Utilize time-saving appliances such as slow cookers, pressure cookers, food processors, and immersion blenders to speed up cooking and preparation.
3. **One-Pot Meals**: Opt for recipes that can be made in a single pot or pan to reduce cleanup time.
4. **Pre-Chopped and Frozen Vegetables**: Use pre-chopped or frozen vegetables to cut down on prep time without sacrificing nutrition.
5. **Multitasking**: Cook multiple components of your meal simultaneously. For example, roast vegetables in the oven while cooking rice on the stove.
6. **Organize Your Kitchen**: Keep your kitchen organized with frequently used items within easy reach to streamline the cooking process.
7. **Batch Cooking**: Prepare large batches of meals and freeze portions for later use. This is especially useful for soups, stews, and casseroles.
8. **Simplify Recipes**: Choose recipes with fewer ingredients and simple preparation methods.
9. **Label and Store**: Label your prepped ingredients and meals with dates to keep track of freshness and reduce waste.
10. **Use Efficient Cooking Techniques**: Techniques like stir-frying, grilling, and broiling cook food quickly while preserving nutrients.

ONE-PAN ROASTED VEGGIES AND CHICKEN

PREP TIME
10 MINUTES

COOK TIME
30 MINUTES

DIFFICULTY

SE4VES
4

INGREDIENTS

- 4 boneless, skinless chicken breasts
- 1 large red bell pepper, chopped
- 1 large yellow bell pepper, chopped
- 1 zucchini, sliced
- 1 red onion, chopped
- 1 cup cherry tomatoes
- 2 tablespoons olive oil
- 1 teaspoon dried oregano
- 1 teaspoon dried basil
- 1 teaspoon garlic powder
- Salt and pepper to taste
- Fresh parsley, chopped (for garnish)

INSTRUCTIONS

1. Preheat Oven: Preheat your oven to 400°F (200°C). Line a large baking sheet with parchment paper.
2. Prepare Ingredients: In a large bowl, combine the chopped red and yellow bell peppers, sliced zucchini, chopped red onion, and cherry tomatoes. Drizzle with 1 tablespoon of olive oil, and season with dried oregano, dried basil, garlic powder, salt, and pepper. Toss to coat evenly.
3. Season Chicken: Place the chicken breasts on the prepared baking sheet. Drizzle with the remaining 1 tablespoon of olive oil, and season with salt, pepper, and any additional herbs or spices you like.
4. Arrange Veggies: Spread the seasoned vegetables around the chicken breasts on the baking sheet in a single layer.
5. Roast: Roast in the preheated oven for 25-30 minutes, or until the chicken is cooked through and the vegetables are tender and slightly charred.
6. Serve: Garnish with chopped fresh parsley before serving. Enjoy with your favorite grain or salad.

Nutritional Information (per serving):

CALORIES: 350	PROTEIN: 35G	CARBOHYDRATES: 12G	FIBER: 4G	SUGARS: 6G	FAT: 18G	SATURATED FAT: 3G
SODIUM: 200MG	POTASSIUM: 900MG	VITAMIN A: 60% DV	VITAMIN C: 150% DV	CALCIUM: 4% DV	IRON: 10% DV	

Beginner's Guide: Simple 3-Recipe Plan

Starting with meal prep can feel overwhelming, especially if you're new to it. That's why this beginner's guide focuses on a simple 3-recipe plan to help you ease into the routine. This plan is designed to be straightforward, requiring minimal ingredients and preparation time, while still providing balanced, nutritious meals throughout the week.

Benefits of the 3-Recipe Plan

1. **Ease of Preparation**: Fewer recipes mean less time spent cooking and more time saved.
2. **Variety**: Even with just three recipes, you can enjoy a variety of flavors and textures throughout the week.
3. **Balanced Nutrition**: This plan ensures a balance of proteins, healthy fats, and carbohydrates to keep you energized and satisfied.
4. **Cost-Effective**: Using a limited number of ingredients can help reduce grocery costs and minimize food waste.

Tips for Success

1. **Plan Ahead**: Choose a day to do your meal prep. Sundays are popular, but any day that fits your schedule works.
2. **Double Up**: Cook larger batches to ensure you have enough food for the week. This way, you can mix and match meals to avoid repetition.
3. **Storage**: Invest in good-quality, airtight containers to keep your meals fresh. Consider using clear containers so you can easily see what's inside.
4. **Labeling**: Label your meals with the date they were prepared to keep track of freshness.
5. **Stay Flexible**: It's okay to adjust the recipes based on your preferences and what's available in your pantry.

Simple 3-Recipe Plan

Here's a sample plan to get you started with meal prep. This plan includes breakfast, lunch, and dinner recipes that arc casy to prepare and delicious to eat.

Recipe 1: Spinach and Berry Smoothie (Breakfast)

Ingredients:

- 1 cup fresh spinach leaves
- 1 cup mixed berries (fresh or frozen)
- 1 banana
- 1 cup unsweetened almond milk (or any dairy-free milk)
- 1 tablespoon chia seeds
- 1 tablespoon almond butter (optional)
- 1 teaspoon honey or maple syrup (optional)
- Ice cubes (optional, for a thicker smoothie)

Instructions:

1. In a blender, add the fresh spinach leaves, mixed berries, banana, unsweetened almond milk, chia seeds, almond butter (if using), and honey or maple syrup (if using).
2. Blend until smooth and creamy. If the smoothie is too thick, add a bit more almond milk until you reach your desired consistency. If you prefer a thicker smoothie, add a few ice cubes and blend again.
3. Pour the smoothie into two glasses and serve immediately.

Recipe 2: Quinoa and Black Bean Stuffed Bell Peppers (Lunch)

Ingredients:

- 4 large bell peppers (any color)
- 1 tablespoon olive oil
- 1 small onion, finely chopped
- 2 cloves garlic, minced
- 1 cup cooked quinoa
- 1 can (15 oz) black beans, drained and rinsed
- 1 cup corn kernels (fresh, frozen, or canned)
- 1 can (14.5 oz) diced tomatoes, drained
- 1 teaspoon ground cumin
- 1 teaspoon chili powder
- 1/2 teaspoon smoked paprika
- Salt and pepper to taste
- 1 cup shredded vegan cheese (optional)
- Fresh cilantro, chopped (for garnish)
- Lime wedges (for serving)

Instructions:

1. Preheat your oven to 375°F (190°C). Lightly grease a 9x13-inch baking dish.
2. Cut the tops off the bell peppers and remove the seeds and membranes. Lightly brush the outside of the peppers with a bit of oil if desired.
3. In a large skillet, heat a tablespoon of oil over medium heat. Add the chopped onion and sauté for 3-4 minutes until translucent. Add the minced garlic and cook for an additional 1 minute until fragrant.
4. In a large bowl, combine the cooked quinoa, black beans, corn kernels, diced tomatoes, ground cumin, chili powder, smoked paprika, salt, and pepper. Mix until well combined.
5. Stuff each bell pepper with the quinoa and black bean mixture, pressing down gently to fill completely. Top with shredded vegan cheese if using.
6. Place the stuffed peppers in the prepared baking dish. Cover the dish with aluminum foil and bake in the preheated oven for 25 minutes. Remove the foil and bake for an additional 10 minutes, or until the cheese is melted and bubbly.
7. Garnish with chopped fresh cilantro and serve with lime wedges if desired.

Recipe 3: One-Pan Roasted Veggies and Chicken (Dinner)

Ingredients:

- 4 boneless, skinless chicken breasts
- 1 large red bell pepper, chopped
- 1 large yellow bell pepper, chopped
- 1 zucchini, sliced
- 1 red onion, chopped
- 1 cup cherry tomatoes
- 2 tablespoons olive oil
- 1 teaspoon dried oregano
- 1 teaspoon dried basil
- 1 teaspoon garlic powder
- Salt and pepper to taste
- Fresh parsley, chopped (for garnish)

Instructions:

1. Preheat your oven to 400°F (200°C). Line a large baking sheet with parchment paper.
2. In a large bowl, combine the chopped red and yellow bell peppers, sliced zucchini, chopped red onion, and cherry tomatoes. Drizzle with 1 tablespoon of olive oil, and season with dried oregano, dried basil, garlic powder, salt, and pepper. Toss to coat evenly.
3. Place the chicken breasts on the prepared baking sheet. Drizzle with the remaining 1 tablespoon of olive oil, and season with salt, pepper, and any additional herbs or spices you like.
4. Spread the seasoned vegetables around the chicken breasts on the baking sheet in a single layer.
5. Roast in the preheated oven for 25-30 minutes, or until the chicken is cooked through and the vegetables are tender and slightly charred.
6. Garnish with chopped fresh parsley before serving. Enjoy with your favorite grain or salad.

Conclusion

By starting with these simple and nutritious recipes, you'll find that meal prepping can be an enjoyable and rewarding habit. This beginner's guide is designed to help you build confidence in the kitchen and establish a routine that works for you. As you become more comfortable with meal prep, feel free to explore more complex recipes and expand your culinary skills.

Intermediate Plan: Efficient 5-Recipe Plan

Introduction: The Intermediate Plan is designed for those who are comfortable with basic meal prepping and want to incorporate more variety into their weekly meals. This plan features five recipes that offer a balance of flavors, textures, and nutrients. It's an efficient way to ensure you have delicious, healthy meals ready to go throughout the week without spending hours in the kitchen every day.

Recipes Included:

1. **Overnight Oats**
2. **Turkey Avocado Wrap**
3. **Sheet-Pan Lemon Garlic Chicken with Vegetables**
4. **Almond Butter Protein Bars**
5. **Roasted Red Pepper Hummus**

Step-by-Step Plan:

Day 1: Overnight Oats

- **Ingredients**:
    - 2 cups rolled oats
    - 2 cups unsweetened almond milk (or any dairy-free milk)
    - 1 cup Greek yogurt (optional for dairy-free, use coconut yogurt)
    - 2 tablespoons chia seeds
    - 1 tablespoon honey or maple syrup
    - Fresh fruit (berries, bananas, apples) for topping
    - Nuts and seeds for topping
- **Instructions**:
    1. In a large bowl, mix rolled oats, almond milk, Greek yogurt, chia seeds, and honey or maple syrup.
    2. Divide the mixture into individual mason jars or containers.
    3. Add fresh fruit, nuts, and seeds on top.
    4. Cover and refrigerate overnight.
- **Storage**: Store in the fridge for up to 5 days.

Day 2: Turkey Avocado Wrap

- **Ingredients**:
    - 4 whole wheat or gluten-free tortillas
    - 1 pound turkey breast, cooked and sliced
    - 2 avocados, sliced
    - 1 cup baby spinach leaves
    - 1/2 red onion, thinly sliced
    - 1/2 cup hummus (store-bought or homemade)
    - Salt and pepper to taste
- **Instructions**:
    1. Spread hummus evenly over each tortilla.
    2. Layer with turkey slices, avocado, baby spinach, and red onion.
    3. Season with salt and pepper.
    4. Roll up the tortillas tightly and wrap in plastic wrap or foil.
- **Storage**: Store in the fridge for up to 4 days.

Day 3: Sheet-Pan Lemon Garlic Chicken with Vegetables

- **Ingredients**:
    - 4 boneless, skinless chicken breasts
    - 1 large red bell pepper, chopped
    - 1 large yellow bell pepper, chopped
    - 1 zucchini, sliced
    - 1 red onion, chopped
    - 1 cup cherry tomatoes
    - 2 tablespoons olive oil
    - 1 teaspoon dried oregano
    - 1 teaspoon dried basil
    - 1 teaspoon garlic powder
    - Salt and pepper to taste
    - Fresh parsley, chopped (for garnish)
    - Lemon wedges (for serving)
- **Instructions**:
    1. Preheat your oven to 400°F (200°C). Line a large baking sheet with parchment paper.
    2. In a large bowl, combine chopped red and yellow bell peppers, zucchini, red onion, and cherry tomatoes. Drizzle with 1 tablespoon of olive oil, and season with dried oregano, dried basil, garlic powder, salt, and pepper. Toss to coat evenly.
    3. Place the chicken breasts on the prepared baking sheet. Drizzle with the remaining 1 tablespoon of olive oil, and season with salt, pepper, and any additional herbs or spices you like.
    4. Spread the seasoned vegetables around the chicken breasts on the baking sheet in a single layer.
    5. Roast in the preheated oven for 25-30 minutes, or until the chicken is cooked through and the vegetables are tender and slightly charred.
    6. Garnish with chopped fresh parsley and serve with lemon wedges.
- **Storage**: Store in the fridge for up to 4 days. Reheat in the oven or microwave.

Day 4: Almond Butter Protein Bars

- **Ingredients**:
    - 1 cup almond butter
    - 1/4 cup honey or maple syrup
    - 1 teaspoon vanilla extract
    - 1 1/2 cups rolled oats
    - 1/2 cup protein powder (vanilla or unflavored)
    - 1/4 cup dark chocolate chips (optional)
- **Instructions**:
    1. In a microwave-safe bowl, heat almond butter and honey/maple syrup for 30 seconds until softened. Stir in vanilla extract.
    2. In a large bowl, combine rolled oats and protein powder. Pour the almond butter mixture over the oats and mix until well combined. Stir in dark chocolate chips if using.
    3. Press the mixture into an 8x8-inch baking dish lined with parchment paper.
    4. Refrigerate for at least 1 hour, or until set.
    5. Cut into bars and store in an airtight container.
- **Storage**: Store in the fridge for up to 1 week or freeze for up to 3 months.

Day 5: Roasted Red Pepper Hummus

- **Ingredients**:
    - 1 can (15 oz) chickpeas, drained and rinsed
    - 2 roasted red bell peppers (store-bought or homemade)
    - 1/4 cup tahini
    - 2 tablespoons olive oil
    - 2 tablespoons lemon juice
    - 2 cloves garlic, minced
    - 1 teaspoon ground cumin
    - Salt and pepper to taste
- **Instructions**:
    1. In a food processor, combine chickpeas, roasted red bell peppers, tahini, olive oil, lemon juice, garlic, and ground cumin. Blend until smooth.
    2. Season with salt and pepper to taste.
    3. Transfer to a serving bowl and drizzle with additional olive oil if desired.
- **Storage**: Store in the fridge for up to 1 week.

Preparation Schedule

1. **Day 1: Prep Overnight Oats**:
   - Mix ingredients and refrigerate.
   - Total time: 10 minutes
2. **Day 2: Prep Turkey Avocado Wraps**:
   - Assemble wraps and refrigerate.
   - Total time: 15 minutes
3. **Day 3: Prep Sheet-Pan Chicken and Vegetables**:
   - Season and roast chicken and vegetables.
   - Total time: 40 minutes
4. **Day 4: Prep Almond Butter Protein Bars**:
   - Mix, press into pan, and refrigerate.
   - Total time: 20 minutes
5. **Day 5: Prep Roasted Red Pepper Hummus**:
   - Blend ingredients in food processor.
   - Total time: 10 minutes

Conclusion

The Intermediate Plan helps you streamline your meal prep process while enjoying a variety of healthy, flavorful meals throughout the week. By following this plan, you'll save time, reduce food waste, and maintain a balanced diet with minimal effort. As you become more comfortable with meal prep, feel free to explore more complex recipes and expand your culinary skills.

Advanced Plan: Comprehensive 7-Recipe Plan

Introduction: The Advanced Plan is designed for experienced meal preppers who want a comprehensive solution covering all meals and snacks for the week. This plan features seven recipes that provide a wide variety of flavors, textures, and nutrients. It's ideal for those looking to maintain a balanced diet with minimal daily cooking time.

Recipes Included:

1. **High-Protein Breakfast Burritos**
2. **Mediterranean Quinoa Salad**
3. **Slow Cooker Beef and Barley Stew**
4. **Energy Bars and Bites**
5. **Veggie-Packed Dips and Spreads**
6. **Low-Calorie Baked Goods**
7. **Dairy-Free and Gluten-Free Options**

Step-by-Step Plan:

Day 1: High-Protein Breakfast Burritos

- **Ingredients**:
    - 8 large eggs
    - 1/4 cup milk (dairy or dairy-free)
    - 1 tablespoon olive oil
    - 1 bell pepper, diced
    - 1 small onion, diced
    - 1 cup spinach, chopped
    - 1 cup black beans, drained and rinsed
    - 1/2 cup shredded cheese (optional, use dairy-free cheese if needed)
    - 4 whole wheat or gluten-free tortillas
    - Salsa, for serving
- **Instructions**:
    1. In a large bowl, whisk together eggs and milk.
    2. In a skillet, heat olive oil over medium heat. Add bell pepper and onion, and sauté until softened.
    3. Add spinach and cook until wilted.
    4. Pour in the egg mixture and cook, stirring frequently, until eggs are scrambled and fully cooked. Stir in black beans.
    5. Divide the mixture among the tortillas, sprinkle with cheese (if using), and roll up.
    6. Wrap each burrito in foil and store in the fridge for up to 4 days or freeze for up to 3 months.

Day 2: Mediterranean Quinoa Salad

- **Ingredients**:
    - 1 cup quinoa, rinsed
    - 2 cups water or vegetable broth
    - 1 cup cherry tomatoes, halved
    - 1 cucumber, diced
    - 1/2 red onion, finely chopped
    - 1/4 cup kalamata olives, sliced
    - 1/4 cup feta cheese (optional, use dairy-free cheese if needed)
    - 1/4 cup fresh parsley, chopped
    - 2 tablespoons olive oil
    - 2 tablespoons lemon juice
    - 1 teaspoon dried oregano
    - Salt and pepper to taste
- **Instructions**:
    1. Cook quinoa according to package instructions with water or vegetable broth. Let cool.
    2. In a large bowl, combine cooked quinoa, cherry tomatoes, cucumber, red onion, olives, feta cheese (if using), and parsley.
    3. In a small bowl, whisk together olive oil, lemon juice, oregano, salt, and pepper.
    4. Pour the dressing over the salad and toss to coat evenly.
    5. Store in the fridge for up to 4 days.

Day 3: Slow Cooker Beef and Barley Stew

- **Ingredients**:
    - 1 pound beef stew meat, cubed
    - 1 cup barley, rinsed
    - 4 cups beef broth
    - 2 carrots, sliced
    - 2 celery stalks, sliced
    - 1 onion, chopped
    - 3 cloves garlic, minced
    - 1 teaspoon dried thyme
    - 1 teaspoon dried rosemary
    - Salt and pepper to taste
    - Fresh parsley, chopped (for garnish)
- **Instructions**:
    1. In a slow cooker, combine beef, barley, beef broth, carrots, celery, onion, garlic, thyme, rosemary, salt, and pepper.
    2. Cook on low for 7-8 hours or on high for 4-5 hours, until the beef is tender and the barley is cooked.
    3. Garnish with fresh parsley before serving.
    4. Store in the fridge for up to 4 days or freeze for up to 3 months.

Day 4: Energy Bars and Bites

- **Ingredients**:
  - 1 cup oats
  - 1/2 cup nut butter (almond, peanut, or sunflower)
  - 1/4 cup honey or maple syrup
  - 1/4 cup flaxseed meal
  - 1/4 cup chocolate chips or dried fruit
  - 1 teaspoon vanilla extract
- **Instructions**:
  1. In a large bowl, combine oats, nut butter, honey or maple syrup, flaxseed meal, chocolate chips or dried fruit, and vanilla extract. Mix until well combined.
  2. Press the mixture into an 8x8-inch baking dish lined with parchment paper.
  3. Refrigerate for at least 1 hour until set.
  4. Cut into bars and store in an airtight container in the fridge for up to 1 week or freeze for up to 3 months.

Day 5: Veggie-Packed Dips and Spreads

- **Ingredients**:
  - 1 can (15 oz) chickpeas, drained and rinsed
  - 2 roasted red bell peppers (store-bought or homemade)
  - 1/4 cup tahini
  - 2 tablespoons olive oil
  - 2 tablespoons lemon juice
  - 2 cloves garlic, minced
  - 1 teaspoon ground cumin
  - Salt and pepper to taste
- **Instructions**:
  1. In a food processor, combine chickpeas, roasted red bell peppers, tahini, olive oil, lemon juice, garlic, and ground cumin. Blend until smooth.
  2. Season with salt and pepper to taste.
  3. Transfer to a serving bowl and drizzle with additional olive oil if desired.
  4. Store in the fridge for up to 1 week.

Day 6: Low-Calorie Baked Goods

- **Ingredients**:
    - 1 cup whole wheat flour
    - 1/2 cup oat flour
    - 1 teaspoon baking powder
    - 1/2 teaspoon baking soda
    - 1/2 teaspoon salt
    - 1 teaspoon ground cinnamon
    - 1/2 teaspoon ground nutmeg
    - 1/4 teaspoon ground cloves
    - 2 large eggs
    - 1/4 cup coconut oil, melted
    - 1/4 cup unsweetened applesauce
    - 1/4 cup honey or maple syrup
    - 1 teaspoon vanilla extract
    - 1 cup grated apple (about 1 large apple)
    - 1 cup grated carrot (about 2 medium carrots)
- **Instructions**:
    1. Preheat your oven to 350°F (175°C). Line a 12-cup muffin tin with paper liners or grease with cooking spray.
    2. In a large bowl, whisk together whole wheat flour, oat flour, baking powder, baking soda, salt, ground cinnamon, ground nutmeg, and ground cloves.
    3. In another bowl, whisk together eggs, melted coconut oil, unsweetened applesauce, honey or maple syrup, and vanilla extract until well combined.
    4. Add the wet ingredients to the dry ingredients and mix until just combined. Fold in the grated apple and grated carrot.
    5. Divide the batter evenly among the 12 muffin cups, filling each about 3/4 full.
    6. Bake in the preheated oven for 18-20 minutes, or until a toothpick inserted into the center of a muffin comes out clean.
    7. Allow the muffins to cool in the tin for 5 minutes, then transfer to a wire rack to cool completely. Store in an airtight container for up to 1 week.

Day 7: Dairy-Free and Gluten-Free Options

- **Ingredients**:
    - 1 cup coconut flour
    - 1/2 cup almond flour
    - 1 teaspoon baking powder
    - 1/2 teaspoon baking soda
    - 1/2 teaspoon salt
    - 1 teaspoon ground cinnamon
    - 2 large eggs
    - 1/4 cup coconut oil, melted
    - 1/4 cup honey or maple syrup
    - 1 teaspoon vanilla extract
    - 1/2 cup unsweetened almond milk
    - 1/2 cup dairy-free chocolate chips (optional)
- **Instructions**:
    1. Preheat your oven to 350°F (175°C). Line a 12-cup muffin tin with paper liners or grease with cooking spray.
    2. In a large bowl, whisk together coconut flour, almond flour, baking powder, baking soda, salt, and ground cinnamon.
    3. In another bowl, whisk together eggs, melted coconut oil, honey or maple syrup, vanilla extract, and almond milk until well combined.
    4. Add the wet ingredients to the dry ingredients and mix until just combined. Fold in the dairy-free chocolate chips if using.
    5. Divide the batter evenly among the 12 muffin cups, filling each about 3/4 full.
    6. Bake in the preheated oven for 18-20 minutes, or until a toothpick inserted into the center of a muffin comes out clean.
    7. Allow the muffins to cool in the tin for 5 minutes, then transfer to a wire rack to cool completely. Store in an airtight container for up to 1 week.

Preparation Schedule

1. **Day 1: Prep High-Protein Breakfast Burritos**:
   - Cook and assemble burritos.
   - Total time: 30 minutes
2. **Day 2: Prep Mediterranean Quinoa Salad**:
   - Cook quinoa and combine ingredients.
   - Total time: 20 minutes
3. **Day 3: Prep Slow Cooker Beef and Barley Stew**:
   - Combine ingredients and start slow cooker.
   - Total time: 10 minutes
4. **Day 4: Prep Energy Bars and Bites**:
   - Mix and press into pan.
   - Total time: 20 minutes
5. **Day 5: Prep Veggie-Packed Dips and Spreads**:
   - Blend ingredients in food processor.
   - Total time: 10 minutes
6. **Day 6: Prep Low-Calorie Baked Goods**:
   - Mix and bake.
   - Total time: 30 minutes
7. **Day 7: Prep Dairy-Free and Gluten-Free Options**:
   - Mix and bake.
   - Total time: 30 minutes

Conclusion

The Advanced Plan helps you streamline your meal prep process while enjoying a variety of healthy, flavorful meals throughout the week. By following this plan, you'll save time, reduce food waste, and maintain a balanced diet with minimal effort. As you become more comfortable with meal prep, feel free to explore more complex recipes and expand your culinary skills.

Customizable Meal Prep Templates

Introduction: Customizable meal prep templates are ideal for those who want to tailor their meal prep to their specific tastes and dietary needs. These templates provide a structured format for planning your meals, making grocery shopping easier, and ensuring you stay organized throughout the week. This section will guide you on how to use these templates effectively and provide sample templates for various dietary preferences.

Benefits of Customizable Meal Prep Templates:

1. **Personalization**: Tailor your meal plan to fit your unique dietary needs and preferences.
2. **Flexibility**: Adjust the plan as needed based on your schedule and lifestyle.
3. **Efficiency**: Streamline your grocery shopping and meal prep process to save time and reduce stress.
4. **Organization**: Keep track of your meals and ingredients, ensuring nothing goes to waste.
5. **Consistency**: Helps you maintain a balanced diet by planning your meals in advance.

How to Use the Templates:

1. **Select Recipes**: Choose recipes from the cookbook that fit your dietary preferences and goals.
2. **Fill in the Templates**: Use the weekly meal plan template to schedule your meals. Transfer the required ingredients to the grocery list template.
3. **Plan Your Prep**: Use the preparation schedule template to organize your cooking sessions, ensuring you efficiently use your time and kitchen resources.

Sample Templates

Here are sample templates that you can fill in with your chosen recipes. These templates are designed to be flexible and cater to various dietary preferences and goals.

Weekly Meal Plan Template

Breakfast:

- Monday:
- Tuesday:
- Wednesday:
- Thursday:
- Friday:
- Saturday:
- Sunday:

Lunch:

- Monday:
- Tuesday:
- Wednesday:
- Thursday:
- Friday:
- Saturday:
- Sunday:

Dinner:

- Monday:
- Tuesday:
- Wednesday:
- Thursday:
- Friday:
- Saturday:
- Sunday:

Snacks:

- Monday:
- Tuesday:
- Wednesday:
- Thursday:
- Friday:
- Saturday:
- Sunday:

Grocery List Template

Produce:

Proteins:

Dairy/Dairy Alternatives:

Grains:

Pantry Staples:

Miscellaneous:

Preparation Schedule Template

Sunday:

Monday:

Tuesday:

Wednesday:

Thursday:

Friday:

Saturday:

Examples of Customizable Meal Plans

Example 1: Vegetarian Meal Plan

Breakfast:

- Monday: Berry Bliss Overnight Oats
- Tuesday: Spinach and Berry Smoothie
- Wednesday: High-Protein Breakfast Burritos
- Thursday: Carrot Apple Muffins
- Friday: Mango Coconut Chia Pudding
- Saturday: Greek Yogurt and Berry Protein Smoothie
- Sunday: Lemon Poppy Seed Muffins

Lunch:

- Monday: Mediterranean Quinoa Salad
- Tuesday: Black Bean and Avocado Burrito
- Wednesday: Asian Sesame Chicken Salad
- Thursday: Hummus and Veggie Wrap
- Friday: Southwest Black Bean and Corn Salad
- Saturday: Veggie-Packed Dips and Spreads
- Sunday: Spinach and Strawberry Salad with Feta

Dinner:

- Monday: One-Pan Ratatouille
- Tuesday: Quinoa and Black Bean Stuffed Bell Peppers
- Wednesday: Slow Cooker Lentil Soup
- Thursday: Cauliflower Crust Pizza
- Friday: Brown Rice and Edamame Bowl
- Saturday: Thai Red Curry with Tofu
- Sunday: Grilled Chicken and Vegetable Skewers

Snacks:

- Monday: Coconut Date Energy Bites
- Tuesday: Matcha Green Tea Energy Bites
- Wednesday: Baked Sweet Potato Chips
- Thursday: Flaxseed and Sesame Crackers
- Friday: Almond Butter Protein Bars
- Saturday: Fresh Berry Salad with Mint
- Sunday: Apple and Cinnamon Fruit Leather

Example 2: Low-Carb Meal Plan

Breakfast:

- Monday: Keto Avocado and Bacon Salad
- Tuesday: Green Energy Smoothie
- Wednesday: Keto Egg Muffins with Spinach and Cheese
- Thursday: Chocolate Peanut Butter Smoothie Bowl
- Friday: Vanilla Almond Overnight Oats
- Saturday: Chocolate Banana Chia Pudding
- Sunday: Turkey Sausage and Veggie Burrito

Lunch:

- Monday: Tuna Salad Sandwich on Whole Wheat (with lettuce wraps)
- Tuesday: Mediterranean Veggie Pita (with low-carb wrap)
- Wednesday: Quinoa and Chickpea Power Bowl
- Thursday: Shrimp and Snow Pea Stir-Fry
- Friday: Chicken and Vegetable Stir-Fry
- Saturday: Beef and Broccoli Stir-Fry
- Sunday: Chicken and Wild Rice Soup

Dinner:

- Monday: One-Pan Balsamic Chicken and Veggies
- Tuesday: Sheet-Pan Teriyaki Chicken with Broccoli
- Wednesday: Slow Cooker Thai Peanut Chicken
- Thursday: Instant Pot Beef Stroganoff
- Friday: Low-Carb Chicken and Broccoli Casserole
- Saturday: Spicy Black Bean and Sweet Potato Hash
- Sunday: Barley and Mushroom Bowl

Snacks:

- Monday: Greek Yogurt Berry Parfait
- Tuesday: Peanut Butter Protein Balls
- Wednesday: Skinny Blueberry Muffins
- Thursday: Low-Fat Chocolate Chip Cookies
- Friday: Dark Chocolate Avocado Mousse
- Saturday: Dairy-Free Coconut Yogurt Parfait
- Sunday: Gluten-Free Stuffed Mushrooms

Conclusion

Customizable meal prep templates provide a flexible and efficient way to plan and prepare your meals. By using these templates, you can tailor your meal prep to fit your specific dietary needs and preferences, ensuring that you stay organized and consistent with your healthy eating habits. These templates make it easy to plan your meals, create a comprehensive grocery list, and organize your cooking schedule, saving you time and reducing stress. Happy meal prepping!

Understanding Nutritional Labels

Understanding nutritional labels is a crucial skill for making informed food choices and maintaining a healthy diet. Nutritional labels provide essential information about the contents of packaged foods, allowing you to evaluate their nutritional value and make comparisons between different products. This section will guide you through the key components of nutritional labels, explain how to interpret them, and offer tips for making healthier choices based on this information.

Key Components of Nutritional Labels

1. **Serving Size**:
   - **Definition**: The amount of food that is considered one serving. This is usually listed at the top of the nutritional label.
   - **Importance**: All the nutritional information on the label is based on this serving size. Be mindful that the serving size might be smaller or larger than the amount you typically consume.
2. **Calories**:
   - **Definition**: The total amount of energy provided by one serving of the food.
   - **Importance**: Helps you understand how much energy you will get from a serving and manage your overall caloric intake.
3. **Macronutrients**:
   - **Fat**: Includes total fat, saturated fat, and trans fat.
     - **Importance**: Total fat indicates the overall fat content, while saturated and trans fats should be limited as they can contribute to heart disease.
   - **Cholesterol**: The amount of cholesterol in one serving.
     - **Importance**: High cholesterol intake can increase the risk of heart disease.
   - **Sodium**: The amount of salt in one serving.
     - **Importance**: High sodium intake can lead to high blood pressure and other health issues.
   - **Carbohydrates**: Includes total carbohydrates, dietary fiber, and sugars.
     - **Importance**: Total carbohydrates provide energy, fiber aids digestion and controls blood sugar levels, and sugars include both natural and added sugars.
   - **Protein**: The amount of protein in one serving.
     - **Importance**: Essential for muscle repair, growth, and overall bodily functions.
4. **Micronutrients**:
   - **Vitamins and Minerals**: Key vitamins and minerals are listed, such as Vitamin D, calcium, iron, and potassium.
     - **Importance**: These are essential for various body functions and overall health.
5. **Daily Values (DVs)**:
   - **Definition**: Percentages that show how much of each nutrient one serving of the food contributes to a daily diet, based on a 2,000-calorie diet.
   - **Importance**: Helps you gauge whether a food is high or low in a particular nutrient. A DV of 5% or less is considered low, while 20% or more is high.

How to Interpret Nutritional Labels

1. **Compare Serving Sizes**:
   o Always check the serving size and compare it to the amount you plan to eat. Adjust the nutritional information accordingly if you consume more or less than the serving size.
2. **Evaluate Calories**:
   o Consider your daily caloric needs and how a serving fits into your overall calorie budget. High-calorie foods should be consumed in moderation, especially if you're watching your weight.
3. **Assess Fats**:
   o Look for foods low in saturated and trans fats. Aim to get most of your fats from healthy sources like nuts, seeds, avocados, and fish.
4. **Monitor Sodium and Sugar**:
   o Choose foods with lower sodium and added sugar content to maintain heart health and prevent conditions like hypertension and diabetes.
5. **Check Fiber and Protein**:
   o Opt for foods high in dietary fiber and protein. Fiber aids digestion and keeps you full, while protein is essential for muscle maintenance and overall health.
6. **Consider Micronutrients**:
   o Aim to get a variety of vitamins and minerals from your diet. Check the DVs to ensure you're meeting your nutritional needs.

Tips for Making Healthier Choices

1. **Read Ingredient Lists**:
   o Look for foods with short ingredient lists and recognizable ingredients. Avoid foods with a lot of added sugars, sodium, and artificial additives.
2. **Watch for Hidden Sugars**:
   o Sugars can be listed under many names, such as high fructose corn syrup, cane sugar, and agave nectar. Check the ingredients to avoid hidden sugars.
3. **Choose Whole Foods**:
   o Whenever possible, choose whole, unprocessed foods that are naturally rich in nutrients.
4. **Limit Processed Foods**:
   o Processed foods often contain high levels of unhealthy fats, sodium, and sugars. Opt for fresh or minimally processed options.
5. **Use Nutritional Labels for Meal Planning**:
   o Incorporate the nutritional information into your meal planning to ensure balanced and nutritious meals.

Practical Example

To help you apply these principles, let's go through an example of reading a nutritional label:

Example Product: Whole Grain Cereal

- **Serving Size**: 1 cup (40g)
- **Calories**: 150
- **Total Fat**: 2g (3% DV)
    - ○ **Saturated Fat**: 0.5g (3% DV)
    - ○ **Trans Fat**: 0g
- **Cholesterol**: 0mg
- **Sodium**: 200mg (8% DV)
- **Total Carbohydrates**: 32g (11% DV)
    - ○ **Dietary Fiber**: 5g (20% DV)
    - ○ **Sugars**: 7g (includes 5g added sugars, 10% DV)
- **Protein**: 4g
- **Vitamin D**: 2mcg (10% DV)
- **Calcium**: 100mg (8% DV)
- **Iron**: 8mg (45% DV)
- **Potassium**: 250mg (6% DV)

Interpretation:

- **Serving Size**: Ensure you measure 1 cup if that's the amount you're eating.
- **Calories**: 150 calories per serving fits well into a 2,000-calorie diet.
- **Total Fat**: 2g is low, and the saturated fat is minimal.
- **Sodium**: 200mg is moderate; be mindful if you're watching your sodium intake.
- **Dietary Fiber**: 5g is high and beneficial for digestion.
- **Sugars**: 7g total, with 5g added sugars, which should be consumed in moderation.
- **Micronutrients**: High in iron (45% DV), which is great for meeting daily requirements.

By understanding and interpreting nutritional labels, you can make healthier choices that align with your dietary needs and goals. This knowledge empowers you to take control of your nutrition and lead a healthier lifestyle.

Complete Nutritional Breakdown of Each Recipe

Understanding the complete nutritional breakdown of each recipe in this cookbook is essential for making informed dietary choices. Each recipe will include detailed nutritional information to help you manage your intake of calories, macronutrients, and micronutrients, ensuring you meet your dietary goals. This section explains how to interpret the nutritional breakdown provided for each recipe and the importance of various nutrients.

Components of Nutritional Breakdown

1. **Calories**:
   - The total amount of energy provided by one serving of the recipe.
   - Helps you manage your daily caloric intake.
2. **Macronutrients**:
   - **Protein**: Essential for muscle repair, growth, and overall bodily functions.
   - **Carbohydrates**: The primary source of energy. Includes total carbohydrates, dietary fiber, and sugars.
     - **Dietary Fiber**: Aids digestion, promotes satiety, and helps regulate blood sugar levels.
     - **Sugars**: Includes both natural and added sugars. High intake of added sugars should be limited.
   - **Fats**: Necessary for various bodily functions and energy. Includes total fat, saturated fat, and trans fat.
     - **Saturated Fat**: Should be consumed in moderation to maintain heart health.
     - **Trans Fat**: Should be avoided as it increases the risk of heart disease.
3. **Micronutrients**:
   - **Vitamins and Minerals**: Key vitamins and minerals, such as Vitamin A, Vitamin C, calcium, and iron, are listed to help you ensure you meet your daily nutritional needs.
4. **Daily Values (DVs)**:
   - Percentages that show how much of each nutrient one serving of the recipe contributes to a daily diet, based on a 2,000-calorie diet.

Example Nutritional Breakdown

To help you understand how to use the nutritional breakdown, let's go through an example recipe:

Example Recipe: Quinoa and Black Bean Stuffed Bell Peppers

Nutritional Breakdown (per serving):

- **Calories**: 350
- **Protein**: 12g
- **Carbohydrates**: 45g
    - **Dietary Fiber**: 12g
    - **Sugars**: 6g
- **Fats**: 15g
    - **Saturated Fat**: 3g
    - **Trans Fat**: 0g
- **Cholesterol**: 0mg
- **Sodium**: 350mg
- **Potassium**: 800mg
- **Vitamin A**: 50% DV
- **Vitamin C**: 200% DV
- **Calcium**: 15% DV
- **Iron**: 25% DV

Interpreting the Breakdown

1. **Calories**: Each serving provides 350 calories, which is a reasonable amount for a meal when balanced with other meals and snacks throughout the day.
2. **Protein**: 12g of protein per serving supports muscle maintenance and repair.
3. **Carbohydrates**: 45g of carbohydrates provide energy, with 12g of dietary fiber aiding digestion and promoting satiety.
4. **Sugars**: 6g of sugars, with a focus on natural sugars from vegetables, keep the sugar content in check.
5. **Fats**: 15g of total fat includes healthy fats from ingredients like olive oil, with 3g of saturated fat, which is within a moderate range.
6. **Cholesterol**: 0mg of cholesterol is beneficial for heart health.
7. **Sodium**: 350mg of sodium is moderate and helps manage blood pressure levels.
8. **Potassium**: 800mg of potassium supports heart and muscle function.
9. **Vitamins and Minerals**: High percentages of Vitamin A (50%) and Vitamin C (200%) boost immunity and skin health, while calcium (15%) and iron (25%) support bone health and energy levels.

Benefits of Detailed Nutritional Information

1. **Informed Choices**: Helps you understand the nutritional value of each meal, aiding in better decision-making.
2. **Dietary Management**: Assists in managing specific dietary needs, such as low-sodium, high-protein, or fiber-rich diets.
3. **Balanced Diet**: Ensures you get a variety of nutrients essential for overall health and well-being.
4. **Goal Tracking**: Supports tracking of macronutrient and micronutrient intake to meet personal health goals, such as weight loss, muscle gain, or improved energy levels.

How to Use Nutritional Information for Meal Planning

1. **Daily Caloric Needs**: Determine your daily caloric needs based on your age, gender, activity level, and health goals. Use the calorie information to balance your meals throughout the day.
2. **Macronutrient Balance**: Aim for a balanced intake of protein, carbohydrates, and fats in each meal. Adjust portions to meet your macronutrient goals.
3. **Micronutrient Intake**: Ensure you get enough vitamins and minerals by including a variety of nutrient-dense foods. Use the nutritional breakdown to identify key sources of essential nutrients.
4. **Portion Control**: Use the serving size information to manage portion sizes and avoid overeating.

Conclusion

Providing a complete nutritional breakdown for each recipe empowers you to make healthier choices and manage your diet effectively. Understanding how to interpret this information allows you to plan balanced meals, meet your dietary goals, and maintain overall health. Use the detailed nutritional information provided in this cookbook to guide your meal planning and enjoy the benefits of a nutritious and well-rounded diet.

Calculating Your Daily Nutritional Needs

Understanding and calculating your daily nutritional needs is essential for maintaining a balanced diet, achieving your health goals, and ensuring that your body receives the nutrients it needs to function optimally. This section will guide you through the process of determining your daily caloric needs, macronutrient ratios, and micronutrient requirements based on your individual characteristics and lifestyle.

Factors Affecting Daily Nutritional Needs

1. **Age**: Nutritional needs vary at different stages of life. Children, teenagers, adults, and seniors all have different requirements.
2. **Gender**: Men and women have different caloric and nutritional needs due to differences in body composition and hormonal functions.
3. **Weight**: Your current weight affects how many calories you need to maintain, lose, or gain weight.
4. **Height**: Taller individuals generally require more calories.
5. **Activity Level**: The amount of physical activity you engage in significantly impacts your caloric needs. More active individuals require more calories.
6. **Health Goals**: Your goals, such as weight loss, muscle gain, or maintenance, will influence your nutritional needs.

Calculating Daily Caloric Needs

The first step in determining your daily nutritional needs is calculating your Total Daily Energy Expenditure (TDEE). TDEE is the total number of calories you burn in a day, including both your basal metabolic rate (BMR) and physical activity.

1. **Calculate Basal Metabolic Rate (BMR):**
   - BMR is the number of calories your body needs to perform basic functions like breathing, circulating blood, and cell production.

   Harris-Benedict Equation:

   - For Men: $BMR = 88.362 + (13.397 \times weight\ in\ kg) + (4.799 \times height\ in\ cm) - (5.677 \times age\ in\ years)$
   - For Women: $BMR = 447.593 + (9.247 \times weight\ in\ kg) + (3.098 \times height\ in\ cm) - (4.330 \times age\ in\ years)$
2. **Determine Activity Level:**
   - Sedentary (little or no exercise): $BMR \times 1.2$
   - Lightly active (light exercise/sports 1-3 days/week): $BMR \times 1.375$
   - Moderately active (moderate exercise/sports 3-5 days/week): $BMR \times 1.55$
   - Very active (hard exercise/sports 6-7 days a week): $BMR \times 1.725$
   - Extra active (very hard exercise/sports & physical job or 2x training): $BMR \times 1.9$
3. **Calculate TDEE:**
   - $TDEE = BMR \times Activity\ Level$

Determining Macronutrient Ratios

Once you know your TDEE, you can determine your macronutrient needs. Macronutrients include carbohydrates, proteins, and fats, each of which provides energy and plays a specific role in your body.

1. **Carbohydrates**:
   - Provide 4 calories per gram.
   - Typically, 45-65% of your daily calories should come from carbohydrates.
2. **Proteins**:
   - Provide 4 calories per gram.
   - Typically, 10-35% of your daily calories should come from protein.
3. **Fats**:
   - Provide 9 calories per gram.
   - Typically, 20-35% of your daily calories should come from fats.

Example Calculation:

- Suppose your TDEE is 2,000 calories:
   - Carbohydrates: 50% of 2,000 calories = 1,000 calories (1,000 ÷ 4 = 250 grams)
   - Protein: 25% of 2,000 calories = 500 calories (500 ÷ 4 = 125 grams)
   - Fat: 25% of 2,000 calories = 500 calories (500 ÷ 9 = 55.5 grams)

Micronutrient Requirements

Micronutrients, including vitamins and minerals, are essential for various bodily functions. While the specific needs can vary, here are some general guidelines:

1. **Vitamins**:
   - **Vitamin A**: 700-900 mcg/day
   - **Vitamin C**: 75-90 mg/day
   - **Vitamin D**: 600-800 IU/day
   - **Vitamin E**: 15 mg/day
   - **Vitamin K**: 90-120 mcg/day
   - **B Vitamins**: Varies by specific vitamin (e.g., B12: 2.4 mcg/day)
2. **Minerals**:
   - **Calcium**: 1,000-1,200 mg/day
   - **Iron**: 8-18 mg/day
   - **Magnesium**: 310-420 mg/day
   - **Potassium**: 2,500-3,000 mg/day
   - **Zinc**: 8-11 mg/day

Adjusting for Special Needs

1. **Weight Loss**:
   - To lose weight, create a caloric deficit by consuming fewer calories than your TDEE. A safe and sustainable rate of weight loss is about 1-2 pounds per week, which generally requires a deficit of 500-1,000 calories per day.
2. **Muscle Gain**:
   - To gain muscle, create a caloric surplus by consuming more calories than your TDEE. Focus on a balanced intake of macronutrients with an emphasis on protein to support muscle synthesis.
3. **Dietary Restrictions**:
   - Adjust your macronutrient sources based on dietary restrictions such as vegetarian, vegan, gluten-free, or lactose-free diets. Ensure you get sufficient nutrients from alternative sources.

Practical Tools

1. **Online Calculators**:
   - Use online TDEE and macronutrient calculators to simplify the process. Enter your age, gender, weight, height, and activity level to get personalized recommendations.
2. **Food Journals and Apps**:
   - Track your food intake using apps like MyFitnessPal or Cronometer to monitor your calories and nutrient intake. These tools can help you stay on track with your goals.
3. **Professional Guidance**:
   - Consider consulting with a registered dietitian or nutritionist for personalized advice and guidance tailored to your specific health needs and goals.

Conclusion

Calculating your daily nutritional needs is a foundational step in achieving and maintaining a healthy lifestyle. By understanding your caloric requirements and the right balance of macronutrients and micronutrients, you can make informed decisions about your diet. Use the tools and guidelines provided in this section to tailor your nutrition plan to your unique needs and goals, ensuring you support your overall health and well-being.

CONCLUSION

Staying Motivated and Consistent

Maintaining motivation and consistency is crucial for long-term success in meal prepping and healthy eating. As you embark on your journey with the Stealth Health Meal Prep Cookbook, it's important to develop strategies that keep you inspired and committed to your goals. This section provides practical tips and techniques to help you stay motivated and consistent, ensuring that your efforts lead to lasting results.

Tips for Staying Motivated

1. **Set Clear Goals**:
   o **Short-Term Goals**: Set achievable short-term goals, such as prepping meals for a week or trying three new recipes each month. These small victories will keep you motivated and provide a sense of accomplishment.
   o **Long-Term Goals**: Define your long-term goals, such as improving your overall health, losing a certain amount of weight, or building muscle. Having a clear vision of your end goal helps you stay focused and committed.
2. **Track Your Progress**:
   o **Food Journal**: Keep a food journal to track what you eat, how you feel, and any changes in your health. This can help you identify patterns, celebrate successes, and make adjustments as needed.
   o **Photos and Measurements**: Take regular photos and measurements to visually track your progress. Sometimes changes are more apparent in pictures than on the scale.
3. **Stay Positive**:
   o **Celebrate Small Wins**: Celebrate your successes, no matter how small. Whether it's sticking to your meal prep plan for a week or trying a new healthy recipe, acknowledging your achievements keeps you motivated.
   o **Positive Self-Talk**: Practice positive self-talk to boost your confidence and keep your mindset focused on success. Remind yourself of your capabilities and the progress you've made.
4. **Mix Things Up**:
   o **Variety in Recipes**: Avoid monotony by regularly trying new recipes from the cookbook. Experimenting with different ingredients and flavors keeps meal prep exciting and enjoyable.
   o **Seasonal Ingredients**: Use seasonal ingredients to keep your meals fresh and varied. This also ensures that you're getting a wide range of nutrients.
5. **Find Support**:
   o **Buddy System**: Find a meal prep buddy or join a community of like-minded individuals. Sharing your journey with others provides support, encouragement, and accountability.
   o **Online Communities**: Engage with online communities and social media groups focused on healthy eating and meal prep. These platforms offer inspiration, tips, and camaraderie.

Strategies for Consistency

1. **Create a Routine**:
   - o **Weekly Schedule**: Establish a weekly meal prep schedule that fits your lifestyle. Consistency in your routine makes meal prepping a habit rather than a chore.
   - o **Prep Day**: Designate a specific day for meal prepping. This reduces the likelihood of skipping it and ensures you have healthy meals ready for the week.
2. **Plan Ahead**:
   - o **Grocery List**: Plan your meals and create a detailed grocery list before heading to the store. This saves time and ensures you have all the necessary ingredients.
   - o **Meal Prep Kits**: Consider using meal prep kits or pre-measured ingredients to streamline the cooking process.
3. **Stay Organized**:
   - o **Kitchen Organization**: Keep your kitchen organized and stocked with essential tools and ingredients. An organized space makes meal prep more efficient and less stressful.
   - o **Labeling**: Label your prepped meals with the date they were made to keep track of freshness. This also helps you quickly identify meals during busy times.
4. **Adjust and Adapt**:
   - o **Flexibility**: Be flexible and willing to adjust your meal prep routine as needed. Life can be unpredictable, so adapt your plans to fit changing circumstances.
   - o **Simplify When Needed**: On particularly busy weeks, simplify your meal prep with quick and easy recipes. It's better to have basic, healthy meals than to skip meal prep altogether.
5. **Prioritize Self-Care**:
   - o **Balance**: Ensure that meal prepping and healthy eating fit into a balanced lifestyle. Avoid burnout by taking breaks and indulging in occasional treats.
   - o **Mindfulness**: Practice mindfulness in your eating habits. Pay attention to your body's hunger and fullness cues, and enjoy the process of cooking and eating.

Staying motivated and consistent with meal prepping and healthy eating can be challenging, but with the right strategies and mindset, it is achievable. Remember that progress is a journey, and it's important to celebrate your successes along the way. Use the tips and techniques provided in this section to maintain your motivation and consistency, ensuring that you achieve your health and wellness goals. The Stealth Health Meal Prep Cookbook is here to support you every step of the way.

I want to thank you for reaching the end and for giving this little manual an opportunity by purchasing it. Do not hesitate to contact me for any reason, or doubt, or advice, or just to say hello. I'll leave you my email address.

And if you liked the book and it was useful in any way, leave a vote on Amazon. Your feedback is valuable and can help me deliver higher quality products. Thank you for everything!

Sam CulinaryKid

rising2dreamy@gmail.com

GET YOUR BONUS:

Made in the USA
Las Vegas, NV
11 December 2024

d9c25b54-96ee-4eb1-8d98-0d50b2483c7bR02